# *Composing*
# *a Culture*

# Composing a Culture

*Inside a Summer Writing Program with High School Teachers*

Bonnie S. Sunstein

Boynton/Cook Publishers
HEINEMANN
Portsmouth, NH

**Boynton/Cook Publishers**
A subsidiary of Reed Elsevier Inc.
361 Hanover Street, Portsmouth, NH 03801-3912
*Offices and agents throughout the world*

**Library of Congress Cataloging-in-Publication Data**
Sunstein, Bonnie S.
    Composing a culture : inside a summer writing program with high
school teachers / Bonnie Sunstein.
        p.    cm.
    Includes biographical references.
    ISBN 0-86709-342-0 (acid-free paper) : $21.50
    1. English language--Rhetoric--Study and teaching.  2. High school
teachers--In service training.  3. English teachers--Training of.
I. Title.
PE1404.S87    1994
808'.042'0712--dc20                                            94-10334
                                                                   CIP

Editor: Peter R. Stillman
Production: J. B. Tranchemontagne
Cover design: Twyla Bogaard

Printed in the United States of America on acid-free paper
98 97 96 95 94   EB   1 2 3 4 5

*To my mother,*
*Janet Schloss Stone*

*who taught me to love people and the art of their language.*
*She is an art teacher, a portrait painter, and a reader of biographies—*
*written and spoken, published and unpublished.*
*For me, my brothers, our children, her friends,*
*and her students—she enables us to become ourselves.*
*She knows how to sweeten the struggle that comes with growth.*
*In this book, I paint word portraits about teachers who enable,*
*create, and learn as they share the struggles of growth.*
*She planted the seeds for this work.*

# Contents

# Foreword

This beautifully written book entices us into becoming figurative members of a transient community of teachers who have come together in a summer writing program in New Hampshire. Bonnie Sunstein moves us into all manner of spaces within and without this gathering of teachers committed to finding their writing selves. We hear and see as if we are there. Confronting the challenges of story and story telling, of dialogue and interchange and theme, readers can reflect with renewed energy on their own projects, particularly if these projects have to do with enabling others to find their voices, to undertake (as T. S. Eliot put it) a "raid on the inarticulate."

Far more than an account of an educational experiment, more than an exploration of what Sunstein calls "ritual" and "culture," the work is infused with the insights of remarkable thinkers and teachers like Thomas Newkirk, Donald Murray, Don Dippo, Victor Turner, Louise Rosenblatt, and others of kindred spirit. The wonderful thing is that they are not used merely as sources. Sunstein makes them present in what she says about language, perspective, metaphor, imagery. Their words (sometimes, in the case of Newkirk and Murray, spoken as part of the proceedings) provide a narrative framework for these teachers in residence in those summer weeks.

It is in no sense an experience of prescription or imposition. The people we meet are distinctively wrought individuals, each of them eager, each of them in quest. We see them in real settings, hear them open up to one another, join them as they go on (often with great difficulty) to choose their modes of expression and their themes. The lessons, as Sören Kierkegaard would have it, are "indirect"; we are not offered a set of propositions "about" a successful summer writing program. In some sense, we are moved to lend the teacher-writers in the text our own lives and, in doing so, to rewrite our own texts as teachers. Certainly, we ponder anew what it signifies to shape experiences in the form of narrative, what it means to translate reality into fiction, how it feels to say something truly—so truly that new dimensions of lived life are revealed.

We develop our own vantage point on what happens in this unique, unresolved summer program in part because Sunstein tells us about it from an engaged perspective. From the moment she arrives and settles into her room, then ventures out to meet the others, to receive assignments, to test the waters, to keep her records, we feel an active, searching, loving mind at work. I am reminded of John Dewey, writing in *Art as Experience:* "Mind is primarily a verb. It denotes all the ways in which we deal consciously and expressly with the situations in which we find ourselves." He says, too, that mind signifies attention and purpose. It is "care in the sense of solicitude, anxiety, as well as of active looking after things that need to be tended." . . . The writer of this book is mindful in the Deweyan sense as she draws our attention closer and closer to her "subjects," the remarkable and varied yet ordinary group of teachers privileged to go in search of themselves.

There is talk of books; there is increasing talk of the participants own writing and what might happen when they return to their teaching. There are the inevitable sounds of frustration and impatience. There are stirring moments of recovery of long-ago pasts, recollections of the growth of diverse people's literacy. And because the journeys the people in this story share can never be complete, there are conversations, sometimes cross-country, when the summer is over.

Then, when the account of the summer is (regretfully) over, the book suddenly and rhythmically opens out to a meeting of the English Coalition Conference, to the voices of people like Peter Elbow and Wayne Booth, to discussions of the condition of the American high school. Sunstein raises the issue of how people trained in traditional English programs (usually to be "answer men") can make the changes an engagement with writing entails. We suddenly find ourselves facing the complex challenges of our own tasks and our own uncertainties. Having lived the summer Sunstein describes, however, we are oddly refreshed, and we may love our questions even more.

*Maxine Greene*
*Teachers College, Columbia University*

# Acknowledgments

This book describes teachers who came together for knowledge in an intense three week community; a collaboration between themselves and those in a temporary world, crafted through relationships and conversations. These acknowledgments reflect another professional community, one in which I have lived and learned intensively for twenty-seven years.

When it was a dissertation, this project involved a committee of six remarkable people who gave me their company as scholars, teachers, colleagues, and friends. They asked tough questions and demanded clear research, thought, and method, but their confidence in my abilities left the creation of the work to me. Like the teachers in this book, they taught me to teach myself, offering guidance and wisdom while they watched and listened. There is a piece of each of them in these pages. And some of them are the teachers in this book.

Tom Newkirk taught me to look for dissonances, reminding me that tensions are sites of growth and centers for effective writing. With humor and insight, he accommodated the awkward ethics of guiding my research while I studied his program. Tom matured my writing and clarified my thinking; with a single word or phrase, he would capture and direct a long line of thinking. Don Graves, master of the perfect metaphor, helped me focus my research with his wisdom and experience. One day he observed that I was "catching a bullet in flight," and that conversation governed four years of research and writing. Jane Hansen's guidance was strong, and ever present. Her memory for details is astounding; she is perhaps the most responsive listener I know. Despite her tight schedule, she was somehow available to listen and think with me.

Burt Feintuch mentored me in the rich treasury of two academic disciplines: anthropology and folklore. He was patient and flexible, mapping a new territory with the routes I chose, always offering one more reference, one more reading. He guided my methodological perspectives and helped me to develop my own techniques of ethnographic writing. Through him, I found my way to the 1992 National Endowment for the Humanities Institute, "Telling Tales" in the anthropology department at the University of Wisconsin where I worked with Jack Kugelmass and another community interested in the study of narrative and human cultures. The study of anthropology and folklore allowed me to jump out of my own discipline in order to see it better.

Elizabeth Chiseri-Strater, Pat Sullivan, and Donna Qualley placed themselves in complex multiple positions in my life, as nurturing, personal friends, devoted teachers, and the very closest of colleagues. Like the writing partners in this book, they have seen this project through from its inception; they are models of professional scholarship, incisive response, love and sisterhood. Elizabeth helped me see the nuggets of truth and flecks of light inside a dark massive muck of data, watching as I sorted out the parts that hold value, reassuring me many times over. Pat's close and honest readings kept me cleaner as a writer, stronger as a woman, and more sure as a scholar. Donna summarized my thinking when I couldn't and kept a sisterly eye on me with a string of outrageous and loving postcards.

Don Murray's friendship, wisdom, sympathy, and humor has influenced my reading, writing, and teaching for twenty-five years. Over many lunches and during my visits to their home, both Don and Minnie Mae Murray listened and helped with thousands of thoughts and details. My siblings in the UNH English and Education Departments were and still are a bottomless source of intellectual and emotional support. Danling Fu, Dan Seger, and Peg Murray, whose brains, logic, love, and three years of weekly study sessions made me feel firsthand how knowledge happens. Tom Romano offered live fellowship for a year, and then kept it growing through the U.S. mail with detailed responses and rallying postcards; his passionate belief in this project made it more important to me. A very special writing group, Donna Qualley, Sherrie Gradin, Cindi Gannett, Elizabeth Chiseri-Strater, and Pat Sullivan continues to read, respond, laugh, and support through distance and conflicting schedules. Other colleagues in New Hampshire offered insights, ideas, and valuable references in every conversation we had: Linda Rief, Susan Stires, Amber Dahlin, Lad Tobin, Jay Simmons, Cindy Matthews, Peg Voss, Kathe Simmons, Cyrene Wells, Judy Ferrara, and Don Jones. A University of New Hampshire Dissertation Fellowship endowed me with peace for a year of writing and analysis; I had the luxury of choosing my own interruptions.

I am blessed also with colleagues from a long history in this profession who offered readership, suggestions, and support: Tom Devine who ushered me in and remains a mentor, my Writing and Learning Center family at Rivier College, Paul Lizotte, the Judiths Summerfield and Stanford, the Kathleens Cain and Lampert, Rebecca Burnett, Phil Anderson, Sharyn Lowenstein, Pam Farrell, and Rick Evans. Dave Wilson of the University of Nebraska shares my investment in the study of summer writing programs. His earlier study influenced my original design, and now his interest and collaborative stance is a relationship most scholars only dream about.

There are two very important "distant teachers" who reside in this book. Although my relationships with them are primarily on the page, their thinking and writing has guided mine. Louise Rosenblatt and Maxine Greene are women whose minds and souls made me look more deeply at what I had always seen. They taught me to study people in the contexts of their literacies, and their writing gave courage to write the way I had always wanted to write. As this book has taken shape, Maxine Greene has emerged from the page into life and affirmed my own scholarship with her sensitive foreword.

My new community of colleagues and students at the University of Iowa quite literally made this study become a book. They welcomed me and offered new perspectives: colleagues Carolyn Colvin, Anne DiPardo, Linda Fielding, Jim Marshall, and Cathy Roller, research assistants Joe Potts, Janet Smith, and Julie Cheville, colleague-students Bill Broz, Jenny Gassner, Cynthia Lewis, Peg Finders, Rachel Russell, Steve Vanderstaay and our energetic and stimulating monthly teacher-group. Most important, Beth McCabe and Sandie Hughes whose help, brains, and computer acumen put the finishing touches on the final manuscript. Each of these people has made a contribution to this book—with careful reading, collegial support, and honest response. In less than a year, I have another academic home.

The Boynton-Cook/Heinemann family has shaped my work for as long as I've been a teacher. Their books cover my office, my courses, and my thinking. Bob Boynton's friendship and guidance over many years came together as this work became a book during the first year of his retirement. Peter Stillman, Toby Gordon, Dawn Boyer, and Philippa Stratton have been and will continue to be colleagues with an eye toward the quality writing that teachers want to read. They are ever present for us all. And for the second time, Joanne Tranchemontagne has turned my manuscript pages into a book.

Most daily, my family allowed me to stay in their universe. Amy and Stephen are able assistants on the phone, the family calendar, at the washing machine, and in the kitchen. My mother, Janet Stone, to whom this book is dedicated, trusted my dreams and nourished my passions. Phyllis Sunstein, my other mother, supported my ambitions with buoys made of supportive words and a dolphin made of silver. Janet Wikler, my cousin-sister, gave me counsel and courage as she has in every stage of our lives. Drew, for years my most critical reader, offered insights from a distance and gave me extra memory for my computer when my mind wouldn't hold anymore.

And finally, nine very special teachers let me into the privacies of their lives. I rummaged around in their drafts, their journals, their rooms, and their memories for three heated weeks and then at school and home for a year while they were engaged in the very private processes of revising themselves. They allowed me to maintain my researcher position, shut my mouth, and keep our friendship and respect. While studying a writing community, we made one. Many times, as I wrote their words and analyzed their thoughts, I felt they were doing the writing for me. Much of this book is quietly theirs.

*We must rely on our scientists to help us find the way through the near distance, but for the longer stretch of the future we are dependent on the poets. We should learn to question them more closely, and listen more carefully. A poet is, after all, a sort of scientist, but engaged in a qualitative science in which nothing is measurable. He lives with data that cannot be numbered, and his experiments can be done only once.*

*The information in a poem is, by definition, not reproducible. His pilot runs involve a recognition of things that pop into his head. The skill consists in his capacity to decide quickly which things to retain, which to eject. He becomes an equivalent of scientist, in the act of examining and sorting the things popping in, finding the marks of remote similarity, points of distant relationship, tiny irregularities that indicate that this one is really the same as that one over there only more important. Gauging the fit, he can meticulously place pieces of the universe together, in geometric configurations that are as beautiful and balanced as crystals.*

—Lewis Thomas

# Introduction

## "A Little Bit of a Cult"

*I'm understanding that to read is to write is to listen; they're all the same thing . . . But what is this? There's more to this . . . I almost felt as though I was in a little bit of a cult . . . I got an uncomfortable feeling after a while, because I thought "These people are teaching us more than this stuff. . . . Unless I make a deep change, I'm not going to be making any change at all" . . . That is scary for me, and I didn't know it until I thought about it . . . just about two days ago.*

—Susan Landon, English Teacher

*A* summer writing program for teachers lasts for only three weeks, but it is an important event, sometimes a turning point in a teacher's career. "It's summer camp for the terminally literate," as one teacher called it. The program functions like a temporary culture, a social institution that itself can become a readable text. It's not exactly a university course; it involves more commitment than that. "I love to drop out from my job, my family, my cooking," one teacher wrote, "It's *not* okay to take a vacation, but it *is* okay to get six credits." For a short time—often for the first time—teachers leave their families and their daily lives, intending to examine and enrich their writing, reading, and teaching practices. Unburdened of their daily responsibilities and away from home and work in a place safe to take literate risks, they find themselves in the company of others doing the same. Another teacher explained it this way:

> The first week is 'Holy shit. I'm a wreck.' The second week is 'I don't know if I'm alive or dead, but I think things are start-

*1*

ing to come together.' And by the third week it's like, 'I'm a writer.'

## The New Hampshire Writing Program

This book portrays a few teachers in three combined New Hampshire writing programs during the summer of 1990: The New Hampshire Writing Program (NHWP), for teachers who have not attended a summer writing program before, The Institute for Reading, Writing, and Learning, (IRWL) for teachers who have already participated in the NHWP or a similar program, and an advanced seminar for those who've attended at least two others, the topic of which changes every year. One teacher described his New Hampshire experience in a single "labyrinthine sentence" (Romano in Newkirk, ed. 1990, Weathers 1980):

> NHWP, also known as English 919, The Teaching of Writing, a graduate level class or program that offers its participants six earned credits in one of the country's leading universities pioneering the writing process examination of the author and text, actually gives out FREE coffee at break and a tee shirt you don't have to BUY and can even design if you have the time between supportive and well guided writing groups that live the philosophy that one should practice what one teaches in order to learn what one can then teach also has the best damn dorm food in the United States, prepared by some of the leading pioneers in mass-produced food preparation who make me want to run to dinner from the library that holds New Hampshire's largest collections with volumes numbering in the hundreds of thousands and has the best looking students restacking the shelves smiling at you from between the rows of books.

In the summer of 1990, there were two hundred thirty-three participants from twenty-seven U.S. states, Canada, Bermuda, and Japan. Female teachers comprised 79 percent of the total participants, high school teachers 19 percent. The forty-four high-school teachers in the combined programs came from public and private, special education, college-preparatory, rural, suburban and urban schools. In the NHWP and the IRWL, each teacher met daily in two groups: a workshop with teachers of mixed grade levels, and a shorter theory and methods group with teachers from her own grade level. The advanced seminar in 1990 was "Explorations in Genre" which Donald Murray taught at his home in the afternoons, reserving morning hours for participants' private writing time.

I had never taught in this program, nor had I participated in it. But my researcher lenses were colored by a long teaching career in New England and doctoral studies under the influences of many colleagues here. I began my study knowing three things for sure from two decades of teaching writing in secondary schools and colleges—quite separated from UNH's influence—working and talking with high school teachers inside and outside their schools:

1. That neither the culture of a high school as an institution nor a public high school's English curriculum supports an approach to teaching writing based on offering time, choice, and collaboration.
2. That the high school teachers I know who feel most comfortable teaching writing are ones who have attended summer programs, and that they will actively resist a prescribed curriculum in order to teach writing their own ways.
3. That high school teachers who want to write themselves have trouble finding time to do it, have little professional encouragement from administrators, colleagues, or students to pursue it.

And so I began to ask some questions. Why does a high school teacher seem to need the support of a summer program in order to teach writing with confidence against a prescribed curriculum? Why don't other kinds of inservice models affect people as much as summer programs? What is the nature of this encounter, and why see it as a culture? What kind of culture does this summer writing program provide for a high school teacher? How does a summer program affect a teacher during the summer, and then what does she bring back to school in the fall?

New Hampshire's program is certainly not unique; a look at writing programs for teachers across the U.S. suggests that they are efficient, relatively inexpensive ways to re-educate teachers in the summertime. The National Writing Project, with over one hundred sixty sites across the globe, began in 1974 as the Bay Area Writing Project in California, a model with a mission to identify good teachers of writing, train them to present classroom practices to other teachers, and then follow up their contact during the school year in inservice workshops and courses. It is based on a few fundamental concepts: that writing teachers ought to write, that the best teachers of writing teachers are other teachers, and that curriculum change must be a grassroots effort—that it come from the "bottom up," from the teacher. Over the past twenty years, the National Writing Project became what James Moffett calls "the most positive development in English education during the 70s" (1981, 81). The Bay Area Project was not the first summer writing program for teachers. Private and university-sponsored summer writing programs have beckoned teachers for decades, but this one gave attention to a mix of pedagogy and practice; it made the teaching of writing accessible to large groups of public school teachers.

The New Hampshire Writing Program, begun by professor Thomas Newkirk to offer help specifically for New Hampshire teachers, differs in its design and philosophy. There were strong resources available at the University of New Hampshire at the time. The English Department had a strong commitment to writing under Donald Murray's chairmanship, with faculty specialists in writing instruction, authors in fiction and poetry, and award-winning journalists. The Education Department was in the midst of elaborate research in the development of writing in schools (Graves 1983), becoming a springboard for much professional activity and publishing in the field of teaching composition in schools across the English speaking world. But these rich resources were missing most New Hampshire teachers. Over the summers, faculty members splintered into workshops out of state. One-semester evening courses couldn't effectively accommodate most working teachers commuting long distances in a rural state, and short inservice programs were proving insufficient.

In his original proposal, Newkirk (1979) documented the public pressures that defined writing as a competence to be assessed, and pointed out that few English teachers were making an effort to teach composition, and most had no formal training. His description of the course outlined three basic features: an "experiential base," a "theoretical base," and a "pragmatic base" that, ten years later, still stand. His words about the experiential base foreshadow much of what the teachers in this book will learn:

> Painting teachers should paint, acting teachers should act, carpentry teachers should saw, and writing teachers should write. Many English teachers do not write. And by not writing they experience both ethical and practical problems when it comes to teaching writing . . . A teacher will have difficulty dealing with students' writing anxiety when he or she is terrified of writing. No component of the proposed program will provoke as much anxiety among participants as the writing workshops, and at the end of the program no other component will have done as much to generate the enthusiasm for the writing process. The workshops provide the energy that runs the program. The purpose of the workshops is not necessarily to produce publishable writers but to help participants to discover (or rediscover) their own voices and to develop their skills. (1979, 12)

In Newkirk's program, participants live the "experiential" base daily, writing and responding to others' writing with teachers across grade levels. The "theoretical" and the "pragmatic" bases become the foundations for the daily grade-level sessions that represent one-third of their class time. After three summers in the New Hampshire program, one teacher confesses:

It's like a luxury, an opportunity to be able to do something that I know is going to be good for me but it's kind of a discipline that I'm a little scared of too. . . . All the years that I've taught writing I would always start stuff but never finish, because that's when my students would need me the most. . . .

One teacher recalls theory from her grade-level instructor: "She made me think about why it is that I taught what I taught, and what was important, what was valuable and what wasn't . . . She didn't tell me what was valuable. She got me to ask the questions." The "pragmatic base" in grade-level sessions applies theory to practice with specific strategies for the classroom, samples of student writing, videotapes of reading and writing classes, and guest demonstrations. In his original proposal, Newkirk wrote, "The very nature of a summer program makes follow-up essential. Its virtue is, in a sense, its defect. . . . teachers can study and work free from teaching responsibilities. Yet this separation can cause teachers to generate unrealistic expectations" (1979, 23).

The "theoretical base" is a hedge against this problem of follow-up. "Without a theoretical base," Newkirk wrote in his proposal, "a writing curriculum can easily resemble a classic definition of 'history'—one damn thing after another" (14). Instructors choose texts and arrange assignments to highlight their own commitment to "the relationship between language and learning and to the special contributions that writing can make to the learning process." One teacher, after three years, told me that she bases her curricular decisions on a gradual understanding of theory:

After the first summer I tried to do everything all at once, and it didn't work. So then I focused on one thing at a time. . . . after the second summer it was better. Now I feel as if I see the writing/reading philosophy more clearly. Before it was broken up, like little pieces of a puzzle that weren't put together yet . . . I'm too easy on the kids . . . I let them give up too easily. . . . sometimes you have to push people, especially teenagers . . . they're not used to making their own choices when it comes to reading and writing.

Neither curriculum change nor institutional transformation is a specific goal for New Hampshire's participants.[1] But the program holds a strong assumption that change will happen in the teacher herself, that it will continue to happen when her own literacy is strengthened and she is invited to become a member of this community. After ten years, Tom Newkirk knows that the experience is not always joyful; it evokes emotion, confusion, and doubt in every person every year. The program excites him and it unnerves him. He looks forward to it as each summer approaches, he told me just a week before the 1990 session began, with "a sense of dread . . . for the thing that's about to come down."

## Summer Writing Programs and Teacher Change

Most people who attend summer programs say the programs have lasting effects. Alumni remain active at conferences and in professional journals. They establish informal and formal networks. All over the country, regional and local writing projects publish newsletters and collections of teachers' writing. The National Writing Project alone offers monographs and papers written by teachers, and *The Quarterly*, a periodical devoted to sharing ideas, research and projects with an increasing international readership. Harvey Daniels and Steven Zemelman's book *A Writing Project: Training Teachers of Composition from Kindergarten to College* (1985) is a comprehensive, book-length manual drawn from eight years in the Illinois Writing Project and written by its directors.

---

[1] In his 1983 English Education article "Is the Bay Area Model the Answer?" Newkirk commends the National Writing Project for the "justifiable euphoria" over its success and praises both programs for creating "an esprit and a continuing bond" different from traditional methods courses and the "enforced captivity of the mandated inservice workshop" (166). As a result of Newkirk's critique, during the following summer, Bill Strong, director of the Utah Writing Project, taught in the New Hampshire Writing Program and wrote a report for the National Writing Project's publication, The Quarterly. It is more like a course, and conservative in that way, Strong observed. It is not specifically aimed at creating curriculum change. The "political message," as Strong saw it, was "one emphasizing self-sponsored writing, integration of reading and writing, and the teacher as researcher," that "the real goal of these teachers was to become more effective in the classroom." Strong admitted that time spent in National Writing Project teacher workshops "holds the schedule hostage. . . . from the activities of reading and writing" (20). He concluded that at New Hampshire, "teachers were participants in an Institute, not owners of it."

The professional friendships and publications are visible, but what about the more invisible "lasting effects" teachers describe? Do teachers actually change? There are a few studies of teacher change after inservice projects. Sondra Perl and Nancy Wilson's *Through Teachers' Eyes: Portraits of Writing Teachers at Work* (1986) studies writing teachers in a suburban New York school system after four summer writing institutes. Nancy Lester and Cynthia Onore's book *Learning Change: One School District Meets Language Across the Curriculum* (1990) accounts shifts after a four year inservice writing program in another New York school district. School change, in this book, involves a group of people with active support from one administration, working together to examine their practices in teaching literacy. Although these books detail teachers and their curricula, they focus on changes in one school system.

Three other recent studies describe teacher change after summer writing programs. Wendy Bishop's book, *Something Old, Something New* (1990), presents college writing instructors during a two-summer doctoral studies program, and documents change and lack of change in each of five teachers' college classrooms during the following school year. Her study shows that teachers' beliefs about what they do are not always consonant with what their students believe they are doing. David Wilson (1988, 1994) wrote a retrospective study of teacher change in writing program alumni, high school teachers, in their classrooms three and six years after the Iowa summer program. The teachers in Wilson's study claim that community and personal writing were much stronger influences than the books they read or the instruction they received, but he does not emphasize this among his major findings. In a study of four secondary teachers returning to their classrooms after a Wisconsin summer writing project, Mary Louise Gomez (1990) found teachers disappointed at not being able to "effect change," that "resocialization" for them would require time to meet regularly, that school change would require collaborative efforts with administrators, and that the isolating environment of a secondary school constrains them from reflection, collaboration, or individual attempts at innovation (in Hawisher and Soter, eds., 79).

These studies examine change in writing teachers' practices and beliefs as they return to their classrooms. Each presents the writing community as a hedge against professional isolation, a support for articulating beliefs about writing instruction and applying them to a prescribed curriculum. All combine researchers' observations with teachers' self-reports of shifts in their own beliefs. But no study investigates teachers in the summer workshop itself. None tries to define what teachers mean by "community," or look at teachers' attitudes about their own writing or reading as they share with their peers. Only two single out the special issues high school teachers face. There are few accounts of informal conversations, personal stories, or views of the environment in which the seeds of these changes take root.

My purpose in this book is not to show teacher change. It is to document a few teachers' experience during one summer. I wanted to listen to their stories, see them as they worked, watch as they read and wrote and responded, listen to their complaints and triumphs as they re-thought their own literacies in the company of other teachers and writers, all teaching and writing. As one teacher told me:

> A lot of why I like this program is that there are no primadonnas
> . . . we are all writers whatever stage we are in at the time. . . . you
> can be who you are, in whatever creative way that you are, write
> what you want using the resources that you have. There isn't a
> formula. . . . I've come away with great respect for elementary
> teachers, and—not a disdain for high school teachers, but I saw in
> them an impatience, an inflexibility, an unwillingness to learn
> something new. And I'm a high school teacher.

Psychologist Jerome Bruner suggests that that education ought to "become part of our 'culture-making.'" We are constantly reconstructing our "selves" as well as our culture

(1986), as this teacher is. Teachers quite literally shape the educational actions for the next generation. It is important to look at them while they engage in their own reconstructions.

## *Writing Programs as Transformation*

Some teachers leave this experience and return to school in the fall reporting feelings of being changed, "transformed." But transformation is not usually an objective of a summer program. In fact, perhaps they are even *more themselves* than they were when they arrived. Why do teachers label it "transformation?" Is it really a *transformative illusion*? Do they credit the program when they begin to write and read for pleasure, when they begin to revise their ideas about teaching? Are they afraid to credit themselves? In the quote that begins this preface, Susan Landon is puzzled, pleased, and a little unnerved when she thinks about her three weeks:

> I'm understanding that to read is to write is to listen; they're all the same thing. . . . But what is this? There's more to this. . . . I almost felt as though I was in a little bit of a cult. . . . I got an uncomfortable feeling after a while, because I thought "These people are teaching us more than this stuff. . . . Unless I make a deep change, I'm not going to be making any change at all". . . . That is scary for me, and I didn't know it until I thought about it . . . just about two days ago.

For Susan and the others in this book, the change agent is herself, but not only herself. It is a complex temporary culture made of herself, her social environment, the language she shares, a poke into her own personal history and a glimpse at her occupational traditions. Her writing creates internal dialogue—she writes to know what she knows. And it creates external dialogue: through colleagues and mentors, constructing and reconstructing shared beliefs, confirming and creating common experience. The program validates movement inward—to explore the self. But it encourages a parallel movement outward—toward a community that offers other people a chance to collaborate in the exploration.[2] She both confirms and revises her knowledge. Here the teacher acts as her own agent for change, inside this culture designed for her, and determines new ways to enable her students to evaluate their knowledge, their changes.

Can we see it as a temporary culture? I think so. Anthropologists define cultures as collections of beliefs, behaviors, rituals, and language which shift as time and participants reorganize them. "Cultures are, after all," writes anthropologist Barbara Myerhoff, "collective, untidy assemblages, authenticated by belief and agreement, focused only in crisis, systematized after the fact" (1974, 10). The unsettling "deep change" teachers report is part of that untidy assemblage which constitutes this culture, informed by agreement and shared beliefs, as Myerhoff defines it. It is focused by a gentle personal and pedagogical "crisis," three weeks of reflexive immersion—turning in upon the self and out again toward her institutions. And she waits to "systematize after the fact" when she returns. Each teacher will impose, in her own way, a systematicity, with recollection and application months and years later.

The summer writing program is a ritual itself. The community makes fellowship by telling stories, sharing artifacts, enacting practices and rites of passage, honoring its elder tradition-bearers, establishing a lexicon, a set of symbols, and a system of beliefs that each year forms a new identity for the people who enter, while it conserves a core of its own. And each year, the summer writing program, although full of its former tradition, reinvents itself. "A society's culture," writes anthropologist Ward Goodenough, "consists of whatever it is one has to know or believe in order to operate in a manner acceptable to its members. . . . Culture is not a material phenomenon; it does not consist of things, people,

---

[2] Tom Newkirk, who has directed this program since the beginning, stresses that his program is "not trying to make this a transformation . . . it is a confirmation, an affirmation of who they are and what they're already doing." (5/28/90, personal communication)

behavior, or emotions. It is rather an organization of these things. It is the forms of things that people have in mind, their models for perceiving, relating, and otherwise inter- preting them" (1957, 167).

But the participants in this culture are each teachers with long career histories who are reading, writing, reflecting, ask- ing questions of themselves and their pedagogies. Together, they form an intense assemblage, full of the colors and tex- tures of literacy and teaching. Alone, each will take away something different, think about it, and apply it to her life at school. This book attempts to peek in on how teachers orga- nize, interpret, and reflect on their histories and literacy prac- tices inside this temporary culture, and in turn, their own per- ceptions of schooling.

In a summer writing program, teachers learn by self-reflec- tion as they write and talk inside a social environment that holds other teachers who read and listen. The essence of human learning is an "interweaving of two lines" (Vygotsky, 56), language and personal development as it works inside a social context. Despite their adulthood and their college degrees, each teacher learning inside this culture works in her "zone of proximal development," the term Vygotsky uses to describe "the distance between the actual developmental level as determined by independent problem solving and the level of potential development as determined through problem solving under adult guidance or in collaboration with more capable peers." (86)

Learning happens too in the company of an equal, a col- laborator, as the teachers in this book discover. Donald Graves (1991), one of the tradition-bearers whose influence is a major force in this program, cautions that Vygotsky's terms "adult guidance" and "more capable peers" imply an intellectual hierarchy. When someone is forming a concept, Graves says, it might be a "less capable peer," or just a capa- ble one, who puts in the missing link. And peer response to drafts-in-progress is one of the program's most sacred shared beliefs. One high school teacher noticed her gradual shift in attitude toward her own peers when she began to know them as writers:

> I tended to put teachers in boxes and label them. . . . I could sort of write them off when they weren't in my group, but I have been repeatedly surprised . . . people who I had felt detached from I became attached to . . . then their writing suddenly looked better! And I came to see a breakdown of barriers. . . . I came to have an enormous respect for junior high teachers who I always thought were lunatics . . . and elementary teachers will always take a stab at something that comes along, they know how to teach kids how to think and how to learn. . . .

For these adults, there are zones of proximal development in their peer conferences, their response groups, and the classes and presentations the program provides. But the acts of teaching and learning are messy here; they mix and brew continuously. They seep around the formal edges of the program. Concepts form and gel in the dorms, in carpools, at the picnics, over coffee, or beer, or ice cream in the local restaurants and on weekend trips to the beach and the mountains. One teacher wrote in her journal:

> We sit in cubbied spaces . . . trying to read gestures. . . . I'm wondering . . . how this brief encounter will work . . . wondering if I'll make a connection to anyone here. . . . Writing is like that . . . a risk . . . it follows you into your bed whispering. . . . I meander up and down the halls in search of a sympathetic ear . . . a door opens and a voice yells, "I can't write, I can't take it anymore, just give me a ditto and let me fill in the blanks." Another door opens and someone shouts "Listen to this, listen to this" . . . the hallway fills with writers sharing, whining, laughing. . . .

## *Twin Laws and an Event that Re-presents*

"Reading" this summer program as a culture means looking at its participants, like this teacher does, as more than a group taking a course. There is a relationship between each person and the event itself. Participants recognize its belief system

*13*

and enact its rituals and practices while the event is taking place. They know they are "in a little bit of a cult," but they also recognize that one of its rules is to "be who you are," as she observes. They mark their own contributions with their individuality as they begin to adapt its cultural system, or as they reject it.

To find a way to "read" this culture, I borrowed two frames from folklore and anthropology. Folklore's "twin laws," as folklorist Barre Toelken refers to them, are conservatism and dynamism. One has to do with conserving, a culture's tradition-keeping function, and the other is its way of reconceiving knowledge, rituals, craft, and verbal art as they are passed on. The conservative core is fixed: "all those processes and forces that result in the retaining of certain information, beliefs, styles, customs, and the like, and the attempted passing of those materials, intact, through time and space in all the channels of tradition and expression" (1979, 35).

Each year at UNH the special sessions change, the formal lectures change, the participants and their interests change. But much remains the same. "I'm conservative about the staff," Newkirk says. "We've made our careers together." In 1981, staff and participants all fit around one long picnic table for their first lobster dinner. By 1990, they used three rooms in the university's largest student dining facility. Of the 1981 staff, five people are still teaching in 1990, and three others have been participants. They are all practicing teachers who write. In 1981, of the staff members who were teaching in public schools, none had published a piece of writing for a wide professional audience. Since then, collectively, the 1990 staff of thirteen had published hundreds of articles over ten years, eight books, and seven other books in press.

Newkirk bases his program on a core of theories of learning from Jerome Bruner, John Dewey, William James, and theories of composition that draw from Donald Murray, Janet Emig, Peter Elbow, James Moffett, and James Britton, and such ancient composition theorists as Plato and Montaigne. He applies careful attention to the maintenance of the rituals

*14*

that he believes strengthen the program. These are as formal as the yearly presentations by composition and literature scholars and writers, the time allotted to writing groups and grade level groups, the formal reading of selected writings on the last day of the program. Other features are less formal, but important conserving traditions: cookouts, an annual tee shirt design contest, a lobsterfest, a daily newsletter, informal opportunities to view classroom videos, exchange visits, and join other summer faculty for brown-bag lunches.

But in the cultural products of a folk group, there is always a part in motion, the dynamic features of the event: the things that change each time the event reoccurs, with each person who is part of it. Toelken places dynamism at the other extreme of conservatism: "all those elements that function to change features, contents, meanings, styles, performance, and usage as a traditional event takes place repeatedly over space and time. Matters of taste, context, art, playfulness, change of function, translation, shift of audience . . . all encourage continual change . . . even when the bearer of the tradition tries to prevent it" (35).

Using this frame from folklore, I saw participants acting as folk groups act. They accepted the program's conservative core: the writing groups, the grade level groups and the functions of both. They learned the established lexicon, attended the formal lectures by writers and poets, tried out the disciplines required of the crafts they were learning: reading, writing, and the teaching of both, the cookouts and lobster dinners. But the dynamic features lurked everywhere: in shifting talk, using tools, swapping knowledge, sharing old crafts in new ways. There were long conversations about pens and pencils, lap desks and computers, literature of the canon and literature of the drug store. There were complex discussions and reconsiderations of such matters as genre, grammatical choices, and literacy histories. Throughout the three weeks, participants told stories about personal school failures, writing anxieties, classroom dilemmas. They shared books they loved and books they hated, and they met some authors—the tradition-bearing elders. Roles broke down as participants watched the tradition-bearers draft their own writing and participate with the group. And as in all cultures, there were moments of deep resistance in unexpected places. This was a culture carefully designed to encourage non-competition, for example, but the competition was fierce for the annual tee shirt design; it took three, forty-five minute meetings to come to consensus. And competition seeped beyond the tee shirt. The program valued process over product, but it issued grades and graduate credits.

I borrowed a way to look at the event itself from anthropology. Don Handelman (1990) describes public events as dense concentrations of rituals and symbols in any culture, often temporary in time and limited in space, occasions "that people undertake in concert to make more, less, or other of themselves than they usually do." The summer writing program serves as an event that re-presents a culture to itself, as Handelman explains it. It allows teachers to be students, to experiment in the crafts of reading, writing, and arranging both classroom and curriculum. Here, they can tinker with the learner-teacher relationship and examine the light and the dark sides of their own learning and teaching histories. Handelman shows that such events can "refract multiple visions of the possible . . . inversions of social reality" which can cause participants to question an existing social order (49). First, the summer writing program offers teachers reflexive glimpses of themselves as learners, as readers and writers. Then it offers them a chance to project those glimpses toward their own teaching. In short, the very structure of the event itself re-presents, to a teacher, another way to look at herself inside the culture of schooling.

## "Being There" on Paper: a Cacophony of Verbal Data

I needed to live this experience to understand it, and then reconstruct it on the page to give a sense, as Clifford Geertz describes, of "being there" (1988). The summer program is a unique kind of event in the education of teachers, and I tried to render this event to reflect its uniqueness. To do that, I drew interpretations from a mixture of academic disciplines: composition and feminist theory, and sociolinguistics, educational philosophy and psychology, anthropology and folklore studies. Geertz offers in his essay "Blurred Genres," the idea of seeing the summer as a readable event, a text of sorts:

> To see social institutions, social customs, social changes as in some sense "readable" is to alter our whole sense of what such interpretation is and shift it toward modes of thought rather more familiar to the translator, the exegete, or the iconographer than to the test giver, the factor analyst, or the pollster (1983, 32).

And so I blurred genres and chose ethnographic lenses to see, read, and describe what I saw. Geertz claims, "now that ethnographies look at least like romances as much as lab reports, ethnographers have to convince us . . . not merely that they themselves have truly "been there," but that had we been there we should have seen what they saw, felt what they felt, concluded what they concluded" (1988, 16).

The event itself called for a special way to represent it which was, to my mind, as important as the research questions. I tried to render it as "artful science," educator Elliott Eisner calls it. For this, the writer needs to be selective as she perceives and discloses. "The making of a fine meal does not require using everything in the pantry," Eisner writes (1990, 90). "Connoisseurship," his term, is a quiet, private act of appreciation (85), with little social utility. But for connoisseurship to have a public presence, we must turn to criticism— "connoisseurship with a public face." If connoisseurship is the art of appreciation, "criticism" is the art of disclosure. An artful ethnographic narrative, according to Eisner, is an appropriate form of educational criticism.

How best might I design a study to write about a temporary three-week experience in which my informants are writing too? How can I "read" this culture as a text so my reader can also read it? What multiple kinds of data sources could I find to let my informants speak in their own voices? How would I design an educationally critical narrative with the sense of "being there," out of pieces of other people's texts and lives? From Geertz's perspective, "How words attach to the world, texts to experience, works to lives, is not a question anthropologists have been asking for very long" (1988, 134). This is a question composition scholars and educational researchers are just beginning to ask (Green, Kantor, Brodkey, Simon and Dippo). I needed to use the tools of the contemporary ethnographer, but adapt them to the special features of this culture.

For my informants and me, the three weeks were only a moment in our teaching and learning lives, but for everyone it was an important moment. Like a good ethnography, it was a moment telescoped in time and space. I began with seven informants and a set of guiding questions. I knew it was important to look for personal stories, mentors and memories of past teaching and learning experiences, "turning" points in people's own literate histories. Stories are crucial links in female knowledge and teacher knowledge (Carter, Barone, Witherell and Noddings), and they enable occupational groups to define themselves (Santino, McCarl, Handelman, A. Green). I wanted to see how teachers engaged or disengaged with others, what they chose to write about, in what ways they felt like members of a quickly evolving culture. Did they take part in shaping it, or did the culture just seem "there" to them?

I collected data day and night: eighteen days, sixteen hours a day, a total of two hundred eighty-eight hours, thirty-two ninety minute tape recordings from two tape recorders, and two large plastic crates full of verbal data—the reading and writing of my informants, a rich collection of ethno-verbiage, a cacophony of verbal data. It included everything they wrote from formal writing to notes I found in wastebaskets, what they said in classes, informal conversations, and interviews. I wanted each voice to tell her version. They spoke and read and wrote. I listened.

Then, the three weeks were over. Suddenly came the quiet, the sorting, the transcribing, the filing, and coding, and recoding. First, down to five informants, then four, and eventually three. And the methodological questions. Where does an ethnography take place—in the field or on the page? As George Marcus says, attention to the language and form of an ethnographic text is the way we synthesize our fieldwork and our theory. It is, in his terms, an act of "deskwork as opposed to fieldwork" (in Ruby, ed., 171).

I've designed this book in two forms to mirror the way I saw those three weeks: three long case portraits and five short intertexts, with impressions from others and myself on both sides. There are three detailed portraits of high school teachers: Therese Deni, Dorothy Spofford, and Joyce Choate.[3] I show them as they each try to "read" themselves inside the texts, subtexts, and contexts of the New Hampshire Writing Program. Each confronts her internal oppositions—interrelationships between her teacher-self and her writer-self, her past and her present circumstances. Each must "read" two cultures as she understands and participates in them—that of her summer, and that of her school. Each teacher shuttles, too, between her personal agenda and the program's agenda for her. Through each person's tensions, her actions, her conversations with others, her formal and informal writing, responses to her reading, and my observations and conversations with her, I try to capture the ways she interprets the summer's academic and social system.

The intertexts are meant as verbal snapshots, landscapes of the culture itself. In each intertext, I attempt to freeze a moment (Rosenberg 1989), stop an action or a person just long enough to examine some of the thinking, pieces of texts, scholarship, and experience that contribute to that moment. My hope is that the intertexts will add flesh and color, that they will offer other smaller slices of the program and its participants, little tastes of its richness.

There is also the question of my own voice. Subjectivity is an inherent part of fieldwork, and I certainly entered this

---

[3] All names of participants have been changed. Unless otherwise identified, they are all high school teachers from across the U.S.A. and Canada. Informants chose their own pseudonyms. Names of program instructors are not changed.

fieldwork with an "insider's" biases. But it is the reflexive perspective that gives ethnography its color, texture, and luster. "To be reflexive," writes anthropologist Victor Turner, "is to be at once one's own subject and direct object" (in Ruby, ed., 96). Like the teachers in this book, I was caught between myself and my objectives. I wondered, "How do I authorize a text that's been authored by someone else? And do it preserving the author's voice?" I needed to preserve their texts inside my text. I had to foreground their own voices, fold them into my narrative. And I needed to write their biases, their stories, their understandings—not mine.

When we work with writers, it is not just the final piece of writing that offers information. It is that cacophony of verbal data that holds the clues. In my analysis, I learned to validate from different pieces of discourse and actions, through multiple perspectives within the same person. Like a good poem, a good ethnographic account ought to present an impression of an event through carefully chosen words, metaphors, imagery, and real field experience—through the lenses of both the informants and the researcher. An "impressionist tale," sociologist John Van Maanen writes, presents "the doing of fieldwork rather than simply the doer or the done" (105). He reminds us that there is a trend these days for ethnographers to study our own institutions, that we are drawn to familiar places "with the slightly ironic intention of making them strange," and to make the familiar strange we use metaphor, "the coke dealer as small businessman . . . the computer hacker as Bohemian artist . . . the congressman as tribal chief or flunky . . . the drunk driver as media fiction . . ." (1988, 126).

My intentions for this book and the metaphors I use may not look as "strange" as the ones Van Maanen cites, but I looked into a familiar place and found a strange irony: the teacher as student, away from her institution in time and space, participating in an event deliberately designed to be different from school. I present it here in an impressionist form to place in the foreground the writing and thinking of my informants and myself. The chronological pattern shuttles, as it must. To present each person's story as a connected whole I must move back to the beginning of each person's three weeks, and then in Chapter 5 they all appear again, back at school during the year that follows.

In this book you will find four deep impressions of the summer writing program culture: Therese Deni's, Dorothy Spofford's, Joyce Choate's, and mine. Others' impressions, the supporting roles, I might call them, appear and reappear as colleagues, correspondents, and writers themselves in the Intertexts. They are meant to fuse a few moments when issues, politics, conversations, and writing comes together, to capture the rich landscape that surrounded us, to flesh out the culture's colors, textures, and lusters. I offer these moments and these portraits as I saw them, as I selected them from millions of moments and hundreds of people. I hope that through the detail—their very particularity—you might find yourself, your colleagues, your story.

# Confessions of a Participant-Observer

When I parked my car at the rear of the dorm, I was not thinking about writing or teaching. I was thinking about leaving my family for three weeks, feeling guilty. I'd grumbled at my daughter because she had forgotten to pack socks for camp and commanded my son to set his alarm each morning for summer school. I waved good-bye to them on the highway as my husband's car headed north and I forked east for Durham, just past the Bedford tollbooth. Three tentative arms, raised through the open sunroof, waved me away.

In the back of the car, my desk lamp rattled against the room fan, and they both bumped against a plastic crate full of books and files. The lamp slid off my pillow and dug into my suitcase as I curved east. It was too late to readjust or to reconsider. My plan to observe and study the New Hampshire Writing Program and its participants meant that I would live it. I had registered as a participant and paid for a room in the dorms. I was about to "go native" in my own culture, to try to "see the familiar as strange," as anthropologists say. My stuff was packed, my daughter's stuff was packed, my family was on its way, and the arrangements were made. None of us was very sure how the three weeks would go.

Forty-five miles later, I turned right at the public television station, passed the equestrian field, the dairy barns and greenhouses of the agriculture department, and glimpsed the white, wooden sign with the blue seal of the university. This wasn't a new drive for me. I'd been a commuting doctoral student for two

23

years. As a public school and college English teacher, I had driven here for scores of conferences and meetings. What was strange was that I had time. I was going to stay. This time, I was not panicked to find a parking place or rush to a meeting or a class. I had time. I drove by my current school "home," the Writing Lab office in Morrill Hall, took a deep breath, and headed past the main campus and around to the dorms.

*     *     *     *

I am surprised to find the three minidorms at the edge of the campus—I've completed two years working at this university and never seen them. Sackett, Woodruff, and Richardson are small, two-story wood sided buildings. The dorms cluster around a common velvet-grass lawn and a well-tended forest encircles them. A volleyball net stands between Richardson and Sackett, clotheslines hang outside Woodruff. There is a circular driveway, a flagpole, and a few giant flat rocks the size of park benches. A long wooden stairway on the opposite side of the lawn connects the minidorms to the parking lot and to the rest of the university. Each is unique among the others. Each views the campus from a different perspective. But the design connects them; structurally they are the same.

I glance at the family cars and vans parked around the driveway. Daughters and sons and husbands and wives move cartons of books, suitcases, wastebaskets, desk lamps. They cradle computer monitors and printers wrapped in blankets and pillows. A fluffy white dog yaps through a car window; three small children wrestle on the lawn. Young athletes carry bicycles into the dorms, nesting them gently into corners and onto posts, wrapping metal cords, securing locks. Everyone is wearing minimal clothing: tank tops, sundresses, shorts, sandals, running shoes. The air is sticky; it is ninety-eight degrees and the forecast promises more of the same. I have lived in New Hampshire twenty-four summers, and I know that mid-July is like this.

Inside Sackett, there is an efficient system for registration. With a flurry of manila envelopes and keys, two young women smile and welcome me to the Summer Writing Program, ask my name and offer me my packet. The lounge is the center of the minidorm, and they sit in the center of the lounge. I sit for a few

24

minutes to watch and listen. The four sofas are upholstered in student-proof blue tweed, armed in oak, and they form a square for conversation. A large square coffee table in the center holds boxes of registration packets and a cooler of cold drinks. Against two walls, there are blank bulletin boards, an old refrigerator, three vending machines, and a table. From the sofa, I can see a kitchenette and a laundry room, a stairway leading to the second floor, and three doorways leading to halls of dorm rooms.

Claire is making posters, squeaking magic markers: red meal times, blue phone regulations, green mail procedures. People shuttle back and forth, accepting keys, asking questions, hauling cartons. "My desk doesn't look like a desk." "I have a broken light bulb." "My window won't open." She promises to assist someone. "I'm getting good at desk assembly; give me two minutes." Claire is young to be a dorm-mother and most of the people she helps are middle-aged. I hear stories: one woman from upstate New York began her trip at 4:00 A.M. and deposited her four children at four different places along the way. Another tells me she cried as she saw three people from last summer hugging on Main Street. The age reversals seem a bit surrealistic and I begin having flashes of my own past.

Kate, who is also in her early twenties, is the program's administrative assistant this summer. She's explaining how to open the combinations on the doors. In five minutes, she explains the procedure seven times. I hate complicated locks. I haven't negotiated a combination since my high-school locker. I find my room, fumble with the lock four times, squeeze it, twist the lever, press the sequence of numbers. Doesn't open. Down the hall, a woman glances at me and chuckles; she shows me how to press the numbered buttons. Her fingernails are bright red, her knuckles are gnarled. Her hands remind me of my sixth-grade teacher; I haven't thought about Miss Irwin in years, but I knew her hands well. I estimate this woman is in her forties, probably about my age. Inside her room, a teenage boy is playing a game on her computer while an older man cheers him on. She has set up family pictures on her dresser and put pink and green decorator pillows on her quilted bedspread. She is here for her second summer.

My car is parked illegally at the rear of the dorm. I discover a side door, just down a rocky slope from my car. A woman smiles and holds the door open as I grab a wedge-shaped rock from the slope; it reminds me of the wooden wedges I've used under classroom doors everywhere I've taught. Together, we jam the door open. Her gray hair is matted and wet, and we share sighs about the heat. I climb up and slide down the slope, taking eight trips from the car to my room, churning dirt with my feet and peeling the sticky knit tee shirt from my back. A large woodchuck waddles across my path and disappears into a metal cylinder leading to Richardson House.

The room is meant for two students: two wardrobes, two dressers, two desks and a bunk bed. I am alone. I hang up my clothes thinking that three weeks of sleeping, reading, writing, cleaning, and dressing will fit comfortably inside this tiny space. Like my dorm room in college—one small rack for ten months of stuff, the little desk that captured my thinking, reading, writing, and managed my social life in brown, cardboard, spiral notebooks. I set the computer gingerly in the center of one desk, arranging my books on the shelves above them. On one dresser I place a photo of my children and my four-cup coffee pot, on the other dresser I place my printer.

The upper bunk is closer to the windows. I decide that maybe tonight there will be some air. I make the bed with my mother-in-law's old blue-striped sheets, and hang my yellow towels on the rack. They were a wedding gift from my father, and they matched the clawfooted bathtub in our first apartment. Alone in the steamy afternoon, I inventory my belongings in this new environment. Stripped of their cluttered context, they represent relationships. Stories. My dead father, twenty-five-year-old towels, my generous mother-in-law, the family picture that's been on four different desks at four different school jobs. My professional books line up above my writing surface, distant mentors and close friends; the texts that shape my own text. A room of my stories for three weeks of collecting the stories of others.

Busy lives gather artifacts with little time to sort or reflect. I am here to study teachers in a summer writing program for three weeks, but right now I study myself. Why do I need time away from home and school? Must I feel guilty about it? But the guilt holds pleasure, nostalgia, and relish for being alone. What makes it feel uncomfortable? Why am I thinking about my sixth grade teacher, college, my early marriage and towels in my first apartment? My dead father? Should I tell anyone about this? How? I will come to see in the next few weeks that I am not the only person asking these questions.

*     *     *     *

The night is hot and lonely. I write a memo to myself. Guilt again. I worry that the printer will wake someone. A train rumbles past my room at ten o'clock, another at eleven o'clock, another at midnight. I stop worrying about the printer and wonder where the bathroom is. At 6:00 A.M., I find the bathroom and take a shower. The shower is hard and warm and comforting; I hear quick breaths next to me, and as I step out, I see a woman about my age. We share an awkward smile again; she is the one who helped me wedge open the door. She is sobbing, and we are both grabbing at our towels. We hold a towel with one elbow as we brush our teeth and speak to each other in the mirror.

She has driven six hundred miles alone, and is ready to write, she says, but is afraid. She can write about anything; her instructor wrote a letter to the class two weeks ago. Today is the anniversary of her husband's suicide, and she wants to write about it, but is afraid to share it on Friday. It's just too personal; maybe she'll just write about her dog. Her honesty surprises me; her willingness to tell me her story, her unwillingness to write about it. Talking to her in the mirror, I try to reflect what I know about helping someone choose a topic and be comfortable enough to write. She decides on the dog, tells me that this is the hardest thing she's ever done, and disappears into her room. Toweled and dry, I climb in my shorts, tie on my sneakers, and pin on the badge that identifies me as someone who's paid for the meal plan.

At breakfast, a table of teachers from last year's writing workshop re-enter their ritual talk before morning writing. They do a verbal sweep of other groups in the cafeteria. I look while they notice. A few elderhostelers fumble with the giant cereal containers, jerking the lucite doors that spill branflakes into their bowls. Pre-adolescent gymnasts eat sugar donuts and drink from the Pepsi dispensers; two bounce to their seats in their fluorescent leotards. At a table of first-time writing participants, there is dorm talk. Sleeping away from home. Trains that pass through the night. Some find them comforting, others complain about the heat and the noise in the dorm. I apologize for my printer. Already, before the first formal meeting, groups are forming and groups are watching: insiders, outsiders, first-time participants and repeaters.

We learn the complex procedure for busing our trays: glasses and coffee cups in the containers overhead, paper trash in the barrel, silverware in the watery bin, scrapings into garbage swirling water trough, dishes and trays on a revolving belt. I joke that it would be great to have a home version of this clean-up machine, including the smiling staff. Someone else jokes that it is a metaphor for drafts we'll create, consume, trash, and recycle. This cafeteria procedure will inspire several pieces of writing within the next few weeks.

As I listen, I remind myself that I am here as a researcher, to gather data about high school teachers as they shape this experience together. I don't hide it from anyone. I have signed on as a participant, but I am an observer. I will be neither teacher nor student. Although I am a "native," I can't "go native" here. And would this be a personal quest for me? Did I want to know about myself, document a transformation I was sensing? Was all my scientific scholarship clouding my own insecurity as a teacher and writer? Renato Rosaldo writes about the awkward view in anthropology that "the optimal fieldworker should dance on the edge of a paradox by simultaneously becoming one of the people and remaining an academic. The term participant-observer reflects even as it shapes the fieldworker's double persona" (1989, 180).

I do have double persona here, like the mirror conversation in the shower room this morning. I am a writing teacher who is studying writing teachers and writing about it, living in my own culture in order to study it. Writing is not just my topic; it is also my method. My personal perspective will render this story, but it cannot smother it. Elliott Eisner suggests that the researcher's

28

perspective is a crucial part of the study, part of the artful science of what he terms "educational criticism."

> In qualitative work the researcher's background can influence the way in which the situation is described, interpreted, and appraised . . . personal biography is one of the tools researchers work with; it is the major instrument through which meaning is made and interpretation expressed. It is not an interference; it is a necessity (1990, 193).

So whose voice am I here to find? Whose stories will I tell? Whose view of reality will it be? Not mine. I don't want to write what John Van Maanen calls a "confessional tale" (1988), in which I put myself in the foreground and whine with stories of self-disclosure. This time, it is not my story I'm writing and this morning, I realize it. I've brought all my personal artifacts into my room to help me record stories of other people. When I leave breakfast, I am quiet, alone with my clipboard binder and the fresh paper that will hold my fieldnotes. I prepare myself to look for stories.

# One

## Distributed Selves and a Divided Front

*Selves are not isolated nuclei of consciousness locked in the head, but are "distributed" interpersonally. Nor do Selves arise rootlessly in response only to the present; they take meaning as well from the historical circumstances that gave shape to the culture of which they are an expression.*

—Jerome Bruner, Acts of Meaning

*W*hether we are beginners or veterans of writing workshops, teachers of twenty years or three, whether we are comfortable with the New Hampshire Writing Program rituals, rules, and language, or whether we are initiates, two-hundred-thirty-three teachers meet together on Monday morning, July 9. It is a Monday not at all like our usual Mondays. For many of us, it began yesterday when we left our families and came to Durham. For all of us, today will be a day to write, talk, think about writing, and immerse ourselves in the present. As Jerome Bruner observes, we are all "distributed selves," immersed in a present loaded with possibility, but rooted in a past we know well. In the daily life of school, we can, in fact, be "isolated nuclei of consciousness," "locked in the head," as Bruner puts it. There, the opportunities to theorize with colleagues are few. School allows little time to develop thoughts, read a whole book, write a finished piece, or tell personal stories. Classroom doors are usually closed.

Here the expectations will turn toward the teacher and the risks will be high. This morning and for the next three weeks, teachers will be in constant touch with colleagues—from their own and others' disciplines and grade levels. And the expectation is that they will write, read, listen, and talk. At 6:00 A.M., after my conversation with one woman in the shower, I noticed another woman cleaning the dorm. I was glad to have nothing to clean, nothing to cook. I smiled and went back to my writing. She wiped her brow with a wet dustrag and shook her head slowly at me, "Gonna be another hot one." It is already ninety-four degrees. I joined the others for breakfast, feeling anxious with possibility myself. In the first two days, I will meet participants, observe carefully, and begin to choose the people I'll write about. The stories will unfold quickly—on the page and in an array of places.

## Presenting a Divided Front

At 8:20 A.M. we are in Hamilton Smith Hall finding our way into a bank of wooden seats. Tom Newkirk greets participants and staff as they arrive. In a side corner a few people fill out course registration forms. One Pennsylvania high school teacher chats with a colleague. They've been corresponding since two summers ago. "I changed my attitude toward teaching. I'm more conscious of what I did before. I drove eight hours to the October conference here and spent a day with my instructor Terry Moher in her classroom. There's nobody in my district who does anything with writing."

Despite the heat, in the dorms, in the cafeteria, and here in the buzzing lecture hall, there is energy to "do something with writing." Even before the formal business of classwork begins, the community is in the business of creating itself. A high school teacher from Massachusetts recalls her first day three years ago with the colleagues she joins again this summer:

> We were all talking. . . . four of us. . . . I showed up with my husband and the dog, bringing in my stuff. . . . We just jelled that very first day. I think in a half hour we were disclosing things that my friends don't know. . . . It's very strange to me that the writing I did my first year is still the writing that I had to write. The stuff was really inventive . . . I had to get it out first.

Themes begin establishing themselves in talk at this first gathering. They will nag at people for three weeks. People will write them down and read them out. Months later when I study the talk, the reading, and the writing, the "I had to get it out first" theme becomes a key. As a researcher, I will discover that in each person lurks an idea, drawn from the past, that she works, reworks, shares, reads about, and writes. Often she tells it as story on the first day. She may not really know it, but it is tied deeply to her knowledge of herself and to her notions about teaching. It shouldn't be a surprise; in theory we know from the work of Moffett, Britton, and Vygotsky that writing begins with freedom to talk and explore ideas. We know from the work of Britzman, Grossman, and Graham that recalling our autobiographies is an important step toward teacher knowledge. And the work of Grumet, Witherell and Noddings, Barone, and Carter reminds us that our personal stories and our professional stories are powerful tools with which to reexamine our teaching theories. Each of these teachers will "do something with writing" in the next three weeks, and I will join some in their lives here.

Newkirk announces that it's hard to believe this is the tenth year of the program, and he introduces the staff. It is 8:50 A.M. His schedule is exact. He wants to "honor the perspective of the teacher," he says, "the teacher's voice informs everything we do." "I hope we present a divided front," he jokes. He mentions some of the traditions of the program and some of the new additions: the barbecues have happened on Wednesdays for ten years, the brown bag lunch talks by local scholars are new this year, created for commuters who can't stay for evening talks. He invites us to an open forum Tuesday night, a chance to ask questions and explore issues together. The meeting has lasted ten minutes. He closes with a quote from Annie Dillard:

> One of the few things I know about writing is this: spend it all, shoot it, play it, lose it, all right away, every time. Do not hoard what seems good for a later place in the book, or for another book; give it, give it all, give it now. The impulse to save something good

for a better place later is the signal to spend it now. Something more will arise for later, something better. These things fill from behind, from beneath, like well water (18).

We look on the blackboard for our room assignments, and distribute ourselves into the morning writing sessions. I will spend the morning with Dorothy Spofford and Therese Deni, the teachers whose portraits are chapters 2 and 3. They are both high school teachers, both here for the first time. They move off to separate writing groups, but after the morning break, they will join a grade level group for high school teachers with instructor Terri Moher.

## Discovering Tension

At 1:30 P.M., less than a mile off campus, a group of teachers gathers outside Don Murray's home as others walk up the street. They are the already initiated; each has come to UNH for at least two other summers, some for a fourth time. There is vigorous talk. "I never understood why people went on retreats until I came here. Now I do." There is laughter. "Of *course* I'm going to live here this year. Home is only an hour away, but if I go, my husband will want sex, my kids will want food, and I'll just want to write." There are professional accolades. One teacher has just heard that *English Journal* is publishing an article she wrote three years ago here, in her first summer writing program.

A few parked cars edge the front lawn and I join several women who are admiring the garden by the mailbox. Rows of tiger lilies border two pear trees beginning to bear clusters of fruit, pink and white carnations bud by the roses next to the driveway. Closer to the house, draped in cheesecloth, there are strawberry patches and two giant bushes jammed with green clusters of blueberries. The growth around his house is well trimmed and functional. It will all be used; for decoration and for consumption. Both Don and his wife Minnie Mae are generous with the fruits of their work. This class of fifteen veterans of the summer program meets at their home.

We walk through the garage door, into Minnie Mae's office, a ceiling-to-floor mass of books, seed catalogues, and paperwork. We gather on the screen porch. A detailed map of Durham hangs next to the sliding glass door, a chunk of blue glass and a set of metal windchimes dangle from the ceiling. "If you get a strange migraine, Barry," Don jokes to the balding man who sits under the windchimes, "just reach up and take it off." We sit on black wrought iron chairs covered in yellow Naugahyde. A long, low, black-painted table offers up a giant lobster claw, a souvenir from the restaurant where one of his daughters waitressed. Minnie Mae is in the kitchen baking a cake we'll have with iced tea during our break.

Don hands out strips of white paper, copies of his motto: nulla dies sine linea, ("never a day without a line"). "The more insecure you are as a teacher, the more handouts you have," he laughs, "and I am the handout king." A week ago he mailed the syllabus and the first assignment to each member of the class, and today he expects them to be ready with drafts and commentaries, the packet of assigned selected readings, and his book *Shoptalk*. He hands out an eight-page collection of his "Daybook Notes" written the previous week. It begins:

> I have found writing commentaries helpful to me as a writer, as a student of the writing process, as a teacher, and I have found them helpful to my students. . . . When students and the instructor share their commentaries they become colleagues and the commentaries become the text of the course. They also often become the agenda for the conference. . . . In the spirit of colleagueship, here are my commentaries for the past week. . . .

Everyone has brought the draft of a written piece and fifteen copies of a commentary about writing it. They share drafts-in-progress with a small group, but they exchange photocopied commentaries that detail and document their daily writing. Murray's plan for "Explorations in Genre" is to devote each week to reading and writing in a specific genre:

nonfiction, fiction, and poetry. He hopes that participants will try using the same topic in each genre, but he will not require it. He begins with a personal story: "I'm sixty-five and I just had a barium swallow. I'm not sick, but I got a poem out of it, and I might get a column out of it, too . . ."

"Why do we write about the same topic in three different genres?" one person asks. Murray answers, "Because it's interesting to the instructor." His laughter booms. "Sometimes these connections are so vague. I would urge all my students to follow their writing first, then my syllabus. Think of the course as a writing course, with an overlay of the genre." Members read the commentaries they've prepared, and Murray talks about his writing and his teaching. In his retirement, he works in all the genres the class will explore. This year, he has revised two textbooks and written another. He writes a weekly nonfiction column for the *Boston Globe*, aimed at retirees, called "Over Sixty." He is currently at work on a novel, actively involved in a poetry writing group, and he continues to lecture and teach regularly.

In the space of ten minutes, he pitches out phrases: "What I really got from teaching is learning from my students". . . . "It is important to lower your standards so you can start writing" . . . "Please don't take me too seriously". . . . "You should be thinking about publication," he continues. "We need to educate the public about education". . . . "We want a fair piece, but not a balanced piece. Take a strong point of view, say one thing, develop it. That point may not be discovered until you draft or re-draft."

But within the first hour, everyone is writing. It is a period of quiet, in his words, to "let the mind reveal to itself what's in it." "Shut up and listen to yourself," he jokes. Around the screen porch, we are fifteen notebooks: loose leaf, spiral, yellow legal pads, small note pads on bare knees. Fifteen pencils and pens, fifteen colors of variously aging legs. We write lists. We search for a fragment that reveals tension, look for something that surprises us. Unlike the other classes, this one meets in the afternoon. Murray's assumptions are clear; these writers will come to the first class with commentaries written, they will write during the morning hours and come here to respond, revise, and comment on the process. They will read assigned readings each night, as well as one anothers' writing. None of the teachers is new to these assumptions; none is new to this program.

Don poises his spiral notebook on his lap desk. It holds fragments of thinking, observations he records during the day. It is his seventy-third daybook, he tells the group, always the kind with the stiff green cardboard cover. He rests his feet on a stool, bites his finger as he "looks for a line" in the writing. "Don't go to a sentence or a thesis statement. It's too long, too conclusive. That should come at the end of the writing. *Look for the line* that reflects the tension. A fragment." Don reads the fragment list from his daybook first: "a barium swallow, spooky room, half-light, two machines, waiting for x-ray, staring into our history." A week later, the details will appear in Murray's *Globe* column and three weeks later other fragments from the list will appear in a poem.

There is a set of new rituals for this class in Murray's home layered over the rituals of reading and writing this class shares from previous years. There will be a formal time at the beginning of class to share the day's commentaries. Participants will assist one another's revisions in response groups. When a writer wants to have a conference with Murray, it is her responsibility to ask for it. He will neither initiate nor assign it. When the small groups meet, Don moves downstairs to his office to write.

These people have learned the habits of writing and responding that this program expects; they share the language and accept the rules. The group is comfortable with the rituals, but not with the writing itself. Anne Valdez asks for a conference. She is the teacher whose writing will appear in *English Journal*. It is her third summer at UNH. She wants to talk about a kernel of an idea she has for her first piece, a nonfiction essay. Don and Anne confer:

Anne: What keeps presenting itself to me is something that would be boring. About my superintendent.

Don: If it's intruding that much, there's probably something that deserves attention. Take a different point of
view. Or person, or historic.

Anne: Do you write about things you don't want to write
about?

Don: I complained about revising a book on revision.

Anne: I don't know that I want to work with conflict.
There's nothing aggravating me.

Don: There needs to be tension: a beautiful day needs to
see a day that's not.

Tension not only lurks in the lines people write; there is
tension in the class itself. Murray, the writer, is frustrated with
teaching and Anne, the teacher, is frustrated with writing. But
he shares it in his commentary the next day: "Relearned the
price of teaching: preparation comes first. Didn't get to the
writing because I was writing my presentation called "How to
Get the Writing Done." Anne's commentary expresses her
tension:

> This is my third summer doing this. I've come to expect that a
> subject will feel right—that I'll know it when it pops into my
> mind. But now I'm dry—and I know why. I haven't written any-
> thing in so long, there's no source to draw from. . . . The topic is
> a neighborhood issue, something I will have trouble seeing from
> the other side. That will be the problem to solve. . . . It bogs
> down the piece to have to keep explaining what the history of it
> is. . . . I need to work on keeping the reader there without telling
> the whole thing over again.

Anne is an accomplished writer; one of her pieces will be
published this fall for a large readership of English teachers.
In this class, she understands the power of a writing community to drive her writing and self-discipline, but she is still not
comfortable. She writes:

> Writing can be such a high for me, I'm surprised I resist it so. Do
> I think it'll be better for the waiting? . . . In fact, just writing this
> has helped me get into writing. I needed to wade in a bit, feel the
> water around my feet, know that I won't drown this time either.

Besides, you'll all make such helpful life guards. . . . Writing works for me when I hear the voices speaking, my own and others. . . . I try to write with dialogue to help the reader hear the voices. Right now, I am sick of my voice.

Although she has attended three other summers, Anne is facing this summer with a mix of desire and dread; she feels the tension between being a teacher and being a writer. This is a group of seasoned, summer, teacher-writers, and Don Murray is a seasoned professor. Anne tells me that her conference with Murray has frustrated her. Her expectations were high; she was eager to work with Murray, but she realizes, as her students should, that she really ought to be working with herself. But she is "sick of her own voice." Despite his collegiality, his handouts, and his own back porch, Murray cannot overcome his stance as an "elder" in the New Hampshire Summer Writing Program community; his only option is to joke about it.

For Anne, despite the congenial sessions, this is the most difficult distance to bridge. She has heard him speak and she reads his publications regularly. Her familiarity with his work makes her more comfortable with the rituals of the writing culture, but it makes her less comfortable sharing writing at his feet, even though his feet are sockless, sneakered, and resting on a naugahyde footstool. Her goal this summer, she tells me, will be to become more independent as a writer, to be less involved in pleasing her teacher—exactly what she knows her students ought to be learning. Murray has designed his seminar to support that; it is clear on his syllabus, in his arrangement of time, and in his words to the group.

## *Administrivia: One Teacher's Journal*

It is still Monday, at 8:00 P.M., still the first night of the program. Alison Clark sips a glass of wine at her kitchen table at home. She is a commuter to the program, a teacher-administrator at a private school, and she checks in at her office every day on her way home. She wants to spend most of the three weeks away from her office so she can drive the extra two hours, keep her house in order, and concentrate on the reading and writing she'll do. She adjusts books and papers piled on the table. One of her cats peeks over the oval pine edge, and she shoos him away. She writes in her journal:

> My professional life is busy. It involves writing comments, writing letters, writing reports, writing to students on papers, writing memos, writing to faculty, writing to the board. I hope my writing is colorful, emotional—precise, succinct, effective, human, sympathetically understanding. I don't write with my students. I want to be told that's okay, but I suspect it isn't. . . . I'm looking forward with some fear to doing more of what I secretly consider to be "creative" writing: stories, descriptions, poetry, personal narratives with a point. I don't know whether I have an eye or an ear for imagery, for detail. I know lots of descriptive words for students' end-terms, for describing kids to colleges. I'd love to know how the colleges view my recommendations. The day to day life I lead is jumping around from moment to moment, task to task, assignment to assignment.

Alison does her required writing jobs for school mechanically and with confidence. She writes memos, end-term reports, college application letters. She "jumps around," as she says, because she's a teacher-administrator. Although she knows her writing tasks for school demand creative competence, she doesn't see them as "creative." Her journal entry illustrates what Michael Apple calls "intensification" in education. When teachers meet all the demands of the curriculum and the community, the quality of their work dwindles into "skill diversification," and they, like overworked laborers, become "deskilled." Apple believes deskilling alienates teachers from their perception of themselves as professionals (1986).

Although Alison works in a private school, has fewer students than most teachers, and uses words like *end-terms* instead of *report cards* and *comments* instead of *grades*, her role as a teacher-administrator fragments her and her skills. There is little time left for her own reading and writing, the acts she secretly sees as creative. She feels that she works "moment to moment, task to task," maintaining a silent one-way partnership in her students' college searches, yielding to genres of memos and letters. Although she writes frequently, she sees herself as "teaching writing without writing." She continues in her journal:

> I hope the reflection time here will also manifest itself in my writing. Can I teach writing without writing? I'm here to see if what I did last year in teaching the writing process was really teaching the writing process. I don't enjoy writing. I don't have a passion for writing. I have a passion for teaching. When my writing flows quickly and easily, I can't even read it myself. Normally, when I've had to write a paper or an essay, I've had to "burfle"—to complain to who's ever around, to drink a drink or eat food, to talk on the telephone. . . . So in this writing process, sitting thinking about doing this homework, I am angry at writing, at all the gurus who say one must write in order to teach writing.
>
> I've done something called teaching composition successfully for fifteen years, and now you're telling me I need to do more. What's been successful? I have to ask myself. What makes a good writing course? Well, for whom? Me or the kids? My confusion may lie in my own perception, my definition of a writer. . . . I recognize my own reluctance to begin. This dichotomy, this separation between self and self-object is easier for me because it's objective. So am I writing in a journal right now? Am I writing a "piece?" Am I beginning something? What the hell am I doing?"

As Alison's journal points out, her school's prescriptions and expectations can define "teaching" as moving students successfully through a system; she becomes their conduit from the private high school to the college. Accepting this definition, she devalues herself as a reader and writer. The voice in Alison's memos blends into the school's background noise; there is no time left to speak of quality in either the products or the processes of learning (Apple, 43). To survive in her job, she must yield to the system's control. Both teachers and students risk becoming mute on the page and in the classroom. Maxine Greene reminds us that schools erect subtle barriers:

> . . . in schools, like other institutions, there are memos, not actual barriers to reflective practice. There are conference and commission reports, not barbed wire fences in the way. There are assured, helpful, bureaucratic faces, not glowering antagonists to growth and freedom and an enlarged sense of being in the world. The 'weight' is only dimly felt . . . (1988, 15).

Alison's journal suggests that it is easy for a teacher in mid-career to accept our culture's idea that the teacher is a "knowledge dispenser," and feels inadequate as such. Alison loves her profession, but she often loses patience with her job. A few days after she writes this entry in her journal, her thoughts turn into the first poem she's written since her college experience, fifteen years ago. In it she gives voice to some of the conflicts she feels about her job:

*administrivia*

phone rings
head requests
student needs
teacher asks
parent wants
colleague suggests
secretary buzzes

I stop—paralyzed.

How to do it all?

Just do it.
Just say no.

white notes, a blur of snow
blue stickies, shingled up the wall
pink phone slips, an open screaming mouth—

the dizzying untrivial demands

of meeting needs and treating egos,

paced by others,
embraced by me.
I wouldn't have it any other way.

Like this poem, the snippets of thought that nag at Alison tonight will show up again as she writes her way through the program. At school, Alison must be an "expert" in the face of a relentlessly demanding public. At school, she receives little response to the writing she does and has no time for reflection. Like the others, Alison worries about writing tonight. She has frustrations she'd like to handle in her writing, just as she encourages her students to do. At her kitchen table, with some time and a sip of wine, her first night's journal explores those frustrations:

> Whence the anger? I rail against I know not what or whom. Getting started . . . I have lots of ditties for my students to get started, but I've no idea where to start. Oh damn, it's because I want to know where I'm going before I start. Will I end up with a piece about my mother? my aunt? my grandmother? my sister? The women in my family? Talkative, strong women with a purpose, a closed ear . . . do we all have a closed ear? I want clearer assignments . . . my students and I are now in the same boat—but they have oars and I have none? No, we all have oars, but I'm used to functioning as their rudder? No, I'm jumping out of this metaphor. It's leaking. A conscious recognition of a nice turn of phrase . . . Does this mean I need to have a purpose before I set to write? Can my purpose simply be to "fill two pages?" I'm uncomfortable with that notion, because I question its usefulness. Yet I'd tell a student it's fine, and I'd go back to find in the writing something to start with. So I have two things: the knowledge that I have direction or think I do, and my leaky metaphor. And yes, I feel better.

It is no accident, Apple observes, that "deskilling" is gender-related because teachers are predominantly female and administrators predominantly male. No wonder Alison's metaphor is leaky; she is in the same boat as her students, and someone else is rocking it. In her first journal entry, she begins to explore her history as a teacher and as a woman. It is no accident that during the first week, Alison will decide to write about the strong women in her family. And this theme will continue for her through the final week when she collaborates with three women to write an essay using cheerleading as a metaphor for collaboration. That writing is the subject of an Intertext in this book.

## Thoughts and Themes

As the first two days unfold, personal stories dazzle with complexity. The program is as intense as the heat. One day's writing can magnify years' worth of personal hidden themes, as Anne finds in Murray's class and Alison finds at her kitchen table. The themes surface on the first day, and by the second day everyone has begun a piece of writing, often the "I had to get it out first" type, as Anne put it. The personal writing isolates, but it is cushioned as teachers learn the collective themes under which the program's culture operates and reshape those themes for their own summer experience. By the second day, teachers' journals, commentaries, and conversations begin to highlight the beliefs they begin to share:

1. *Writing happens best in a community of writing peers.* We are all colleagues, we are all teachers of reading and writing. The boundaries here at New Hampshire blur between teacher and learner. We learn because we have set time for writing and reading.

> The laundry is laundered. The ironing is hidden. The garden is hoed and mulched. The fridge is full. Writing is not tidy. It clutters things up. . . . Where did I leave that envelope with ideas written in brown crayon? . . . Do you see my folder in the downstairs bathroom? How can I finish this draft with spaghetti sauce all over it? . . . After a year of forced writing I am anxious to write for myself again. . . . Now I worry that I have nothing of my own to say. That's what this is for. To loosen up again. And I'd better loosen up or the kids will pay in the fall.

2. *Observation and information takes time to craft into writing.* The purpose of writing and reading is to share ideas, observation, and information. And to do that, we must constantly write and read. In literate communities, we learn from our students and our students learn from us.

> Writing about writing? . . . Or how I can write about my writing when I haven't written much lately? Cold reality. . . . During the school year I write sporadically with my students. Scribbled drafts, journals, bits and pieces, but then nothing is ever brought to completion. . . . Summers at UNH are a brief respite from the "not writing" syndrome. . . . This is summer number four and I fear my last possible attempt to overcome my malaise. Discipline, where are you?

3. *Reflection makes learning and leads to theory-building.* There are important ways to build reflection, that metacognitive step in all literacy: response groups, daybooks, journals, portfolio collections, and writer's commentaries.

> On one level I know I have plenty to say, but on another level, a deeper one, I don't know how to say it. Maybe I should find a pen that moves more slowly? For some people, not having words makes it hard. Having dyslexia makes it hard. Having a left-handed desk makes writing much easier. It's amazing. Fear, lack of confidence. Lack of direction. Physical environment. Forced time. Time of day.

4. *Writing isn't easy.* For everyone, writing is disciplined work. An important part of the time allotted in a formal class ought to be spent writing, reading, examining, and documenting the strategies and details of doing it.

> My writing process includes demons, stoppers. For example, meet the No family: no time, no audience, no discipline, no energy, no coffee. The Nos do not live alone. There are others. I have also tangled with the Critical Censor who chants: "You have nothing to say and who are you kidding anyway and you call that a poem?" After I had greeted and named these process creatures I hoped I had slayed them and they'd move it along. Well . . . not yet. I am satisfied with peaceful co-

existence, but they constantly lurk in the corner of my confidence. To my demons I say, I'll write badly even when I have no time, and little energy but never without morning coffee.

5. *Stories are powerful teachers.* The stories of our own histories, the stories we hold from our own cultures are stories worth telling others. With personal choice of genre and subject, we can write what we know, learn more about it, and let it link us to further investigation.

> I am a storyteller. I started telling stories when I was three years old and invented a purple grandmother. . . . I am a reader. I was read to and started reading when I was very young. . . . [At fifty] I am getting ready to become a writer. I collect pocketfolders full of partially written drafts. . . . I am beginning to look at how authors develop a piece of writing. . . . I still spend more time talking about my writing than writing. I read books about the craft of writing but I hate to put myself on the line.

There is a shared dilemma about how to be a writer and teach writing at the same time, about how reading fits into writing, and how students fit into it all. These teachers' writings from the first two days highlight the topics that they will ask and answer, discuss and revise, accept and reject for three weeks. But this time, they will not be alone. The program itself will provide a place for professional discussion on the second night. After dinner, participants gather for the open forum, an event that is new to the program this year. I walk through the woods with Joyce Choate, the subject of Chapter 4.

## *The Open Forum: A Consciousness of Possibilities*

At 7:30 P.M. on Tuesday, the second night, we pour into Murkland Hall's Richards Auditorium. It is an old lecture hall with walls painted the color of eggshells. Banked seats face a scuffed wooden stage, and a dusty black curtain is the focal point of the room. The long windows are gridded with old glass, and a few layers of colored paint show through the chips in the wood moldings. The hall holds about three hundred people, but its age and shape suggests the intimacy of a New England town meeting. And like a New England town meeting, this room offers a site for the tough, passionate, grassroots business of community decision making for teachers. In this room over many years at the University of New Hampshire, audiences have responded to speakers, speakers to audiences, students and teachers to one another. Much writing about thinking and thinking about writing has been begun, shared, argued, and fleshed out in this room.

Tonight I sit sweltering among colleagues. We don't look like the conventions of teachers who fill this room in October and April. There are no suits, no ties, no stockings no high heels; not even briefcases or totebags full of students' papers. We wear shorts, sundresses, tank tops; we are chewing gum. The auditorium is heavy and hot. We use spiral notebooks to fan ourselves and we peel our bare legs from the seats.

The summer staff members sit on the edge of the stage, legs dangling. Tom Newkirk begins, standing on the floor. Above him on the stage, the wooden podium is empty. One shirttail hangs over his jeans, and he smiles. Tom jibes each staff member as he tailors an introduction. The staff has been together for ten summers; a few began as participants, all are teachers. "It is here we honor the teacher," he says. Teaching, he adds, is "putting our ideas and processes into procedures; we need to be alert, attentive, and wise on our feet." There is no pressure here tonight to make decisions; we can ask questions and play with answers. At Tom's suggestion, we take a few minutes to write a question we want answered. We think and write. The room is silent.

As in a town meeting or a faculty lounge, this room becomes a place to consider possibilities. I recall the philosophical work of Maxine Greene as I look around the room. No one achieves freedom without a forum in which to speak, she claims. A teacher is marginalized in the system of the schools; she must muffle her voice most of the time. The freedom to grow comes only when there is a "consciousness of possibility" (1988, 16). Tonight there are spaces and possibilities. Here teachers can play a little and speak a lot. For two days, everyone has been writing, thinking, reading, and reconsidering. In classes, outside of classes, and on paper, a consciousness of our power as teachers and our voices as writers begins to develop.

The writing stops and the questions begin. First, the dilemma of evaluating writing and using standardized tests. "I am trying to find a way to deal with standardized tests. I need help" comes a plea from the middle of the room. Someone yells: "Standardized tests should be burned." There is roaring laughter.

"Suppose they make 'em faster than you can burn 'em?" Newkirk asks. The room moves. Dozens of hands shoot up. For the next five minutes, we take a national tour of writing assessment practices:

"We give 'em every year for a week at grades four and eight. . . . My class doesn't dread them as much as I do. I'm the one who resents them."

"It's my job to choose a measuring device for pre- and posttesting. How do we measure writing?"

"So you're asking for us to recommend one? Can't do it; we don't know your school."

"Michigan and Illinois have been working hard."

"The California Writing Assessment has eight 'domains.' Kids have to know the domains in grades three, six, eight, and twelve, and they are given a "prompt" in each one and then they have to write an essay. It is scored automatically."

Brows furrow, glances speak, and eyes roll across the room. Teachers want their students to read and write freely, yet they know the public pressure to measure and define literacy achievement with standardization. Around the country, there are assessment commonalities and assessment differences. Teachers read the national reports, hear the politicians, and spend their time in the classrooms. The "they" and the "we" in those statements point to the stance teachers take between the communities they serve and the students they teach. It points, also, to a group identity that is beginning to develop in this room.

Newkirk stops the sharing and summarizes. There are clearly two issues, he says: the state's need to require an assessment, and the school administration's need to be accountable. Assessments won't go away. They are a bother to those who teach writing because the results are too often interpreted as markers of students' progress. For people who practice formative evaluation, knowing a student in the process of growth, the summative evaluation suggested by American standardized testing practices is a dilemma, he concludes. Assessment and evaluation hold complexity and politics.

The talk of tests highlights the teacher's irony; she is perched between a public's institution and each of her students as a single, literate, growing person. And this meeting highlights that dilemma. Some people are attending this program supported by school money, and their schools expect them to return with ideas. It is the second night and most people are not collecting ideas; they are just beginning to take time to write for themselves. But this meeting raises the questions they brought here from school. Can we incorporate the "process approach" system-wide? What do we mean by the "process approach?" What happens when a system "mandates" an instructional approach? How do we "get people" to "do it?" The room moves into action. Themes emerge and colleagues talk:

*Be conscious of each teacher's work and highlight those who are working with writing:*
"Go slowly, build up the few people who are already doing things. Show what people are doing."
"Give out a few articles."
"The computer is a gentle way of promoting writing."
"We've got about 40 percent of our teachers working with writing."
"Want to trade jobs with me? Your percentage is quite high."

*Publicize the products and practices of teacher and student writing:*
"I let people know that there are a lot of things going on."
"Daily, weekly newsletters from principals to staff."
"Send out a bibliography. To staff members. To parents. Include kids' writing."

"Share writing at faculty meetings, parent meetings."

"I know one teacher who spends Saturday mornings in her classrooms for kids and parents to come with their writing."

*Provide time for teachers to write and teach together:*

"We were just teachers in our districts. We were released so that we could go around and work in other peoples' classrooms with them. It helped to work with our colleagues."

"We had developed a morale problem in our school. At one inservice day, we worked out our problem by writing."

"One year, our inservice budget paid us to have afternoon writing groups. We had no outside consultants or workshops that year. We'll do it again; those who did it really got a lot out of it."

"During faculty meetings, share a piece of writing by a student. Everybody's going to say, 'He did that?' or 'I saw her conferencing with you.' It's a slight subtle message that you're being supported."

Muffled responses wave through the auditorium. These are not so "subtle" messages; they are ways to nudge the edges of the system, to encourage without forcing everyone to change. There is a consciousness of possibility here as teachers examine their own practice. Tonight they speak in a forum of people who share their language. They raise shared questions and consider them without giving answers. There is no pressure to produce a report or a curriculum.

But as the meeting continues, a tacit assumption is forming that there is one way to teach, and that is the "process" way. I squirm in my seat, feeling the forum is shifting into a religious-sounding testimonial session. One person cites a principal she knows who hires with an eye to balance "process-oriented" staff with traditional teachers: "You can't force people to teach writing this way." I squirm more as a longtime independent writing teacher when I remember phrases linked to the people associated with UNH: "the Atwell model," "The seven-step Graves," and "the Murray method." With the ritualized behaviors and some of the "elders" teaching, there is a danger of replacing old orthodoxies with new ones, and the staff knows it well. Tom Newkirk speaks quickly. He grabs the microphone: "I think it's really easy to fall into *a conversion syndrome*." He glances behind him at his staff sitting on the edges of the stage. They comment:

> "A teacher has a right to reject this. . . . The real key to being a good teacher is the relationship with the students."
>
> "Parent education is good. In New York, for instance, fifth grade parents are demanding that their teachers go to Columbia to learn writing."

Newkirk's term "conversion syndrome" touches a sensitive spot. In Graves' words, "the enemy is orthodoxy." Orthodoxies are substitutes for thinking, he wrote in 1983, and issued his own list of nine "orthodoxies" of "the Writing Process Movement." He warned that there are no shortcuts, that we cannot "cloud the issues with jargon in place of simple, direct prose about actual children" (1984, 185). Tonight, Tom both redirects the discussion and gets to the heart of it: "Can we talk about the student?" he asks. "And how do we examine ourselves as writers? Writing takes so much work."

> "Writing and reading are just tools to make them honor their own brains."
>
> "Should students have diverse writing experiences?"

Tom's staff members look at one another and smile. It takes a minute to decide who will speak first. Ellen Blackburn-Karelitz answers: "First graders feel that they can write. I like to help them diversify, and a lot of little pieces of real writing accumulates. They write notes and observations. *That's a genre.*"

Jack Wilde, a fifth grade teacher, is finishing a book about diversity in writing. He answers. "All of us are committed to single-draft writing occasions as periods of reflection, but the biggest mistake is to think words are the only way to communicate. . . . I have a problem with the notion that students should always choose what they do. I'm going to make them write it, sometimes," says Jack. I wonder how many people share his assumptions and recognize his language: that an "occasion" can just be a ten-minute period of writing to "reflect" about an idea—maybe in science or math or social studies—that "ways to communicate" can be through art, music, mathematical and graphic notation, that students who "always choose what they do" won't know how to follow assignments. Embedded in Jack's short answer are assumptions that people will call into question often during the next three weeks.

> "At the beginning of the year, they start out with one sentence and no focus in their writing."

> "I focus on focus first, then go to content. By October, it might be more."

> "I let a lot of things go by in kids' writing, but I can't stand letting certain things happen: should I let my standards be lower? What should I do?"

> "If I have to slice it up, then that piece is history; it's not theirs anymore. . . . I bring in good pieces of fiction: why did this work?"

> "The answers come down to knowing the students well—more and more I'm working with them individually."

Newkirk summarizes: "Sometimes I wonder if our models of success show only the classroom *working*. When it's written in a book, it looks so successful, there seem to be breakthroughs on an hourly basis. Our image of success is unrealistic."

Jane Kearns, staff member, smiles and retorts. "Yeah, *we* don't have those perfect kids and perfect classrooms from the Heinemann books in *my* school system." Laughter, relief. The conversation shifts to reading. "What about remedial readers?" someone asks. An active rumble runs through the auditorium.

One participant asks the staff: "If each of you were stuck on a desert island with the kids you teach, what one book would you take? Someone yells *Lord of the Flies*. More laughter. What follows is an interesting, uncategorizable book list, revealing diverse private and professional reading:

any guide to Ireland
*East of Eden*
*Bridge to Terabithia*
*Charlotte's Web*
*Huckleberry Finn*
anything by Ezra Jack Keats
*One Flew Over the Cuckoo's Nest*
"I'd rather have them take pencils and paper and write their own."

No canon appears here. No curriculum. Only teachers' passions reflecting their personalities. Someone calls out "But what about *teaching* reading?" What everyone has in common is the classroom.

"I have response groups for reading, just like in writing."

"I had high school juniors sit together, grouped by genre. The main characters had to meet; some came up with junk, but they solved problems in the thinking of other centuries and the understanding of genre differences."

"How about children's literature with junior and senior high schoolers. Kids can read them quickly and enjoy them."

## Turning Up the Rocks

With the perspectives and experiences of the people in this room, we hear that the "orthodoxies" are not "orthodoxies" at all. We reaffirm that "there is no one right way to teach writing." New England gardeners know that when the soil freezes each year, it pushes rocks up from below. When the ground thaws, the soil shifts, and a new crop of rocks surfaces with the spring. Tonight, like cycles of freezing and thawing, like the rocks that emerge annually, many of the foundational assumptions of the writing program are unearthed, turned over, and reexamined. In Newkirk's words, tonight's purpose was to "honor the teacher," to "think about putting ideas and processes into procedures," to be "wise on our feet." We have picked at the dilemmas of "the process approach" turned over the paradoxes as our intuitions meet our institutions. Teachers want to offer students time and choice for writing and reading, but we know curriculum mandates. We want to use writing as a tool for thinking in all disciplines, but we are each slotted into school subject categories. We recognize that our personal reading choices do not draw from school-recommended book lists, but we work in an educational system that imposes book selections. Newkirk ends the evening, "We must recognize that genuine change takes time. Pseudochange is easy. It took ten years to get us to this point. Remember that the turtle always wins. There's no version of that story where the rabbit wins. The turtle always wins."

The open forum allows some dilemmas to emerge and us to see them. Like the New Englanders who work the soil, we will continue to remove the rocks and they will continue to come up; the soil shifts slowly. Each person tonight examines a self among possible selves: as adult, as teacher, as writer, as reader. In this place we reconsider, reaffirm. Each person attempts to place herself as an insider; she works her own experience into the language and belief system that is taking shape. To some, it appears cultish, "conversion-like." Tonight marks the beginning of, in anthropologist Victor Turner's term, "a flash of communitas" (1982, 45). People come together, form a set of experiences, share rituals, memories, and knowledge to reexamine and reconstruct an existing social structure—their roles in school and their roles on the page. Like a church retreat or a therapeutic vacation, it is a flash that is temporary in time and space, intensive in reflection and self-examination.

And it provokes us to think in possibilities. In the long tradition of progressive education, learning is a constant, slow movement, enriched by experience and reflection. When a teacher searches for her own freedom, it will enable her students. Maxine Greene writes, "A teacher in search of his/her own freedom may be the only kind of teacher who can arouse young persons to go in search of their own . . . children who have been provoked to reach beyond themselves, to wonder, to imagine, to pose their own questions are the ones most likely to learn to learn" (1988, 14).

It is two days into the program, and Tom Newkirk's progressivist stance holds tonight's open exchange. Genuine change takes time, he said, and the turtle always wins. Progressive thinking moves teachers toward "a new conception of literacy, a different way of looking at their world and their work," observes Patrick Shannon, "It can help them to celebrate teachers' often courageous movement away from the scientific management mainstream and from the cultural imperialism of the renewed humanist approaches" (1990, 179). The forum tonight invited us *not* to settle on answers. It marked the beginning of the time here, not the end. It defined dilemmas and raised common interests. But it affirmed, too, that each teacher is separately one person, a reader and a writer with her own quirky tastes and her own topics to work with.

Outside, the lawn glows green and misty under the university lights; the night is dark and humid. Sandals click, sneakers squeak, and people continue conversations as they pour out of Murkland Hall and disperse to their cars and dorm rooms. In the parking lot, a woman says that she had left her computer keyboard at home in Connecticut. Her husband drove it three hundred miles, had a cup of coffee with her, and returned home. A man from New York complains that he has come to get teaching ideas, that so far he has none, and he'll leave if he doesn't have "devices" for his notebook soon.

I walk down the moist wooden steps to the dorm, and I see silhouettes of people swapping books. Six teachers pass papers to one another in the lobby of Sackett around an open box of donuts. Five teachers in pajamas—from Vancouver, Massachusetts, New York, and Missouri—consider the values of hyphens, dashes, and semicolons while they hold their toothbrushes and towels. Standing in a doorway, a second grade teacher wearing a tie-dyed tee shirt recalls a college writing experience with her freshman English professor: "He told us we were stupid. He said 'green.' We wrote 'green.' That was the end for me. I haven't written since."

At forty-five, that teacher is writing tonight. It is Tuesday, the second night of the program. There are sixteen nights left. This evening's forum has opened possibilities and pushed barriers aside. It has honored multiple solutions to our dilemmas. Despite what may appear as a single "process approach" to teaching, there are as many approaches as there are people writing and reading. There are stories, there are new rituals shaping themselves, we are sharing in the artifacts of a culture developing, and there is common language growing to talk about it. Books and papers shift from room to room. Computer keys click. Printers chunk into the night. Here, there will be writing, and the writing will be read.

# Caring Away From Home: Poetic Sanctuary

I cross the street in a cool, early morning drizzle, past Kingsbury Hall, the engineering building, past the Paul Creative Arts Center, on to a damp footbridge over a summer stream. The rocks are darker than usual and I delight in the drizzle on my nose and back. Today the pine needle beds make the campus smell pungent, like a forested New England resort.

Ahead of me, a young woman twirls patterns with a red checked umbrella. Her backpack sags with books. It is covered with plastic buttons. I quicken my step to catch a peek. There are two photobuttons of a little boy and girl, and a photo button of a man playing with them: her husband, their father, I imagine. Another button encases a child's crayon writing: "This is a mom," and one shows a crest of a high school in Ohio. She walks briskly in her sneakers, thick socks rolled over them, her green jumper flopping in the drizzle. She moves toward the library, and I am still behind her, inventing my version of her story. She's away from home, perhaps, for the first time since she's had her children, and she teaches high school. The buttons encase snapshots of pieces of her life, artifacts of identification. They dot the bag that sags with her current efforts. Is she lonely or refreshed or both? Is she writing about her children or her husband or her students? I wonder.

She is still twirling her umbrella when we top the hill. A sleek, older woman greets her, folding her arm around the young woman's shoulder, squeezing under her umbrella. The older woman is casually elegant in her pink and gray sweatsuit, pink quartz earrings

57

swinging under her grey hair. "Hi honey, were you cold last night? Did you sleep without a blanket?" The blankets were locked in a building and no one had yet found the key. I had noticed stacks by the window next to the locked computer room, unavailable to those who had traveled a distance. "We'll be sure to get you a blanket tonight," she says, and together they walk into their morning. Just like a mother, I think, or a teacher. Teachers and mothers handle daily glitches: locked closets, locked machines, broken machines, broken spirits, missed paperwork, unavailable materials, injuries, sickness. They merely notice and act—detail after detail.

Away from home, this young teacher wears her story on her bookbag, and in the thin morning mist, an older teacher reads it. She is the "one-caring" for "the cared-for," as Nel Noddings suggests, a female way of relating. Noddings describes the "ethics of being cared for" as reciprocity; an attitude natural to both parent-child and teacher-student relationships, "mutual inclusion," a "climate of receptivity." Accepting "the gift of responsiveness" is an act characteristic of both mothering and teaching (1986).

But there is a paradox in this situation. This young teacher-mother is away from home. In another way, though, she is closer to home than her home usually allows. Both the older teacher and the writing program itself offer her a temporary sanctuary, placing her in "cared-for" role so that she can have the peace to reflect on her role as the one-caring at home and in school. "The teacher as "one-caring," observes Noddings, "needs to see from both her own perspective and that of the student in order to teach—in order to meet the needs of the student." Just as caring is dependent on being cared for, teaching is dependent on learning (67). Over time, this young teacher explores the double-bind of her double role. Two weeks after this casual encounter, the young teacher/mother with the buttons on her bookbag submits her poem to the final New Hampshire Writing Program (NHWP) publication:

### Sanctuary

*Hunched under the fluorescent glare*
*I slump*
*Present day Quasimodo*

*A freak of nature born of stress and fatigue.*
*Lips stretched white over clenched teeth,*
*Deep ridged brow over spastic lashes,*
*Ears ringing, I hobble to his room to find my sanctuary.*

The moon, half hidden by clouds, covers his walls with
    shadow and light.
There on his sheets he lies, arms stretched outward, opened
    to the breeze.
I lie beside him.
He unconsciously folds toward me,
    his small hand just touching my arm.
I study his face
    the creamy smoothness of his lids and brow
    the stillness of his lashes
    the wafer of air between his lips.
If I am patient, he will move and fold himself toward the
    moon patterned wall.

And I, his disciple
    can follow.
I conform to his body,
My jutting neck realigns to fit
    his downy head under my chin.
My spine slowly straightens as I press my chest against his
    back.
Together we form a C
    as
    our legs curve in unison.
My knees serve as the pedestal for his tiny feet.
I listen. I follow.
He breathes.
I breathe.
My heart slows to his steady beat.
I lie in sync
with his slow
    waltz
    time.

# Two

## Therese Deni:
## Finding Authority on the Inside

*The universal and the unique are entwined aspects of existence.
In the course of growth, children are powerfully influenced by
the living patterns of their family and community while also
being subject to a common, species-specific trajectory of development. . . . the contradictory pulls of necessity and choice.*

—Vera John-Steiner, *Notebooks of the Mind*

The basement is cool in Hamilton Smith Hall where
Terry Moher's class of high school teachers gathers for the
first time. It is a traditional college classroom: wooden chairs
with notebook-sized arms lined in rows, a beige speckled
linoleum floor, aluminum-edged rectangular windows, and
two dusty walls of blackboards. I join them, hoping that as the
three weeks unfold, this group will help me determine some
key features for high school teachers having this summer
experience. We scrape the chairs as we form a wide circle
around the perimeter of the classroom.

"No one sits outside the circle, please," Terry demands.
There are seven men in this group, a number disproportion-
ate to the New Hampshire Writing Program as a whole. Most
are English teachers, some are department heads, and two
teach social studies. Twenty-seven of us. Along with the twenty-three high school teachers in the class, there are also two
sign interpreters and me. Four teach in a school for the deaf;
one is hearing and the others are deaf themselves. They take
positions in the circle directly across from the interpreters.

"There's a lot of experience in this room." Terry smiles, opening her slender arms and hands. "I will be willing to share what I've done, what I've learned from my mistakes, what I plan to do. There are twenty-seven fine teachers here, and we ought to look to one another." She reads a paragraph from Natalie Goldberg's *Writing Down the Bones*, "go back again and again to books. . . . it frees up the writer to let loose" (1986), and then we write for ten minutes about issues we want covered in the course. At the end of ten minutes, she asks us to summarize what we have written into one line. She asks for introductions: where we teach, what we teach, and why we're here.

She begins by describing her own teaching. "The kids are great, the system stinks," Terry says. Her voice is resonant; her brown eyes dart around the circle. "I'm here to be enlightened. I need to come back year after year." She began the NHWP ten years ago as a participant, and has been here every summer since. The introductions move around the circle. "I don't feel like a good writer. An imposter, in fact," Arnold signs while he speaks. He laughs a little, and looks around for approval. His colleagues jab him in the arm at the word "imposter." More introductions follow, admissions of inadequacy and not "fitting" in. "I want to synthesize all the methods and techniques I've read about into a coherent whole. I am the black sheep of my department," sighs a woman from upstate New York.

Another middle-aged man speaks up, "I'm here to figure out how to get people to write across the curriculum. How to make writing the job of every teacher in my school." He has been an English department chair for twenty-four years, and now feels responsibility for all the writing in his building. Heads nod toward him, implying that they share this pressure, confirming.

"I have had a year of failures. Deadlines and demands," admits a young first-year teacher from a New England prep school. "I have all this literature to cover, and I don't know when to teach writing." He flits a smile, nods at his colleagues around the room, and then his head darts toward his notebook. He is silent.

"I want to turn the 'ughs' to 'awesomes.' I've gone from being a traditional lecturer to a collaborator with my kids, from reading to reading and writing," adds a woman from Ohio. She wants collegial support, she says, to find people who want to think of themselves as collaborators.

"I am the least comfortable teaching writing, and am looking for techniques," another man confesses.

"I have been teaching twenty-three years, only three as an English teacher," Linda signs with deft and precise hand movements although her oral speech is barely audible. The others hunch toward her. "I want to make English my friend. I've had problems with English as a language, and I need to make it a better tool for deaf students. *It is not* their first language." The two interpreters look at each other and smile.

"Students are the same at all levels with writing. Only the sizes change," an older teacher adds. She has taught most elementary school grades for over thirty years, and this year, because of staff reductions and state budget cuts, she will be teaching high school for the first time.

Around the large circle, these introductions could be religious testimonials or pleas for therapeutic healing. These high school teachers share their professional pressures with others who share the same jargon and worries: staff reductions and grade level changes, writing in the face of other departments' demands, handicapped teenagers who must "befriend" the English language, writing about literature in order to "cover" the demands of a curriculum, initiating approaches without administrative or collegial support, feelings of failure and pressure. In twenty minutes, these high school teachers frame their problems, a process Donald Schon identifies as an important step for a reflective practitioner. Theories muddy themselves when they are applied to practice; they become the "swampy lowlands" in the work of real life. And, as Schön has observed, practitioners are able to reframe problems when they work in a "studio," with mentors or peers as guides (1987).

## The Courage to Arrange a Circle

I notice Therese Deni in the circle. She is squirming like a student, nervous. Her brown eyes, large and terrified, follow each speaker around the room. She looks down occasionally, clasped hands covering her mouth and nose. Her head moves slowly from side to side, and her dark hair moves with it; tiny white earrings peek out from under the curls. She is wearing a pink cotton top and crisp white shorts. She crosses her feet at the ankles; her pink socks are cuffed like a little girl's. Her long, sinewy legs seem out of place. When it is her turn she introduces herself, a teacher from California, entering her second year in a very traditional high school. "I *don't know how* to teach. I am frustrated. I want to convey my love of literature to them, and I don't know how."

Terry acknowledges Therese's dilemma, and explains that she will spend time talking about "how to give up control in the classroom so you can gain it." She confesses to the class, "I controlled because I lacked control." Therese writes rapidly in her notebook.

Terry assigns books: Don Murray's *Expecting the Unexpected*, Tom Romano's *Clearing the Way*, and Tom Newkirk's *To Compose*. Over three weeks, participants will join these authors as they teach and write, grill hamburgers, eat lobster, swim, and climb a mountain. Her choice of books is deliberate; it is important to Terry that teachers see one another as people and as writers. She recommends Toby Fulwiler's *The Journal Book* as well, as she assigns a journal about teaching. Therese shakes her head and wrinkles her brow. "I'm vague on purpose," she explains. "In school, I want to find ways to get my students to do things their own way, especially honors students." Terry says, "Why am I in that classroom every day? To have them do well on their SATs?" The class asks her to stop and repeat the assignment.

Terry asks the class to write again for a few minutes about "What makes writing hard? Take this opportunity to use writing to think it out," she suggests. Therese writes:

> I am frustrated because I know what I want to say but I can't find the words to say it. I know I have a story inside to preserve, but it won't come out. Writing workshops are scary things for me because I'd rather not reveal my stories. I want to, but I always fear revelations.

During the next three weeks, Therese will reconsider herself as an adult, a writer, and a teacher. Therese's story will be a solitary one cushioned in a context of people and events. With the help of her colleagues—in her classes, on the page, in the dorms, and at leisure—she will begin to reveal her stories. Two weeks later, on the Sunday before the final week, she reflects on what she wrote that first morning as she reads it in her journal:

> So I'm thinking . . . school and life experiences shouldn't be separated. Check this out. . . . You know what this means, don't you? If I want to afford the same environment of trust and support in my classroom, I need to do some modeling. Do you realize how much courage I am going to have to find to arrange my classroom in a circle, establish writing groups, carry on conferences?

For three weeks she asks and answers her own questions, following and breaking the rules she sets, writing about her reading, reading her writing, and reflecting on what she does. Therese is not alone. In this group there is resistance and eloquence. Empathy is both self-directed and student-directed; the frustration is clear. "It is tough working with secondary teachers," says Terry to her class. "We are cynical and skeptical. We feel comfortable with our professional content, but we don't know much about how people learn." Therese writes Terry's remarks on the left side of a notebook. She will keep a double-entry journal for three weeks. On the right side, after each week passes, she'll comment on each entry. The journal is meticulous, dated on each page. It will furnish Therese with a record of her thinking and me with a document of a young teacher's internal struggle. I decide to follow her closely.

## Getting Permission

It is 10:30 P.M. on the fifteenth of July, the Sunday night after the first week. I knock on Therese's door and open it a crack. The beam of light from the hall hits her in bed. Her eyes pop open, and I wonder if she'd rather sleep. "Oh no, it's fine," she croaks and switches on a light, "I really wanted to talk with you." The air is muggy, and she has no fan. It's okay, she tells me, because she's taken two showers. Her nightgown is buttoned up to the lace around her neck. She arranges the limp sheets around my tape recorder as I plug it in.

I notice a Bible angling out from a corner under her bed. An iron stands on the shelf next to a few folded cotton shirts; a skirt, two blouses, and several pairs of shorts line up on hangers. Her shoes are placed in pairs on the floor of the wardrobe closet: running shoes and a pair of white high heels. She has not brought her computer from California, but her desk is set up neatly with notebooks, paper, and writing utensils. Her required textbooks are ordered by size on the shelf above. "Make yourself at home," she invites me, "take off your shoes." When I flip off my sandals, I have an urge to place them in her neat shoeline.

"It's small in here, but that's okay. I don't stay here." By now she has arranged her personal routine as carefully as she has arranged her possessions. A commuter in her class has told her where she can get "really good" coffee, so she spends early mornings alone in Durham's Bagelry writing in her journal before her morning class. She has found an aerobics class for the late afternoon, and after an early supper in the cafeteria, she writes in the computer lab every evening. Yesterday, Saturday, she took a trip to Boston with a few people from her writing group, and this morning she walked to Durham's Catholic church for Mass. I see that she's feeling settled as she invites me to sit on her bed.

Framed snapshots of family members stand next to her notebooks. She speaks proudly of them all; she has moved to northern California to be near her sister. "She got a job first. I wanted to live in California with her. I liked the climate. Not the school system." We swap stories about siblings in southern California. I mention that I was there recently for my brother's third wedding and joke about Hollywood romances. She looks distressed. "Oh, I can't imagine what it must be like to get used to three different sisters-in-law!" Her comment jars me; I'd never seen my brother's succession of wives as a problem for me. I realize that even extended family is very important to Therese. During the week just passed, she's phoned her parents and her sister several times.

Therese grew up in a suburb of a large eastern city, the daughter of an engineering professor at a university. She talks with him often about teaching. She attended Catholic schools for twelve years. Aside from her father, I wonder, did she have any other mentors? "You know what?" Her eyes widen, "I wrote my way through high school: literary analysis and journals. I trusted Sister Mary. She was my teacher both freshman and senior years. She is still my friend now. We just had a special relationship."

She majored in English education at a state university, a two-hour drive from her home. She loved writing in college; "We always had a topic. We always had a 'This is what you need to do.' All you had to do was look at the books." She first read Donald Murray's *A Writer Teaches Writing* in her course on the teaching of writing and was eager to see him here. She taught junior high and went to summer school herself the summer she graduated from college. A year later, she moved to California where she has taught in a public high school for two years.

Last summer, after her first year of teaching, Therese was selected as a "teacher-consultant" in a summer writing project in California. "The way I got in was you had to send them a copy of a personal statement describing a teaching process you use. I wrote to them about how I teach *Lord of the Flies* to my grammar class, and how I integrated the writing with it.

The teachers all had to share their ideas the whole morning and part of the afternoon was presentations." She did some personal writing, too, about a failed relationship "that opened my eyes to the world of dishonesty and distrust," and she wrote about it to "preserve my lessons on paper." Most of her writing last summer came from the teachers' presentations, exercises mostly devoted to curriculum. Therese found a comfortable routine there; a table at a gourmet coffee shop and writing time on the beach. With the other teacher-consultants, she published writing in a magazine and shared a favorite book.

Her major assignment was to write an "I-Search" paper, a model described by Ken Macrorie (1988), written inquiry more subjective than a formal research paper, but full of information. As Macrorie describes it, an I-Search paper is a "story of a quest that counts for the quester" (56). Therese's instructor "just gave me the permission, and I just went away with it. And that's why it wasn't hard for me." She wrote about the eight California writing domains in the state writing assessment, a personal source of worry in her teaching that she explained here at the open forum. This year, her students did "I-Search" papers, and she is proud of what they wrote. In a journal entry she notes, "the reason why the I-Search paper turned out so well is because I didn't etch directions in stone."

She came out of her California summer with a bagful of ideas and teaching strategies, eager to plant them in her classroom. But other than the "I-Search" assignment, she emerged from her school year with an enormous sense of personal failure. She sees her stories of student failures as stories of her own failure as a teacher. "Unfortunately, these tell me more about myself than about the kids in my classsroom."

> Mark, a member of my senior American Lit section, was tremendously verbal, always contributing to discussions, even joined my forensics team. We always had a lot to share, verbally. Mark hated to write. Because he rarely turned in assignments, he finally flunked my class. Mark gave up—literally, because I never bothered to listen.

Steve radiated downright hate. He never understood why I had them doing interior/exterior monologues. I saw his lack of effort and he earned a D instead of a C. His mother wanted him OUT. He cried during that conference.

Amy's parents were convinced I didn't like her. She missed deadline after deadline, and was earning an F. I didn't slow down for her, and my "consistency" was interpreted as "not caring." Amy ended up dropping my class fourth quarter without a grade. She was removed—at her parents' request.

Therese aches over the discrepancies between knowing each student and assigning grades, over their parents' disappointment in them and in her. "Probably last year I perceived myself in a different way as a teacher. I can't begin to tell you. I really came close to saying I don't want to go on. But I'll go back to it. Because, you know, I won't quit. . . . And in my heart I love teaching as much as I did last summer. I can hear all the teachers in the world give all the presentations in the world, and I don't think right now that's going to be the answer for me. I can read all the books . . . I really think I've got to figure it out for myself, and I don't know if I ever will. . . . I still question whether I'm a true educator. Do I belong in the classroom? I don't know after this year. I've got to find out for myself."

She has been in New Hampshire one week. "Straight writing was not expected last summer to the degree that it is here," and after a week she says this summer is hard for her. "I'm finding it very much of a struggle. I'm mad at myself this year, because I want it to be like it was last summer . . . I didn't have any trouble writing." Here, this summer, there are no specific assignments or exercises. In writing group, she must design her own piece, revise it each day, and share her drafts. The mix of the "straight writing," immersion in new readings, responses, and stories from colleagues are at once exciting and provoking. She sees her colleagues as mentors; their writing is her reading. She is thinking about rules and authority, both personal and professional. She shuttles forward and backward between listening and talking, reading and writing, answers and questions, student and teacher.

In her room, we discuss Tuesday night's open forum; I thank her for explaining the eight California writing domains. The night made her feel professionally connected, she confesses, not alone. "People complained because they had work to do, but I loved that forum. I would do anything to have things like that all the time, where we can just ask questions. Just ask questions. And have people talk all around." She enjoyed Jane Kearns' joke about the Heinemann books: "Maybe there should be a Heinemann book out on how those teachers went about handling the kid who says 'This sucks!'"

Therese asks a lot of questions and she admits guilt about it. I tell her she's brave. "I don't know as I'm a brave woman. I just want to find some answers. But I don't think I can keep reaching out for them. I think it's just got to be internal. I'm glad we have to do all these journals."

## Following Rules, Fearing Revelations

During the first week, Therese spent a lot of time looking for "internal" answers. She questioned external authority in her personal life and in her learning. Her search fell into two main categories. First, her personal writing focused on a conflict between a male friend and her parents' expectations for her: Whose rules should she follow? Whom does she really love? Can these loyalties co-exist? About whom is she most guilty? Second, because she resisted sharing her writing in a group, she questioned her concepts of trust, audience, and authority. Will they laugh at her morality? Will they devalue her writing because it's personal? Whose ideas should she follow when she re-drafts a paper? Who exactly is the teacher in a roomful of teachers listening to her draft?

While her writer-voice drafts its way through the week, her reflective journal-voice notices that the people in her environment are influencing both her thinking and her writing.

On the very first afternoon, five hours into the program, she wrote:

> Monday July 9, 2:15 P.M.: Sharing requires trust. I admit, I am no longer the trustful person I once was, but today, my group taught me to let go just a bit. . . . Through all this sharing, I learned much more about myself through the stories revealed by others. . . .

Her first draft, written Monday night, was a one-page litany of four romantic memories—a sparkling climb near a waterfall, giggling as she lurches forward in a car with manual transmission, waving goodbye from an airplane as it flies over the Sierra foothills—and it ends with the "pain that continued to grip" into February when it became "a celebration of friendship." Before she shared it with her group Tuesday morning, she writes in her journal:

> Tuesday, July 10, 8:04 A.M.: I am fearful of penning a story I don't want misunderstood (I have no trust). I know what I want to say, but I haven't a clue concerning how to say it. One thing I know— my subject concerns a very special friendship and the tinge of sadness, rebellion, and misunderstanding. One subject? Two subjects? I really don't know.

The next day, she works on another version of the first draft. She collects details from her personal journal— February's entries. "I kept him company, listening to his story, dancing when he asked. . . ." She lists incidents and sketches a triangle diagram: "Family-Me-John." She documents her struggle, and surveys what she sees about her writing:

> Tuesday, July 10, Draft 1:00 P.M., Second attempt: I can't seem to begin this piece. I'm stuck. I don't like what I wrote this morning at all. It is full of clichés, and the clichés cloud what I have to capture. What do I want to say? Implications: (1) Although writing is natural, it is activated by enabling environments; (2) Character of these environments: SAFE, STRUCTURED, PRIVATE, UNOBTRUSIVE, LITERATE.

"The subject matter bothered me," she writes to herself, "It bothered me so much I couldn't sleep. I was worried about being a faithful friend to John, and guilt-ridden because I didn't feel like a faithful daughter." Therese called John at 2:30 A.M. "He didn't know where I was. Thought I was visiting relatives. Weird. Interesting. Don't judge. I didn't call my parents." Her writing breakthrough came after the phone call. She produced five pages. At this point, quantity was valuable to her and as she scans her journal a week later, her reflective voice notices: "I wasn't pleased with what I had produced. I was also bothered by the subject matter. . . . I called my friend, thinking I could ease the discomfort . . . he didn't even remember where I was. Translated—DID NOT CARE. It made me write more. . . . What came out was a piece about transitions—transitions between childhood and adulthood." And the following day, knowing her response group would be waiting for the written piece, she developed it further:

> Thursday, July 12, 8:30 A.M.: I wrote constantly yesterday but am still unhappy with the fragmented product. I dread sharing the work today. I am embarrassed . . . it is because of the various conflicts—the incompatible emotions. I am not trying to assert my grown-up independence, but I keep asking inside "Mom and Dad, quit smothering me with your opinions, your beliefs." . . . I haven't called them yet.

Her Monday draft began, "My shadow is fear. I fight my shadow" . . . it continues for eight lines of poetry echoing the fears in opposition: "I fear my parents, so I seek their approval/ I fear, so I fight. . . ." and then several pages of personal narrative: "The blond-haired stranger said goodbye. It was a foggy evening, and I envisioned the Christmas tree I knew we would never decorate. The man was now a stranger. I finally let go. 'God? God? This is a dream, right?'" By Thursday the draft is five different pages, and she reads it to the group. Her response group has listened, offered suggestions, and enabled her to revise. In her Thursday journal, she notes:

71

Thursday, July 12, 10:19 P.M.: Yes . . . I changed the damn thing again. I scrapped the poem, the God supplications, the first person narrative. Why? Comfort. Because I have to read it aloud tomorrow. Because I am afraid of hurting and alienating people I love. The writing stuff grows more difficult with each passing day. . . . I finally printed out, knowing I had to set the writing aside. I walked back in the drizzle without an umbrella, missing sunny California, missing my parents, missing my friends. . . . That's me, that's always been me (or "I," if you are grammatically oriented). I walked to the dorm, straight to the phone. "Hi Mom."

By Friday, she shares a five-page story called "Fragments of Fear." Now the five pages have new names, fictionalized characters, added dialogue, and conflict drawn from her group's suggestions. In her writing, she has learned to achieve distance with four techniques: fictionalization through character details and changed names, attention to dialogue and conflict. In her personal life, she has examined her dilemmas about rules and authority. And Saturday she will take a trip to Boston with three colleague-friends from her writing group. None of them has been to Boston before, they are all teachers, all different ages. They will be tourists together. The events of that day will move her toward the next week's project.

## Setting the Stage for Stories: A Progression of Trust

On the bus, Therese remembers, her friends scribbled ideas in their journals while she looked at the scenery. A walk through Boston's Italian North End made her think of family. In an Irish Pub, she heard a storyteller sing "Take Me Home, Country Road." While she listened she jotted down the words of the song on a slip of paper, and next to the words she listed places, family expressions, and names.

Saturday's trip recalled her Italian heritage, thoughts of home, and the storyteller's song: the nucleus for a memorial character sketch of Therese's Italian aunt Rosa. Her drafting process began on Sunday. "I got up and went to Mass this morning and couldn't wait to get back to write. Delete. Delete. Delete. I'd write something. Delete. God, I mean, I only had a page and a half done. I hate it. I'm starting all over again." Four days later, she shares her writing as she examines her past:

> Thursday 7/19/90: It was difficult to share my third draft. . . . I am feeling badly even now. Today I worked on my fourth and final draft, and my heart ached. I missed everybody—my grandmother, Aunt Rosa, my sister and friends. I missed us the way we used to be—if that makes any sense—and all week long, I struggled to capture those people on paper. But I failed at that. . . . I've gone through four drafts and three titles. . . . Is it okay to feel tired? Is it okay to wonder if I really am a writer?

Her journal documents herself as a writer. She is not over her fear of sharing. But during this week, writing about her own behavior activates her thoughts as a teacher, her curiosity about students. A few hours before I meet her in her room, she has written:

> Sunday, 7/15/90, 7:30 p.m.: I press the delete key too often. . . . I delete words, sentences, paragraphs. I wonder if I really have lost part of myself over the past year. . . . Look, I really think we better take a closer look at the "sharing" clause in the process approach. . . . I can also see another can of worms opening—kids taking advantage of the fact that sharing is optional.

When I interview her that night, she talks about her fear of sharing drafts. "What's the matter with me? It's because I need to share." I ask if she has shared her writing in other courses. "They didn't make me. And I didn't want to. It wasn't like it is here. They didn't make you. And you got away with it." Does she feel that anyone here would force her? "I'm sure no one would force me. It's just the pressure of the group." I ask her if the group is supportive, if she'll have the same group this second week. She doesn't know, "it's another thing I'm worried about." Would she force a student to share who won't? "When I was writing tonight, that's what I said. I stopped myself and I said, Oh, yeah, but then the kid can keep saying 'I don't want to share, I don't want to share' and never share. I know. I know. What if they can't find freedom of expression because they're under this constant 'I have to share it' pressure?"

She connects her fear of sharing with her fear of the classroom: "As I read over my journal entries, I realized that the foundation of my impulse to overload the student is nothing short of fear. Question is—what the hell do I fear? Easy enough—REBELLION, loss of control. Ironically, this happened to my senior American Brit Lit class in a silent way. My class shrunk half the size from first to second semester. . . . I lack spontaneity in my classroom, and I am fearful. Ah, but even that is connected. I am fearful, so I lack spontaneity. I am fearful, so I plan."

Therese feels last week's writing was connected to her confusion about her own authority—as a woman, a daughter, a teacher, a writer. And it was in her writing group that she came to make the connections. "My group revealed this, since I was struggling to write about a friendship very special to me, and the choice to continue the friendship despite family disapproval. I had to deal with the guilt of not telling the truth and the responsibility of making my own decisions.

"As I write, I realize I'm scared to death of teaching . . . the climate of my class is all wrong. . . . The writing is happening outside of my classroom. Because in the classroom, I don't give them time to express themselves. It doesn't have to be a spoken rule. They know it. . . . The majority of kids do not walk out of my classroom feeling good about their writing. It's because of the way my classroom's set up. I use a lot of planning. I plan everything. I totally structure my plan. And they follow what I plan. . . . Yes, I can tell you all about the theory of this wonderful writing process. I've got so many books on it, but I can't make the leap from theory to practice. *I don't know how to do it.*" She shakes her head slowly and looks down again.

Therese may not "know how to do it," but she is experiencing it "being done to" her. She marvels at her teachers here. "There's something about the way they run this—I mean, they don't do much, but you know they're doing something. . . . At the beginning of the week when we started writing? It's like, what's going on here? I mean, it's hilarious. It's like I'm looking for this structure. And I'm sure they have their lessons written down somewhere. They know how to do it so that we don't know." And she has seen her instructors work hard—at planning, listening, and responding to each student—on paper and in classes. Over time, she watches her instructors in both classes to see how they do it, and what exactly it is that they do. On the Monday of the final week, she writes:

> Monday, July 23: Lesson? Classroom = Students/Teacher. Don't tell me there's no place for the teacher. Look at last week's progression of trust. . . . But what do we do when outside forces ruin what we attempt to create inside the kid? Terry tells me I'm a wonderful student, welcomes my questions. My writing group welcomes my writing. Carol hugged me because I shared my composition on Friday. I was invited to eat dinner by three people yesterday. Ming who works at the desk knows my name at the aerobics center downtown. Bonnie takes time to listen and record. I get it. It's more than academics. It's environment. It's welcoming—accepting. It's the opposite of rejection. It's more than tiptoeing carefully. It's knowing where to tiptoe.

Over the three weeks, Therese's work evolves in a dialogic pattern, and just like the daily routine she establishes, she forges her work to suit her needs. She has two voices, and they converse constantly. One doubts, the other explores. One follows rules, the other tests them. One takes risks, the other doubts her own abilities. One tells stories, one fears revelations. One is a wide-eyed student, the other is a cautious young teacher. The dialogue in her double-entry journal is a record of these two voices, what she sees and learns from her colleagues, her writing, her reading, and her observations.

Sunday, July 22: As I read over my July 9 journal, I realize just how much I've trusted since I've been here. . . . This past weekend, I can't say I was frustrated at all as the words flowed from pen to paper. Something radical is going on inside my mind. . . . Carol Avery says "build community." Terry Moher says "give time." I am beginning to realize that a lot of this trust is established through environment. You have to set the stage, right? I even said "writing workshops are scary things for me because I'd rather not reveal my stories. Well, hell, everyone else was revealing their stories in our group. . . . That's another thing, see. If you get it to be the norm and not the exception, then you have a community of trust.

Therese recognizes her "community of trust" in a letter written to her writing group. She chooses it to publish in the collection which will go to everyone in the program:

Lest I Forget . . .

Dear Writing Group,

One week from today, we will find ourselves home again. I've decided that it would be wrong for me to forget you. I do not want the memory of this circle to fade, because, you see, I will need to recall you and your stories at some point during the coming year . . . let me record the way it is, so that in the future, I will clearly remember the way it was. . . .

She offers back to them the details of their stories: a hearing-impaired daughter, a sister in childbirth, a great-grandmother's bowl of cornflakes, newlyweds too hot to sleep, a mother too cold to visit her child, a lost three year old, a struggle with bigotry and racism, and ends: "When life brings the stuff that clouds my vision, I will remember these stories, recall this circle, and reread this letter, lest I forget that this is the stuff life is made of. . . ."

She has chosen this as her best piece of writing, "I wrote it right through, without much struggle at all. And I just remembered everybody in the class, and then when I read it to my friends, I thought it was soppy sentimentality, but I thought, 'Yeah, this is me, at least now." Therese is afraid that her audience might not like this piece, but it represents herself to herself, and she is pleased to have the authority to evaluate it that way. "Okay, I can write academic papers which are still going to have *me* in them, but I said, well, here I am, I've got to, and I did . . . it summarized everything I got from the program."

The environment that has been so critical is made of more than her two classes. "I have to start celebrating the surprise. . . . Is it true that this whole thing goes deeper? . . . Is it true that what happens in your personal life connects to what happens in the classroom? . . . See, it's getting too big for me. . . . It goes deeper than education . . . this is a societal thing . . . this spills over. . . . When you go to the Bagelry, there's Don Murray, reading the paper, and there's Tom Romano, stopping to say hi . . . and they're all working very hard. A community of people who are all working toward writing and writing."

## Celebrating the Surprise: A Silent Encounter with Don Murray

Therese uses her class journal to hash out dilemmas, to plan her own writing, and then to reflect on her changes. But she also uses Don Murray as a teacher-god. She has been reading his books throughout her college and professional life; he is, for her, the tradition-bearer. She reveres his books; to her his stature is legendary. She is jarred when she sees him flipping burgers at the picnics, reading the newspaper at the Bagelry, and sharing drafts with students. She reads his *Expecting the Unexpected*, sits a few rows from him at the open forum, and asks questions during his formal presentation called "Pushing the Edge." She giggles when Tom Newkirk introduces Murray, "my dog Jessie thanks him for being featured in three columns in the Boston Globe." He becomes accessible and human while he remains a mythic model. His books bear the traditions she is trying hard to accept.

Most powerfully, she holds a continuous silent conversation with his work in her journal. Her reflective responses to his quotes are marked with diagrams, arrows, and little heart-shapes. She watches herself moving forward as she traces her own dialogic pattern of questions and answers based on Murray and his work:

> Tues., July 10 8:04 A.M.: Murray terms his book "A Celebration of Surprise." My immediate reaction was—Surprise. I am not a spontaneous teacher. Now I know why I plan excessively. In *Expecting the Unexpected,* Murray explains his own experience (1989, 128): "I needed that power at first. I was scared in front of the class." I fear my students will turn both me and the subject matter off. . . . Murray's words ease some of my own writing pains. I feel a celebration inside of me, but I can't find the words to express it.

> Wed., July 11, 1990, 8:20 A.M.: Last night, I delighted in meeting Don Murray at the Open Forum, but I had a difficult time understanding him. This morning, while reading Chapter 5, I know he was making a point about bad writing leading to good writing. . . . Murray may laud bad writing, but I loathe mine. Why does "unclear thinking" lead to good writing? From personal experience, this hasn't worked for me. My structured nature commands me to write only when I have something to say. On page 102 he comments that "most people believe writers know what they are going to say before they say it. They do not know that writing is a thinking skill." Perhaps I am not a thinking person. Perhaps I plan too much. Perhaps I lack spontaneity. Perhaps I could discuss this with him."

She writes five quotes from his chapter in her journal. One week later, in Richards Auditorium, she asks him about "unclear thinking." Murray answers her, "If it's all thought out, it's not worth writing. You'll end up with boring little essays." The question and answer period after his talk raises much that intrigues her. "I do a lot of foolish talking, foolish playing, playing with language," he says. "The point is not the audience or the voice; it is to liberate people from the idea that one is right and one is wrong." She is confused and delighted. A week later, Therese looks back at her notes from Murray's talk and writes in her journal:

Sunday, July 22: 'Writing is thinking' needs to be a productive unclarity—a confusion. He made us laugh, but I finally understand what he was talking about. (This is exactly what I myself was doing with John's story . . . calling my attention to transitions.) Wow! It still blows my mind . . . I need to afford the opportunity for surprise in my classroom. LET GO . . . BUT PLAN HOW TO DO IT CORRECTLY."

She is thinking about "letting go" during this final week, but still expects to learn a correct method for doing it. Two days of thinking about Murray's book and his talk led her this far. In the mornings at the Bagelry, while she watches him read the paper and drink his coffee, she writes a letter she doesn't send, and two weeks later she reflects on how his work has affected her work. Without Murray knowing it, he is both a "distant teacher" (John-Steiner 1985) and an intimate colleague:

Thurs., July 11: I can't believe what I'm reading in Chap. 19. It's almost like Murray read my thoughts. 'Writing as therapy' for this writer also. I used it as such last summer; I use it as such now. . . . I wish I could talk to Murray again. I need to tell him I understand exactly what he is talking about . . .

Fri., July 12, 8:00 A.M., The Bagelry: Dear Don, Funny how people are, huh? . . . Our instructor Terry asked us to read Chap. 19 of your book. I read "Writing is therapy for this writer and for most others I know. We should certainly allow life in the classroom when it walks though the door. Some of our students will find it healing to write about pain and anger in their lives. And it is, after all, the raw material of art" (185). Last summer, Don, I experienced this on another campus. . . . I wrote, and healed a wound that left a scar and built a callous. . . . I have never been in external combat, Mr. Murray. I have only experienced the internal combat—the tugging and twisting of emotions, the struggle to accept reality. . . . Sincerely, Therese

Mon., July 23: Perhaps there is a way to use writing as therapy. Murray's composition on his daughter reminded me of the book *All Quiet on the Western Front*. Couldn't this work in reverse? Couldn't the book remind the student of something he had to

deal with? Murray said in his talk on July 16 that "autobiographical writing is not confession." Come on, Therese Deni, try it. I
know that man would push me to the edge. You see, I am struggling once again with issues in my personal life—incompatible
emotions. . . . someone I felt intensely for. . . . growing up and
making my own decisions. Aren't these the same issues our students are also dealing with?. . . . I continue to have the vision of
a workshop-classroom where the environment will be conducive
to this type of introspection. I see writing groups in a circle, I see
a class not afraid to take risks. What happens when this type of
thing happens to a student—a tenth grade "skills" student instead
of Don Murray?

On his pages and in his public talk, Murray has mentored
Therese at a distance, shared his own teaching fears, encouraged her to use writing as therapy, confused her about taking
risks, writing badly, and "pushing the edges." But he is not her
only extra source of introspection, confusion and delight in
this community. Two days after Murray's talk, she attends a
special session given by Tom Romano, and learns to "Break
the Rules in Style." I join her.

## *Breaking the Rules in Style: into Wishin' About Intuition*

Tom Romano draws the material for his session from
Winston Weathers' book *An Alternate Style* (1980) and his
own experience as a high school writing teacher. Weathers'
"Grammar B," as Tom describes it, demonstrates a non-tra-
ditional way of arranging words, "boundary-breaking written
expression, and above all, glorious human diversity"
(Romano, 1990). With these exercises, Tom encourages students "out of the SAT English Usage Hoop" and into "syn-
tactical promiscuity, linguistic anarchy." He affirms with
Emily Dickinson, John Dos Passos, Walt Whitman, e.e.
cummings, and Virginia Woolf; they have all used "Grammar
B" effectively. With examples from students, he demonstrates
techniques: the list, the sentence fragment, the labyrinthine

sentence, orthographic variation, double-voice, and repetend, repetition, and the crot. (Weathers, 1980) We try a few and share them.

Romano hands out a packet of examples of his students' writing, and tells a story about each piece. One was written by a school superintendent's daughter. Therese reads it and rocks back and forth in her seat. Her mouth is wide open and her eyes smile. Tom shows more examples, gives a few directions, and commands "Give it a shot, let go, be licentious on the page!" "There is no pure language, there is no pure grammar. These are options for composition." We all try more, enjoy each others' products, and that evening, I find a note under my door:

> Dear Bonnie,
> I had a blast writing this in Romano's session today. I had to share it!
>
> Sincerely, Therese

Attached to the note is a page of explanation to her writing class: "Grammar B presents an alternate syle of grammar—a style that plays around with structure and syntax, and breaks the standard rules of style on purpose. The writer delivers a message through the unconventional use of grammar. Don't worry—Emily Dickinson and Walt Whitman did it also. . . ." She describes Tom's examples from his American Lit class, her own American Lit class, her five weeks at a university in California, and her enthusiasm and failure returning to school. She details the six techniques she uses in the piece, and ends by saying "I normally don't use swearing in my writing, but I'm normally not realistic about things either. These were my seniors. This is how they talked." Her poem reads:

### Crash Course in Reality

UC. I don't see.
Oh God. Fourth period. They're coming in the door.

Why did I eat yogurt for lunch? Why did I eat anything?
Ok, OK. Calm down. Clam up. The hand outs are in order.

-The note to the students
-The sillybus
The Writing Goops

Oh God. You got Deni? HaHaHa.
Talk to last year's fourth period. She'll work your ass off
—no kidding. She has a thousand hand outs.
Hand out the note first. Don't rush—don't talk too fast.
Remember last year's fourth period. Write—Right.
UC . . . Integration . . . Intuition . . . Into wishin'

Here she goes. The first hand out of the year.
Handout. Hand up. Question.
"Miss Deni, I have a question about the sillybus."
Hand up. A question—Oh God help me—a question.
"Will you give us the writing topics?"
Complain. Explain. It's plain. They don't understand.
"No. You see, it's like baseball." (But we play football).
"I'll pitch out the stuff. You catch what you want."
I pitch. You catch. We match. (I thought).

What the hell is she talking about?
"I don't understand what you're talking about."
I catch? You pitch? You bitch. (He thought).

The Writing Goops. Explain the Writing Goops.
Writing? I thought this was literature.
Integration. Into wishin'
I wish I was out of here.
It's all so simple.
UC. I don't see.

—July 18, 1990

Therese expressed delight in breaking linguistic structures
to express her frustration. She tells me, "You have no idea how
many times I cried over that situation. And then as I wrote

that poem—it will never be the same again. I'm telling you, now I look back, I think of that first day. But see, the things I talked about in that poem happened over and over again. I was too thickheaded to figure out what to do about it. So what did I do wrong last year? Did I have definite strategies in mind? Some, from the teacher presentations at UC. But was it student-centered? I don't think so, or I would not have had such a severe "Crash Course in Reality."

Romano's session gave Therese permission to "break the rules in style," and it helped her give herself permission to break her own rules about looking at her teaching. But this poem did not just flow out, even if she thought it had. The kernels of thought formed the week before. In the two previous days, she had critically examined some of the words she plays with in the poem. In her journal the night before she wrote the poem, Therese had written:

> 7/17: Terry just told me that I was a wonderful student—a perfect example of my lack of intuition. It is me, you see, not my students. I need to get in touch with myself, because I know my lack of intuition—spontaneity—etc. is all related to my fear.

In Terry's class, they were talking about conferences and having them. Therese looked in her teaching journal from the year before, and saw herself a new way. She discussed it with Terry: "They would come, I'd do all the talking, they'd come to my desk and sit at a little seat. . . . Terry, how did you get to where you got?"

Terry explained that she used to walk to the students' desks and "skootch" down. Now she has two old wing chairs and a special table: "so it doesn't look like a teacher." She assured Therese that it took ten years for her to make this shift. Her comment struck Therese deeply: "The purpose of the conference is to get rid of the kid—to give him a reason to go back and write."

Therese was upset when that class ended. She wanted to continue, had more questions to ask. Her classmate Alison scribbled a note to her, Therese nodded her head, and later I asked permission to remove the note from the wastebasket. On the note Alison had written, "It's not physical, I think. It's an attitude. You sort of have to give yourself permission to screw up a little—because no matter what, they're writing. It's practice—Let's talk?"

Therese wrote back: "Oh, I'd love to. But listen, I talked last summer, too, but then the kids came in the classroom, and I SCREWED UP. It was dictatorship. My way of control. But yes—let's talk." They sat in the room through lunchtime. The subject of their talk? Intuition, and conferences:

Alison: What do you mean you screwed up when you tried conferences last year?

Therese: I never had intuition. . . . I was going to ask Terry what to do if you don't have intuition.

Alison: But I bet you do have intuition. You just haven't practiced it a lot . . . let yourself get in there and listen and ask questions. I mean, human beings have intuition, you've been teaching how many years?

Therese: I'm going into my fourth.

Alison: Okay. That's three rich years of experience. You've been a writer here. . . . it's really scary but it's a matter of letting yourself try things and not worrying about "Uh, I'll screw up" or "Uh, this isn't going to work this peri-od and I don't have time. . . . So what happens in a con-ference if you say you don't have intuition?

Therese: It was pitiful . . . there were no questions, because I had already told them what to write.

Alison: So what if you just stop talking? One task for a con-ference. Just say "What's it about?" Let them talk . . . (Therese says she thinks they won't answer, that her classroom will get "chaotic," that this is luxurious think-ing, and Alison can do that in a private school . . . ) If you start right off with a dialogue instead of a lecture, the atmosphere will shift . . .

Therese: I'm too structured. I don't blame them. There is not flexibility, I struggle with that . . .

Alison: What are you afraid of, in the structure?

Therese: Chaos.

Alison: Assignment chaos?

Therese: I'm afraid, I don't trust them . . . to be talking about what they're supposed to be talking about. That makes me walk around the room like a policeman, which they hate. I don't trust them to write out of class, because I think somebody else is going to be doing the writing.

Alison: Why don't you trust them? What's going to happen if somebody else writes it for a kid? And you start asking questions about where did this come from, why did you write about it, he's not going to be able to answer it, so then you say, go back and try this, try this, he's not going to be able to do that if somebody else did it.

Therese: How do you reach every one of them in a conference?

Alison: I don't know if you even try. If you start out thinking "I'm going to reach every one of these kids and have a miraculous change," you'll be so discouraged before you start, you'll never get there. (They talk about the projects Therese's students have done.) See, you're doing a lot of good stuff, you're doing a lot of good stuff, but. . . .

Therese: Yeah, but it lacks the essential element, the stuff is in there but . . . the atmosphere is not relaxed.

Alison: But it might come down to the whole issue of trust. Think about why you don't trust them, what will happen if you let some of that stuff go, and just sort of mush that around in your head for a while.

All that day Therese "mushes it around in her head"—Terry's comments and Alison's colleagueship. Then, in Tom Romano's session, she produces a poem that explores her self-image as a teacher and her perceived failures with her classes. She plays with language and "breaks the rules" for effect. A week later, thinking about how she's produced this herself, she writes in her journal about how learning comes from language play: "So you teach them backward? Is that what Romano does? You teach them so they recognize a fragment by using a fragment so that they'll know what a sentence is. If they're inducted enough in using fragments, in playing around with language, then they're going to want to know how to do that again."

She applies it to her teaching. "That kind of relaxed rapport happens for me the last six weeks of school. And it's BECAUSE it's the last six weeks of school that it happens. And like, you know, well I can afford this now. The big stuff's over. I can talk to them. I can hear what they have to say. It's a shame . . . they're human beings and they have so much to share. You know, this poem is humorous but there's a seriousness behind it." She is recasting her definition of the "big stuff," thinking about what her students offer. And behind it, there are three days of critical self-examination inside a community of people doing the same.

## *Warming Up to a Cold Reading*

Once Therese has written her poem with Tom Romano, she uses poetry as a form for synthesizing her readings, her confusions, her company, and her experiences. During the second week, she struggles with an issue that nagged her since the first day of the program, one she labels the "cold reading." In Terry's class they have been trying "cold readings," looking at poetry and passages of fiction that they've never read before and sharing their responses (Newkirk, 1990a). On the third day of the workshop, they had read the poem "Stargazer's Death" by Vasko Popa. A roomful of high school teachers yields a roomful of interpretations. "In a hundred years, I wouldn't have come up with all these literary connections. I see what we do to our kids," Alison says. "Yep, we intimidate the hell out of them," echoes Terry. Dorothy is entranced with the language and examines a few key words, "crystals," "done," and then makes a connection to Galileo.

Therese says "I did it wrong!" She is upset. Terry suggests that each person write a quick "memo to the poet." The memos show multiple interpretation and taken together, they provide a rich reading of the poem. Again, Therese sighs, "I did it wrong!" The week continues. "I've never taught poetry because I'm so afraid I don't understand it." In her journal, she writes:

> Now, here's a neat but scary thing to me . . . Terry asks the class for poems they really didn't understand, and then they go over them together in a group. But she's never read them before. They all figure it out—That's a "cold reading." WOW. It blows my mind. I need to ask my dad if he's ever done a "cold math problem" in front of his engineering students.

The night before, her father had told her on the phone, "I still believe in the traditional way. A kid has to know the facts before he thinks on his own." She tells me: "I can't come to grips with the fact that the teacher hasn't read all the books." In her journal she writes:

> What strategy do I use to GET THEM TO ASK THE QUESTIONS? YEP. THAT'S IT. If you do this kind of stuff with poetry, you can do this kind of stuff with short stories, novels, plays, etc. . . . Ah, but the teaching world looks pretty from here, my friend . . . It looks so pretty . . . but for the voice that whispers 'Be Careful. Be Realistic. Remember last year. Learn from your mistakes.'

The next day is Friday. Terry has invited her friend Mary, a teacher and poet, to class. Therese is intrigued with Mary's approach to teaching poetry. She asks more questions:

Therese: How do you know they're reading in the class?

Mary: They're writing about it in class, too, and writing their own poems.

Therese: What happens if you don't understand a poem at all?

Therese freezes when she asks this question. Her hand is clenched, holding up her forehead. Her legs are crossed at the ankles, feet tensed in her sneakers, pointed up straight. Mary offers some examples of exercises and poems from students and professional poets and a bibliography. "I try to keep the exercises very concrete." Mary's positions are strong: "The single event resonates outward," she says, "after kids bring up the details of experience—memories, visions, smells—classroom sets of books are silly," she observes, "they need to read lots of poems. . . . Kids should have a varied diet of exercises and poems. After cooking something, if it tastes good, you eat it. . . . .Everything has worked for somebody, not for everybody. . . . In a read-aloud of finished poems, there ought to be no time for comments. Just listen, no judgments."

Therese moves her head back and forth slowly, thinking, reviewing. She blurts questions: "What will you do if a kid needs a grade?" "What if the kid next to him doesn't do it the same way?" After class, Terry and her poet friend Mary invite Therese to join them for lunch. Therese is astonished, and that night writes in her journal:

> Friday, July 20: Terry, I almost didn't take you up on that lunch offer, but like a starving pauper, I still didn't have enough. I thought, "In a week you will be away from all of this—standing on your own again." So I joined you and Mary . . . tonight, while I wash clothes, I am going to write about this strange and beautiful concept—Time—Mary said "You know, Terry and I didn't just decide to do the workshop approach and implement it in one day. We've been working on this for ten years." Perhaps I am expecting too much too soon. I've made that mistake in my personal life, so I could have made it in my professional life. "You set the environment for the student the first day?" I asked Mary. "Yep—I set the rules—and they are few—and I keep reinforcing them. I walk around, I get to know the student. If they like sports, I find some sports poetry." . . . Now, in class, she spends two weeks—one to read, and one to write. The kids choose their own poems from various books, record the poems and respond to them . . . they move on to the writing section and, of course, they write poems. Those that are good, she attempts to get published, those that are mediocre, she rewards for effort. . . . Mary also has them keep vocabulary collections. Look, I'm trying not to get excited, but internally I'm screaming with enthusiasm."

In this journal entry, Therese reviews her discussion with Terry and Mary and tries to situate herself in her classroom.

She links it to other moments she's had. By now, she has written a poem with Tom Romano and listened to Tom Newkirk and Pat McLure (1993) talk about "cold readings" with first graders. "I still hear Pat saying 'I believe in having kids make their own choices and then holding them accountable for those choices,'" she tells me. "So you go to the library and grab all the literature you can find concerning the genre you're working with, and then you spread them in the classroom table, do a booktalk, and say, "OK, Kiddies, CHOOSE!"

## Looking for Trouble: The View is Much Too Lovely

Following up this obsession Therese reads Tom Newkirk's article, "Looking for Trouble, A Way to Unmask Our Readings" (1990). Newkirk illustrates ways to allow students to explore meanings in text, to "open" a text to student response, as he puts it. With scholarly support and examples from students, he asserts that a single text ought not have one interpretation, that when we assume one way of reading a text, we may lose what we and our students can learn from it. The article calls for "teachers and students . . . to drop the masks that can inhibit learning. We can all act as the fallible, sometimes confused, sometimes puzzled readers that we are. We can reveal ourselves as learners, not always the most graceful of positions" (220). Therese is intrigued with the whole article, especially with Polanyi's idea of "granting allegiance," that a learner can "believe before he can know," and on her second Friday night in New Hampshire she reads the article several times.

Saturday morning she takes another trip. Tom Newkirk had invited workshop participants to hike Mount Chocorua with him and his six year old son Andy, an hour's drive north of Durham, and Therese joined. Sunday, after Mass at the Durham church, she took her seat at the Bagelry for her solitary morning coffee writing ritual, and crafted this poem:

## *Looking From Chocorua*

Looking for Trouble . . . climbing Mt. Chocorua
Hey Newkirk, where do I go now?
The trail, you see, has forked
And little Andy's legs are tired.

Looking for Trouble . . . OK OK
I'll follow the yellow and find the top.
But what happens if I fall?
Will my students be there to catch me?

Looking for Trouble . . . these damn rocks.
I just scraped my knee; My foot slipped.
Oh, where's the top? What did you say?
Drop our masks? But what if I fall?

Looking for trouble . . . my heart is pounding.
This isn't easy. I never climbed this mountain.
Aerobics aside, I have no training.
I'm learning, too, just like my students.

Looking for Trouble . . . my eyes are lowered.
I'd rather not look up. The view is too tempting.
The scene is lovely, but I can't afford to stop.
You can, for you climbed the mountain before.

Looking for Trouble . . . I've got to make it.
Hey Newkirk, I'm almost there.
The turtle always wins; I chose the right trail.
Little Andy's in the lead again.

Looking from Chocorua . . . First Andy, then me.
Hey Newkirk—we finally made it.
The rock is hard; I lay down, but cannot rest.
The view is much too lovely from here.

—July 22, 1990

She senses the series of encounters that enabled her to write this poem when she writes in her journal:

Sunday, July 22: Remember when we were all climbing to the top of Mt. Chocorua yesterday and I wondered out loud if I would make it? I told Ruth "Yeah, you do things and know you can. I do things to prove that I can. . . . The "cold reading" will be like wondering if I can get to the top of Mt. Chocorua. Oh, I have a long way to climb, and my heart is beating so hard it might crack. . . . But I want to climb this mountain, and I want to understand what I am trying to accomplish every step of the way. . . . Today I ache all over, but I know I made it to the top. And you know what? The view from the peak was more than worth it.

She reconsiders her definitions of affirmation and trust when she watches Tom climb with his son, and links it to his article and her class questions about reading. She recalls it to me:

I asked "Are you all right, Andy?" Tom confirmed "You're doing fine, Andy." Do we ask—intending to show concern but revealing insecurity, like I did? Or do we confirm, like Tom did—do we say "You're a hell of a human being, you don't need my concern. Could it be that this response was released because of a developing "personal allegiance" (Newkirk 1990). 'A passionate pouring of oneself into untried forms of existence. . . .' Newkirk, you have a good point here. . . ."

In her journal two days after the poem, she connects her thinking to the three articles she's read in *To Compose*. Besides Newkirk's "cold reading," she quotes Sondra Perl's explanation of Gendlin's theoretical "felt sense"—"when writers pause and seem to listen or otherwise reach to what is inside of them," and Murray's article about the writer's "other self" (in Newkirk, 1990):

I love this! First Newkirk proposes cold readings. Now Murray suggests daydreaming and wasting time. . . . I really got worried when I began deleting entire pages of this poem. But when the subject emerged, I couldn't stop laughing. I really had fun with the poem. A connection between Newkirk's "granting allegiance" to the writer-reader-learner and Perl's "felt sense." Once a learner believes in his own ability, he is much more in line with what's going on inside of him. He believes he has something to say. Once he finds himself in an environment that validates rather than condemns, he is much more comfortable looking inside. You know—the picture is all becoming very clear now. Trouble is, I have to implement it beginning one month from today. . . . Terry, Bonnie, Tom R, Tom N, Carol, how did they do it with me? . . . Hey, Therese Deni, that paper needs to be autobiographical. It needs to describe what's happening to you—what you're realizing about the connection between self-worth and writing. It's becoming very clear what these people are saying and doing.

When we talked on her bed with my tape recorder on the Sunday she wrote her poem, Therese knew she had been in what she described as "an environment that validates rather than condemns:" "I suddenly found this link between climbing the mountain and reading Newkirk's article. It's exactly like it. I kept saying 'I don't know if I'm going to do this. I don't know if I can make it to the top. I really don't.' Because Tom kept saying, 'There's the top. There's the peak. There's where we're going.' And it looked so far away, and he said 'It's only three miles.' And I kept thinking 'I don't know if I can do this. I really don't know. I don't think I can get up there.' And then when I got up there—Well, of course, I even wrote in the poem, 'Aerobics aside, I've no training.' Meaning that all of what I learned previously aside, I have no training in what that article was talking about. I have never gone in there and done cold reading. And then I finally made it. And I was tired. The first thing I did was throw myself down—nobody was there—I lay down and I looked up and said 'I don't believe I'm here.' And then I wrote in the poem, 'because it's hard. The rock's hard.'

"And see, I couldn't rest. And that's how it's going to be. Even if I get this down in my classroom. Even now I can't rest. I can't. These ideas are swinging around in my mind. And I can't stop writing and I can't stop reading. I keep reading and writing and reading and writing. I have to start talking instead. (She begins to laugh.)

"I know when I get home, I can't share this with my dad. He's going to freak out. I know he is. Even on the phone. And that's going to influence me. That's going to influence me. It's going to draw me away. He says 'I don't care what's going on,

I still think that you have to tell a student what to do before he can make choices on his own.'" Therese tells me that only in the past few months has she decided to stop talking to her father to get his advice about teaching.

Therese is beginning to look inside herself for authority, not toward her father or her teachers or her books. She is making connections between her own learning and the knowledge she needs to enable in students. Therese is saying that teaching and learning are both complex and interrelated. She is sensing that by reaching inside for her own responses that she can understand other people in her environment— and draw boundaries for her authority and theirs, for herself, and her students.

In this writing program, she sees herself as well as her mentors in multiple roles. In her eyes, they are the tradition-bearers of the UNH culture, the authors of her books, the thinkers of the ideas she is trying, the practitioners of the strategies she wants to master. But as she humanizes their god like stature, she learns about discipline in literacy. "I mean, we go down to the Bagelry and there's Don Murray just sitting there reading the paper. And there's Tom Romano who stops to talk. And Terry Moher and her poet friend invite you to join them for lunch. And Tom Newkirk climbs a mountain with you. And I think, these people are people! They are really people! This is not where you have the gods and the peons. It's something where you have a community of people who are working toward something. . . . That's why I made the correlation with the mountain. . . . I wrote it after church. . . . Everything happens after church . . . just out of nothing. You know? Maybe I'm making too many connections. I don't know. But it was exhausting; it was just a little mountain. I was, like, 'Okay, Okay,' I figured 'This is exactly what's going on in your life right now. You've got to start with a little mountain. And then you can climb the big one.' I don't think I realized that. Not for a long time. Last summer they accepted me into that program, so I thought I was a good writer. But in reality, I didn't know the first thing about teaching . . .

and that was to work from the inside out. Get them to writing. Trust them."

## Living with Ambiguity

Like her other poem, Therese thinks she made this one "just out of nothing," it is clear that her three weeks enabled her to begin to look inside for her learning. She is beginning to trust herself. Dewey (1938) describes education as the progressive organization of knowledge, that community and conversation blend with the internal motivation of the individual to create a culture for learning. It is continuity and interaction intercepting and uniting, "the longitudinal and lateral aspects of experience." (44). Therese explains:

> This is getting too big for me. I've got to think about it. It goes deeper than education . . . the community, the trust, the environment—this spills all over into personal life and to professional life, and I keep thinking that family life and . . . unfortunately, it's going to be over real soon. And I won't have this anymore.

For Therese, her double-entry journal was a tool to survey and interpret her progression. For me, the journal was a guide to analysis. Her questions in class, conversations with mentors and colleagues, interview time with me, and trips around New England constitute a three-week moment in her development as a teacher. She knows it's temporary, that these three weeks are different from the ones she had last summer, but she knows she might be able to re-create pieces of this for someone else. In her journal during the final week, she writes: "After talking with Bonnie Sunstein and Tom Newkirk and experiencing these three weeks, I begin to understand the difference. In a few days, I will walk out of here knowing exactly what it means to be a writer in a writing community. In other courses, when I walked out, I had a binder full of ideas but no clue as to the practicality of those ideas. My juniors and seniors were quick to show me." Perhaps this was the year Therese was ready to draw more from her theoretical binder;

perhaps this summer she was ready to notice her surrounding community. Vygotsky (1978) describes education as the blending of mind and society, internal development in touch with external action. It is this kind of blending that Therese works hard for, whether she knows it or not.

The very last time I use my tape recorder is to talk with Therese. I've promised to drive her to the airport bus, and she arrives in my room on time. She has been packed since the night before. I'm packing my clothes, cleaning my dresser, and dumping my trash as we talk. She tells me two stories about students:

> One boy, through his "I-Search" paper, discovered who his real father was . . . he ended up saying I'm really glad I did this because this has helped me figure out something I've wanted to figure out all my life. And then the other—a girl who never talked about friends, she'd been abused, a friend molested her as a child, and she finally wrote about it, finally let it out.

These are the only school success stories I've heard her tell in three weeks, and it is an hour before she will catch the bus on the day she leaves. She continues. "SO—that's what I want to get kids to do, through teaching writing and teaching literature, I want to get them to take a good look at themselves. I don't think it's egocentric. I don't think it's wrong to look within yourself. I think that's the essence of teaching, of education, and if you're at peace with yourself you can find peace with the world even if you haven't found it for yourself yet. I mean, if you're like me, and you're looking, and you're trying to figure out the answer anyhow." Therese is still "trying to figure out the answer" for herself and for her students.

Therese's experience here is a solitary struggle inside a context rich with people and ideas, and she moves back and forth between the rituals she establishes and those established for her. Her story is one of productive tension that never gets resolved. But the most important thing that happens is that she learns that we live and teach with ambiguity. There are no set ways to follow the rules or to break them. Each case presents a different set of criteria, each class presents a different set of students, each text presents a different set of words. There is no one "process approach," but there are many single people writing and sharing their strategies with others. No one authority can determine the interpretation of a text, but many readers can provide a vigorous and rich response. There will be more failure and more success. She will choose for her students and let them choose, just as she will pull away from her parents and draw close to them. The dialectic relationship Therese achieves between herself and her community helps her to actualize herself as a teacher. She trusted externals: books, teachers, people. She negotiated authority from the outside to the inside. Now she begins with the inside. This is not a transformation; it is an actualization, an affirmation by context.

As I zip my suitcase, I happen to notice my watch. She is telling stories, thinking about what she's done and what she'll do. I have four minutes to get Therese to the bus stop in Durham. We gasp, and then we separate. I charge across the lawn and up the wooden stairs to get my car, Therese dashes to her dorm for her suitcase. I careen my car around the corner, throw the suitcase into the back, and gun it toward Main Street. We reach the intersection just as the bus does. Unaware that we want him, the bus driver sees our panic, nods, and motions for me to go ahead. I hold the bus in my rear view mirror, in a temporary state for about a mile. We breathe relief, grasp hands for a minute as I stop the car. Therese snatches her suitcase from the back of my car, jumps on the bus and heads west.

# Getting the Words Second Hand: Deaf People Can Do Everything—Except Hear

"Everything you hear directly is what we hear second hand." As we sit in the lobby of Sackett Hall, Lee explains to a few of us how it is to be deaf in a hearing world. She and her colleagues, Ruth and Linda, live down the hall and I see them daily in Terry Moher's class with Therese and Dorothy. As temporary neighbors, we've shared food, drink, dorm woes, and writing. They are here with two other colleagues this summer from an English department at a high school for the deaf. As a hearing teacher who has spent a long professional lifetime in public schools, I learn much that I never knew about the languages, culture and politics of deafness.

The university has hired several free-lance sign interpreters for each day of the writing program. They are not always the same people. Every week there is a new crew of interpreters, probably because it is summer and many of them teach or go to school. Few of the rest of us know how to sign, but we can see there are differences in the interpreters' interpretations. Lee explains to me that there is American Sign Language (ASL), considered a language, and Signed English, a coding system. Each interpreter appears different as we watch, but, like translators, their job is to interpret spoken text as closely as possible. To an outsider, the interpreters are performers. As hearing observers, we enjoy watching the texts of our spoken words dance in their hands and on their faces. It adds a poetic dimension to the summer and some dramatic physical action to all our talk about writing. The language of Sign is an artful mix of letters, facial expressions, and gestures.

But the complexities are more than poetic for those who must rely on the interpreters' work for language. As in all languages, we discover, translation is not exact. It is a special verbal literacy that requires quick and careful thinking on the part of the hearing interpreter as well as the deaf recipient. I ask Lee if it's difficult to get oriented to so many different interpreters, and mention that I've noticed major differences in them. "Of course," she signs while her mouth forms the words, her oral English a bit blurry. "You are very observant." In this encounter, we talk about language and writing with a twist I hadn't considered.

On the lawn in front of the dorm, we lie in the bright sun together, pick at the grass, and talk about how crucial it is for all students to maintain the connection between reading and writing, especially those who are "at risk" with physical disabilities like deafness that block mainstream language acquisition. Lee and I watch each other's mouths carefully and we secure our notebooks under our legs. We do not need an interpreter. Occasionally, we need to write out a word that one of us doesn't understand.

## Deaf Students are Bilingual Interpreters

Lee shows me a record she keeps of her students' "malapropisms." Until now, I have not thought of her students as interpreters. To me, their approximations in using English written language are both amusing and poignant. They remind me of all teenagers as they pursue making their own sense of the adult world. But Lee's students' written words illustrate the extra job a deaf adolescent has as she interprets Sign into writing:

"Oh, thank gosh."
"A shovel slaps the snow."
"Going camping, I wear my pack-back."
"There was a terrible plane crush."
"It is time to clam down."

"When I went to my girlfriend's house, I rang the door bellring," and
    then we had an "argumen."
I put the words in "alphabetable order."
There is a "broadwalk at Ocean City."
I found a "secret passway."
"After the argument, my mouth was wild open."
" I had to go to the hospital to get an x-tray."
"The police arrived in a helicopper"
"The weather is short of warm"
"The dance was wowderful, fan-static."
"I ran the lawnmotor"
"I saw a hummerbird."

In each of these little misuses, there is inherent logic and
figurative language. The words illustrate creative understanding
of meaning, as well as contextual interpretation. "Wild-open"
mouths and beachside "broadwalks," weather that is "short of
warm," and crushed planes and police in helicoppers conjure up
lucid poetic imagery. We must understand that deaf students are
bilingual, and, Lee believes, given an environment rich with reading and writing, they thrive.

## We Read with Our Eyes, of Course

Lee is deeply aware of the unnecessary disenfranchisement her
students suffer. She and her colleagues tell many stories to support this position. Because her school is a demonstration school
in a large city, her students are often "on display" to administrators, politicians, foreign diplomats, and other interested people.
The visitors are not always enlightened. She incorporates one of
those stories into her own writing about disability and power. In
her paper, Lee writes:

   . . . This spring, one of my classes was visited by a South American
   dignitary from a country where educating deaf people is not the
   norm. My students had just finished reading *Sounds of Silence,* a
   young adult novel by Marilyn Levy that includes a mainstreamed deaf
   teen as a major character. The dignitary watched with visible awe as
   the class worked individually and in teams writing an additional
   chapter to the novel, drafting invitations for the character to come

to our school and experience the Deaf culture the students themselves enjoyed.

Our visitor could suppress her confusion no longer. "You mean these deaf students have all READ this book? But how?"

Julie, a junior, confidently stated what was to her the obvious. "With our eyes, of course." And Julie was perfectly correct. . . .

Lee's story illustrates a moment that is at once embarrassing and triumphant. As I see it, this is a story of all marginalized populations in school: the foreign language speaker, the ghetto dialect speaker, the person who is "educable mentally retarded" or physically handicapped. Like Julie and her classmates, our marginalized students deserve *more* fully connected language opportunities in school, *not fewer*. A rich mix of reading, writing, speaking, and listening in the company of other English language users is critical for their literacy. This means reading and writing literature, not executing grammar worksheets. (Sunstein in Stires, ed., 1991)

## Deafness as Deficit: A Self-Fulfilling Prophecy

Lee and I discuss the "deficit model" thinking that we see in curricula for students who carry the label "disabled." As long as schools see human difference as deficit, difference will always be sorted out. On the other hand, schools *could* view difference as opportunity, we agree. The mere act of living in the mainstream demands that "disabled" students develop extra abilities: interpreting and signing, jumping comfortably between two national or ethnic cultures, or understanding the biology of a physical or mental handicap. Students with difference have extra information to contribute.

"If our deaf students cannot read and write literature on a level with their hearing peers," Lee writes, "it may very well be that they've never been exposed to real literature at all. . . . Too long, we have been making deficit assumptions and spoon feeding (sometimes force-feeding) our students with a conceptual mash unable to create or sustain intellectual or linguistic growth. By thinking deaf students incapable of reading and writing real literature, we've created a self-fulfilling prophecy. . . . Reading and writing are power, and empowered students are hooked for life on their own learning."

It is not any lack of intelligence that prevents a student from fuller literacy; it is often the self-fulfilling prophecy of the "dis-ability testing and remediation" she must endure. If these students are given little pieces of language to exercise their broken parts, they will never have a chance to use English whole, or to see how others use it. As these teachers experience reading and writing for themselves here this summer, they rethink their own teaching practices and reflect on their teacher-training histories. Lee's colleague Ruth writes:

> Teacher training programs set the pace for the field of education of the deaf. When I began teaching deaf children over twenty years ago, I took classes towards a certificate that showed I understood deafness and how it made deaf children different . . . in Language Development I learned ASL was to be ignored . . . in Speech and Speechreading the hearing professor was embarrassed about having deaf students in his class . . . in Audiology we learned about how language development is affected by degree of hearing loss . . . in Psychology of Deafness, we learned certain personal traits deaf children have, and that the teachers were martyrs . . . there was rarely a course in American Sign Language, the language that most deaf people used . . . but there were newly developed systems of signs to help children learn English. . . .

Ruth explains that many educators of deaf students still have a clinical, pathological point of view. As a deaf person herself, she writes "We prefer to be seen as a culture, with a rich heritage passed on by children of deaf parents. . . . It will be a long time before my rage is completely gone. Like Toni Morrison said of white people, 'historically, we were seldom invited to participate in the discourse even when we were its topic.'" (Morrison in Zinsser, 111)

## Language Forbidden

Although Lee grew up struggling as a deaf child in a hearing home, her colleagues Ruth and Linda are among the 5 percent of the deaf population who come from deaf families. The deaf child born into a deaf family has a distinct advantage in literacy, Linda tells me, a home environment rich in language. Their "home language" is American Sign, and English is a learned second language. Linda's parents and grandfather signed stories to her when she was a child, creating a context for learning much the same as in any privileged home. But for deaf children like Lee born into hearing homes, there is minimal communication.

Linda observes that Don Murray's term "inner voice" was a new idea to her (1990). She tests herself: "I noticed that I do have a 'deaf voice' based on the dreams I dream. The characters in my dreams have conversations in ASL. With the interpreters, the ones who signed in ASL, I received the messages very comfortably and directly whereas those who signed in Signed English, I had to translate into ASL—especially the phrases, idiomatic expressions, sounds, and puns, and then into English." Linda writes:

> For most of us whose first language is ASL, writing is a laborious chore. We have to translate our native language into English and then put it down on paper. In order to write well, we must read a lot, so we can switch our language into English comfortably when we write.

One of Linda's pieces during the three weeks is a poem called "The Forbidden Language." It details her "seven solid years of battle" during the nineteen-fifties, in a residential school in which ASL was prohibited. At night in the dorms, one student would stand in the doorway, watching for the housemother: "A circle of kids would watch another kid, the storyteller, signing, secretly" and then they would scatter when the housemother came. Although they were punished severely, they "dared to continue the risks." The scars on her sister's thigh clued Linda's parents to the hairbrush beatings they received for signing stories together. A formal, legally filed grievance and a subsequent victory placed Linda and her sister in a different school where signing was respected. Had her parents not been deaf, Linda and her sister and their classmates might have stayed there for more years, deprived of their native literacy.

## A Bond of Stars: The Plastic Spots of Difference

On one night during the first week, Lee, Ruth, and Linda sit in a circle on Lee's bed in their pajamas, eating candy, drinking Diet Coke, joking, and reading one another's writing. Linda is wearing her favorite tee shirt. It is black with white letters across the chest: "Deaf People Can do Everything—Except Hear." Lee's computer is printing out her latest piece of writing, her cloth-bound journal sits inside her folded legs, and the floor is messy with wads of discarded drafts. They are signing wildly to each other when I walk by.

Ruth invites me to take a walk down the hall with her. She has just discovered a planetarium in her room. She points upward and then turns off the light. The ceiling is covered with plastic stars, affixed in configurations that reproduce a few constellations. They don't twinkle; they glow plastic yellow-green over our heads. We can't talk in the dark, but we jab each other and laugh together at the hidden legacy from a recent college student.

When she turns the light on, the stars disappear. It is a fitting metaphor for the shared literacies we are all experiencing this summer. When the lights go on, the eerie spots of plastic difference disappear. But they become a bond between us, the knowledge that each of us has a secret in the dark worth exploring together. Whether we get the words "straight" or "secondhand," it is in talking, reading, and writing about those differences that we can celebrate our human abilities to communicate.

 *Three*

## Dorothy Spofford: Distance, Resistance, and Response

*The alternative to monologue is conversation or dialogue. Bakhtin called dialogism a "merry science," because it has to do, not with formal concepts existing outside of history, nor with prescriptive language imposing "truths," but with talking, interrupting, writing, rewriting, communicating as living and diverse beings in the midst of life.*

—Maxine Greene

I find a note from Dorothy Spofford taped to my door on the Sunday evening before classes begin. "Bonnie: Building H. Come see us." I've known her for a year, visited her classroom, and hoped to include her in my study. She is not living in the dorms with the others. For these weeks, she will be renting a university apartment with her friend Colin. So I walk across campus. Eight doorbells guard the inside foyer of the two-story red brick cluster, and the outside door is locked. I stand on the wet grass under the final purple wisps of sunset, tip my head, and yell Dorothy's name toward the second floor. I hear a printer and I see a fan in the window. I wonder how many people I've disturbed. With my little tape recorder dangling from my wrist and my head facing the twilight, I feel like a bumbling cartoon sleuth. And, although she's agreed to cooperate, the fan and the printer behind the window make Dorothy feel distant and inaccessible.

Eventually, Colin waves, runs down the stairs, and invites me up. There are piles of books on the two coffee tables in the living room, a computer and printer on the desk, and a large tote bag with beach towels and bathing suits in the corner. The bed is unmade and there are stacks of books next to it. "We can keep things messy here. It's not home," Dorothy laughs and talks of their plans for the beach, daily swims in the university pool, and deep-sea fishing. Colin is also a high school English teacher, a veteran of this writing program. While Dorothy is in classes, he will read in the library and write. His presence in her life has recently shifted from colleague to lover and housemate. For the first time, they are together without Dorothy's two small children.

The window fan makes a thin breeze in the hot night air. Dorothy and I sit at the kitchen table with my tape recorder, pouring Diet Coke on mounds of ice in disposable cups, a ritual we will repeat nightly. She pads in her bare feet from the sink to the refrigerator to refill the ice tray. Her skin is evenly tanned and her legs are tight from exercise. She moves like a cat, fluid, quiet, sure of foot. Despite the humidity and the hour, the collar of her shirt stands straight up, and its tails are still tucked inside the waistband of her shorts. Her thick dark hair is caught in back with a tortoise shell barrette. She is "tucked in" in so many ways.

My time with Dorothy will be different from my time with the others. We decide to meet at 9:30 each weeknight in her apartment for a half hour. I'll attend both her classes, join her for special events, collect her writing, but I will not interrupt her time alone with Colin. Dorothy wants to participate, but she participates on her own terms. By living with Colin, she has already made some personal choices that disengage her from the rest of the group. I ask what appealed to her about this program, why she decided to come, and she reminds me that she'd seen the writing program from a distance last summer:

> I heard so many people raving about it . . . watched them through the windows of the cafeteria last summer. . . . sitting in circles with notepads on their knees, talking and enjoying themselves. I saw barbecues. I knew I could get six credits in three weeks, and I wanted to have some time to work on my own writing, because

I'm having a hard time fitting that into my life. Time . . . I can't keep going by sketching an idea down on an envelope and maybe finishing it three months later. . . . My commitment to recycling at home is to use every bit of trash. But to do that I have to set up my cellar in a series of boxes. I have to be in a frame of mind that I'm going to do this. Time boxes, this is how I'm going to do it. Time boxes.

She admits to a "guilt-insecurity syndrome:" "I feel that I'm never doing a good enough job. Writing, anything to do with school, I can never be good enough. But then again, I can never be a good enough mother either." Dorothy's personal history suggests that the "need to be good enough," as a writer, a scholar, a teacher, a woman, and a mother is not new for her. It is a tangled mass of events, places, and relationships. The tangles will loosen in her writing and in her talk as conscious craft and unconscious surprise for her during her three weeks here.

She is a cheerful skeptic full of paradoxes, an interesting mix of guarded enthusiasm, stiff confidence, intellectual energy, and self-doubt. She is an English teacher who majored in linguistic anthropology and speaks four languages. She is a beginner with experience, a writer who doesn't want to share her writing, a participant who has arranged for only partial participation. She talks directly and cheerfully but she's not afraid to tell me what's on her mind. Her tiny frame contrasts with her robust opinions and strong words. Her eyes are soft and dark, but they strike through the thick lashes that guard them. She does not intend to prepare for tomorrow morning.

## *The Writing Group: Listening for Stories*

At 8:30 A.M., after the opening meeting, Dorothy joins Ellen Blackburn-Karelitz's writing class in the English Department faculty lounge. It doesn't look like school or feel like it. Some of us nest in wing chairs and bowed-back windsors, others curl on leather sofas. Our sneakers and sandals rest around the floor and bare feet peek out of the carved oak chair slats. The glass coffee table holds stacks of handouts, a clipboard, and books about writing: Natalie Goldberg's *Writing Down the Bones*, Eudora Welty's *One Writer's Beginnings*. The lights are off and outside the sky sogs gray with humidity. The fan blades buzz gently overhead in the still air; their puffs are lost to the high ceiling.

Above us there are four hanging chandeliers with brass curls and white glass globes. An enormous arched window breaks one wall, white painted molding framing little square panes. It is wide open, begging a breeze. Ellen looks around at the polished leather, wood, and glass: "I think we forgot to see who'll bring the cigars!" She welcomes us to New Hampshire and invites us to take a few minutes to think of a small story to tell about ourselves, not related to our teaching, "so we get a feeling for each other as people."

Ellen tells me later in an interview that this is her way to "set a community." Each person can mark her uniqueness by choosing a personal anecdote. Her opening serves several important purposes for Ellen's teacher/students and for herself as an instructor. In a writing class composed of disparate people who teach grades from kindergarten through college, each person needs to be able to say "don't judge me by my writing," and the stories allow Ellen to think about how she'll arrange response groups for the afternoon. "If somebody is scared to death," she tells me, "I don't put them with an authoritarian or a critical person. I can tell by the stories they choose to tell about themselves."

For me today is like a first chapter in a thick novel. I try to keep the characters straight. Ellen is quiet and calm, dressed in gauzy white cotton. Her hair and eyes are deep brown. Gold chains gleam against her summer-tanned skin. She jots down a few notes on her clipboard, looks, smiles, and tells her own story first. She will sing this summer with her dentist-husband's rock group, "a bunch of middle-aged guys who only perform once a year." They'll perform at a clambake in August, and she's not looking forward to it. "Their lyrics are pretty raunchy, and the music is so loud I can't hear myself sing." She scans the circle of seventeen, waiting for someone to speak.

I am surprised when Dorothy volunteers. She describes the new house she's bought in rural Maine, and her first vegetable garden, "a place to put dirt and green things." She'll return on weekends to check the tomatoes and broccoli. "I haven't seen any critters yet. Everything is growing so far." She is straight and trim, guarded, and hers is more a personal statement than a story. She sits alone in a high-backed leather wing chair. Her shirt collar stands tall around her neck, her thick hair clipped as tight as her sentences. Dorothy's demeanor itself appears a sentry. I discover later that "watching green things grow in dirt" and "keeping the critters out" is a fitting metaphor for Dorothy's history as a teacher, as a woman, and as a young mother. Her final piece of writing will be a fictional account of a disturbed little girl who achieves peace at her aunt's farm in Maine, watching things grow.

Dorothy's response partners will become crucial to her story here. Susan is one of them, and when she introduces herself, she shares her frustration as a single mother. She lives with her two adopted Asian children in Philadelphia, but she teaches in the suburbs: "I give a better education to the kids I teach than to my own," says Susan. "There is a chasm between the suburbs and city. I bridge the gap every day. The suburban kids are afraid of the city kids; the city kids think the suburban kids are boring." Her opening statement highlights a passion for her own children and her interest in the politics of a multicultural society. Her voice is velvet. Her cheeks glow pink. Her short gray hair is a surprise against her smooth face. She is neatly pressed in a white button-down shirt and striped seersucker slacks. This week she will write a very personal piece about adopting her first child, but she will discard it in favor of writing a modern fairy tale with a political message. By the third week, she'll return to the piece about her daughter.

Lenore listens intently to all seventeen stories and waits. Her chin points toward each speaker. She is fiftyish, slim, and chiseled. Her mouth is straight. Her notebook lies open on her lap, her legs set primly to hold it. Her neck tightens as she talks, the words brief and efficient: "Writing is not something I like to do—at all. I do not like to reveal things about myself. I do not have many intimate friends, but I am close to my family."

Ellen's response to Lenore is her first as an instructor, and a lead-in to her conclusion: "Just as you're not comfortable, Lenore, you have children who aren't. It's a wall of censorship that goes up. With opportunities to write in different genres, people begin to feel more comfortable." Over three weeks, Lenore will always volunteer last. She will defer to everyone and respond to their writing enthusiastically. She will ask that her sessions not be taped, and request privacy in the dorm. For three weeks, her writing will explore lifelong family ties: her dead father's stories, two elderly sisters who travel away from home, and her own lifelong investment in the trees that grow around her home.

Ellen will assign Lenore, Susan, and Dorothy together as a group. They will meet this first afternoon as they will every afternoon for three weeks. Beginning with their first drafts, these three women will shape one another's work and they will draw on one another's images, ideas and information. Why did Ellen arrange these women together? Dorothy, a stiff high school teacher who watches dirt and green things? Susan, a serene junior-high teacher who reaches out with a political ethic? And Lenore, a second-grade teacher who is afraid to write and is tied to the world of her home? Ellen made a conscious choice by listening for the stories they chose to tell.

The morning session ends with Ellen's summary: "We are all storytellers—that's what gossip is—writers are receptive to their own lives and what goes on in them." The ninety minutes have been smooth and natural, meticulously planned. She concludes with a reading from Eudora Welty, reminding us to listen *for* stories rather than listen *to* them:

> Long before I wrote stories, I listened for stories. Listening for them is something more acute than listening to them. I suppose it's an early form of participation in what goes on. Listening children know stories are there. When their elders sit and begin, children are just waiting and hoping for one to come out, like a mouse from its hole. (1984, 16)

The writing class disperses at 10 A.M. Each teacher will spend the remainder of the morning talking about theory and practice with others who teach at the same grade levels. Dorothy and I head upstairs for our first daily coffee break in Room 218. But there is no coffee. Room 218 is the place to borrow books, grab the daily newsletter, meet for brief conversation and logistical connections. There are message boxes for instructors, sign-up sheets for books, chalkboards for last-minute communications. There is much talk about having no coffee. The square of tables is covered with a professional lending library, copies of past summer program publications, stacks of newsletters, notices of video showings, optional performances, and New England maps and travel guides. The break time is brief, and I head downstairs with Dorothy.

## *A Two-Headed Woman and a Jangling Horsecart*

Dorothy is one of the twenty-seven teachers in Terry Moher's high school grade-level group. She sits across the circle from Therese. Terry announces that the point of this course is to learn "how to give up control in the classroom so we can gain it." Her eyes dart around the room as she drinks from a thermos of coffee. She jokes about coffee; the class groans. "Tom can't afford coffee this year, so I'm not sure how many people will convene upstairs in 218." The coffee ritual marks one time in a high school teacher's day when she can meet with colleagues. Outside in the bell tower, the UNH carillon bells ring the half hour. I've heard these bells often, but today I hear them in contrast to the buzzers that pierce the time periods in a high school day.

Terry recalls her own experience ten years ago as a participant in the first New Hampshire Writing Program, and as a high school English teacher for fifteen years: "We're a cynical lot, skeptical. We get comfort from our professional content. We don't know a lot about how people learn. . . . I had never been exposed to elementary teachers as colleagues before I came here. As secondary teachers, we are isolated from them.

Elementary teachers know how to get kids to learn." She assigns a teaching journal, and asks people to write only on one side. "I'm not sure what I'll do with the other side yet," Terry says.

In this class, Dorothy introduces herself by describing her school as "a public school although they think it isn't," and says she sometimes feels that she's running "behind a jangling horsecart of ideas" with so many pressures from school and "fads" to follow in the profession. "Why am I here? To get graduate credit—to have time to work on writing." Terry asks the class to write again for a few minutes about "What makes writing hard? Take this opportunity to use writing to think it out," she suggests. Dorothy writes:

> What makes writing difficult? I think it might be the unbalance between physical act and psychic focus. We need to have both going—both tuned in—getting down every time an idea occurs to me—it's easier to file it away, say while I'm driving, and promise myself time later. The time never comes unless I force it. I am too easily distracted by my children, clean clothes, and it's always easier to read than to write. I know that with discipline I could write good stuff, if I kept my needs simple.

In our nighttime interview, Dorothy complains and tells me she's disappointed: "It's a huge group. I certainly wouldn't want to teach it. I feel pretty uncomfortable . . . If I come away from this with some tips and some new ways of trying things, I'm going to be satisfied, because that's what I expect." But she is dissatisfied today. "I didn't learn anything. Terry was unprepared. She didn't address anything directly. It was all so vague."

In that first class, I had watched Dorothy from across the room. She laughed and shook her head at times when others weren't doing either. I wondered about her notetaking patterns. *Why* was she writing when she was? *What* was she writing? The little notebook wasn't new, and it was the first day of class. Odd, I thought. She's writing in the middle of the book. It was what she calls her "compost journal," a half-sized loose-leaf. I'd seen this book of hers before. It was a conglomerate of class notes, personal reflections, and ideas for teaching. She'd kept it for a year already. "What I'm writing about isn't so much what we're talking about as what I see Terry doing. I want it to be a model for me. . . . I wrote things that occurred to me when somebody else was talking . . . nothing to do with what they were talking about."

On the top margin of today's entry, she's doodled a Janus-like female double-head with curly hair and earrings (see Figure 3–1). One head faces forward, mouth open, laughing, and one faces toward the other page of the notebook, pensive. Another paradox. On a page near the two headed woman, she wrote:

> Do I live two jobs? The tense, tired commute to work . . . the bells ring and I face over and over that circle of young people. This year's freshmen—funny, energetic, very willing to work on the tasks I get rolling. . . . I can't define teaching . . . I am never done running behind some jangling horsecart of ideas. . . . All it takes is a casual word, and I realize "I, my God, have forgotten to "do" conferences in two weeks". . . .

The irony in her notes is as two-headed as her doodle. The "circle of young people," a shape she sees them in, is one she must "get rolling" with tasks. She feels pressure to shape them in a "circle," to "do" conferences, and guilt that somehow this is teaching which she "can't define." She feels singularly responsible for controlling her students' class shape, their momentum, their energy, their humor, and their learning, "getting them rolling" with "tasks," "conferences" and "teaching." And she is suspicious of and exhausted by both her mythical horsecart and her real commute. I wonder where these paradoxes will take her in the ensuing weeks. She writes in her compost journal:

> The lessons I spend the most time planning never work out right. . . . I know I'm a good teacher. My students learn, read, write, think, and argue with me until we all get mad. But they come back, say "Hi," share a book, lend me music, whine over

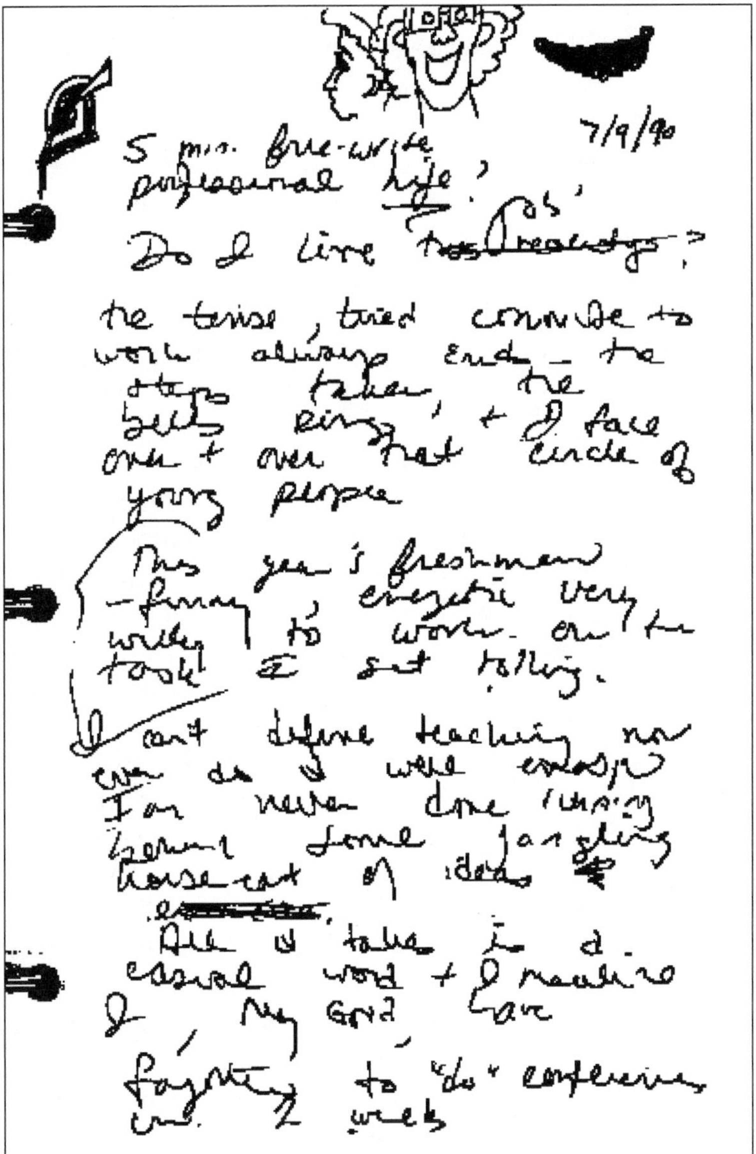

Figure 3–1 *Dorothy's Journal Entry*

assignments. I don't know why I'm a teacher, except that I love the kids and I love finding words and ideas with them. Why am I here?

Dorothy entered Terry's class looking for tips, but already she's found that Terry's goal is not to give them. It is to conceive a classroom as a place in which the teacher must "give up control in order to get control," as Terry said. Dorothy is writing about a school culture in which *she has* control: lessons of her design that go wrong, freshmen who are willing to do tasks she sets, a definition of success that involves her getting students to "read, write, think, and argue until everyone gets mad." She expresses disappointment in Terry's class which she labels "unprepared," that asks her to reconceive her role as a teacher and tells her she's going to give up control. But she "loves finding words and ideas" with students. Her passion for words and ideas will be the personal intellectual themes with which she will explore her work here with colleagues as well.

The second night, Tuesday, after the open forum, Dorothy tells me she's disgusted with the writing program's jargon. She is unwilling to become an insider and keenly sensitive to the "insider's" uses of language here. "I'm sick of the word 'abandoning.' There must be another way of saying that. I can think of several. *Stop writing*, for one." She laughs. "And sharing, '*group sharing*.' And "That really *works for me*." She laughs and groans. She mocks the language of "process approach." I am more intrigued.

In two days this program has established a group identity through a lexicon of special terms and phrases. Dorothy recognizes them as emblems teachers use, and she's not sure she wants to wear them. "I think my bullshit meter is pretty accurate. . . . I noticed that one of the people in the secondary group picked up a phrase of Terry's in five minutes. I thought it was amazing how fast that happened. . . . I'm sure it's totally subconscious."

But she is immersed in one of Terry's assigned readings, from Paulo Freire's *Pedagogy of the Oppressed* (1970). Dorothy hasn't thought about issues of cultural control as they apply to the classroom. "My background leans toward sociocultural things," she tells me, "I'd like to read more Freire. I liked the sentence Terry read that educational reform will never happen until the basic student-teacher relationship is transposed. Altered. I really like that idea. . . ." Although she won't "buy in," Terry's class urges Dorothy to reflect on herself, not only as a teacher of a body of knowledge called English, but as a teacher of adolescents. Days later, in her journal she writes:

> . . . . most significant is my own lack of motivation. . . . It is very hard to "do writing process". . . . Sometimes it's just easier to teach a whole-class lesson, assign a reading. I don't want to always be interactive, acting at my best. I'm not in love with the adolescent mind, nor their hormones. Sometimes I don't want to be nice to them. . . . I guess there are two reasons I'm experiencing failure: (a) I'm not doing it right or consistently; (b) I'm trying to do too much. I should go for success in one or two techniques, rather than limited success in many.

She criticizes herself as harshly as she does others, and inside her criticisms lie her paradoxes. Dorothy recognizes she needs "close personal contact," but she resists it. She feels that "it's hard to *do writing process*," assuming that it is something *to be done*. Intellectually, she endorses the summer program's underlying precepts: that students and teachers can be co-learners, that reading-writing relationships can be "altered, transposed," as she reads Freire. She believes in the collaborative nature of writing but isn't sure how it works. She wants to "succeed with her students," but she knows what it is to be unprepared. She feels antisocial and exhausted. She knows that learning requires guiding students to pace their own work, but she likes the clean, academic structures of teaching formal lesson plans. She complains that Terry's high school class is too big to form relationships. She rejects its jargon and its ritualistic features; her internal "bullshit meter" beeps at everything that bothers her. The class is "anecdotal and self-inflating." and people are superficial, "bitching about things like spelling."

Teachers' portrayals of classroom success annoy her. "A part of me that is growling not to sound so optimistic. . . . sometimes I'm cheerful and bubbly but sometimes I go into class and I want to kill the first kid that crosses me." One night during the second week, she has a dream and describes it in her journal:

> It was the first day of school of this coming fall. . . . In the room were all the worst students I've ever had. Foremost among the crowd was Darryl Perreault—my devil from my first year. They were all over the place, writing graffiti on the bulletin board, throwing papers, sassing to me. I was screaming at them, begging them to stop and pay attention. I wrote the assignment on the board: "Read pages 1-100 in Annie Dillard's *Pilgrim at Tinker Creek.*" I handed out the book amid laughter, but they started to read right away. The magic of literature took over. Silence while we read—except for exclamations. Suddenly the bell rang—except instead of a bell, . . . the 1812 Overture was blaring over the intercom. Kids jumped up and began marching out of the room in single file, in time to the music. Smiling boys started to 'high-five' each other with their paperbacks. I was left alone in the room, watching the kids march out. I sat shaking, exhausted, and happy as the music died away.". . . I have only met two or three kids who like *Pilgrim at Tinker Creek*. I must remember that all teachers love to describe the successes. We try to forget the failures.

Dorothy tells me stories of her personal teaching failures, stories of being "not good enough." It is difficult for her to listen to the success stories in that class of high school teachers while she is thinking of her failures and reconceptualizing her classroom at the same time. Complete with triumphant music, her dream shows a swarm of resistant boys in calm compliance reading one of Dorothy's favorite books written by a female. They haven't lost their masculinity. They are still "high-fiving" each other as they march out of her classroom in a line. Dorothy is exhausted but satisfied. They got what she wanted them to get. It is her dream of control and her concept of a successful classroom.

Dorothy had no formal preparation as a teacher. She relied on colleagues, her own literacy, and her intellectual intuition. When she says she's not "good enough," she is competing against a model of "good enough" which she hasn't really defined. Like many English teachers, she thrived in the traditional academic model. Her history as a student is full of successes. She admits with a sly smile that she never officially graduated from public high school, but her scores were good enough for college admission. Her parents were traditionally educated. Her father is a physics professor at an Ivy League university and her mother a chemist. They divorced when she was a pre-adolescent, and Dorothy lived with her father in a New England suburb. She spent her junior year in the Caribbean living with her mother and attending a bilingual private school with textbooks in English and classes in Spanish. Her father's sabbatical in England gave her a high school senior year inside British academic standards, and she enjoyed the competition. And she followed her passion for language to two colleges majoring in linguistic anthropology. This summer, eight years later, she encounters learning and teaching models that are less familiar.

## Women's Voices in an Academic Community

Her goal this summer is to learn how to use journals in the classroom. Dorothy loves her journal which was born last summer in a month-long institute in women's studies, six credits underwritten by a large national endowment, a stipend, and free tuition. It was her first full-time study since college, her first time away from her children. She lived in the dorms with other women and studied women writers of the nineteenth century. Although the institute dealt with a topic new to scholarship, its method was traditionally academic. She read voluminously, began the compost journal, and wrote a scholarly paper:

I had never considered women's studies at all. . . . We had a huge amount of reading, six hours a day, and then lectures and group readings. I was really entrenched in the community. . . . By the end of the week, we were having beer fests at night and going to the beach to read. . . . A lot of times, ideas would just spring into our conversation. . . . I realized how much I wanted to be part of an academic community. And how much I really love being in school, taking classes.

Dorothy's knowledge of women writers grew "a hundred percent. . . . I knew almost nothing, except for the traditional ones in the anthologies." She credits the institute for a shift in her teaching during the past year. She championed women's writing in textbooks and women's rights in school. "Now, every time we read something by a dead white male I throw in a female." She sat on a department textbook adoption committee and counted women writers in anthologies. She provided opportunities for students to read about women writers, keep journals, and write about women as they are treated in literature.

She highlights female characters in traditional literature whenever she can. On Halloween, she dressed as Hester Prynne, carrying her daughter's baby doll in a baptismal gown. Her students read slave narratives and diaries of pioneer women. She is passionate about the value of journals as they are associated with women: her own, her students', and those written by others. Dorothy tries to amplify the voices of her female students, sometimes at the expense of the males:

> The one thing I know I did differently, in addition to teaching women writers, was I made sure I addressed myself . . . pointedly, to the girls in the class . . . I had really been listening to the boys because their voices are deeper and louder. If a boy started to interrupt a girl, I would cut him off for her . . . it's taken some real effort on my part to get them used to not doing that. . . .

She laughs about a male student who wrote about "*Ms.*" Havisham in *Great Expectations*. They love to tease me about being '*Ms.*Spofford, *Ms.* Woman's Lib.' Although she is determined to be a feminist in her teaching, Dorothy's own mentors were almost all male, but the one she remembers most fondly was a woman:

> I had a dynamic teacher when I was living in England. I can see her. She was tall, in her late thirties, with short blonde hair, very modern and hip. She could read Chaucer with a real authentic accent. . . . she made Middle English come alive for me. In fact, I loved it so much and studied it so hard and took private lessons from her, that I got the highest grade on the Chaucer exam. Out of all those kids, those English kids, I got the highest grade. I was so proud of that. I really loved Chaucer because of her . . . her voice reading it, and the sound of the language.

Dorothy is twenty-nine, younger than her British mentor. And her personal academic history has deep roots in mainstream academic traditions of argument and competition. Her classroom model is traditionally male, like the Chaucer exam she took. She teaches in "a public school although they think it isn't," as she described it in Terry's class. Her comfort in the culture of schooling is based on learning through argument. As she told me, "my students learn, read, write, think, and argue with me until we all get mad." But she feels unprepared as a teacher: "I don't have that old American school background. I'm always winging it. . . . I'm aware of gaps . . . I was overseas in high school, so I never read the traditional American Lit canon: *The Scarlet Letter, Moby Dick*; I wasn't in America for it."

She questions reader-response theory, and the notion of a "cold reading" bothers her when she reads about it in Terry's class (Newkirk 1990). Dorothy comments, "supposedly I could read none of the books and get along just fine, but I think there are times when I need to know where this fits into that, so I can help them make connections. I agree that in theory I can just be a co-learner, but I also think I need to know at least where to find the stuff. And it's kind of fun to be a know-it-all, too, you know? I like telling them about obscure authors that knew so-and-so and said something. It's part of what makes it fun."

## *Journals and The Transfer of Control: Rewriting Last Summer*

Before she arrives, she knows that journals will be her focus. In her compost journal she writes:

> I really need help with journals . . . some kids just give me some-thing that they wrote for five minutes during lunch. . . . kids totally blew this journal off. . . . It seems like any time I give them freedom, they will just shirk their responsibilities. It seemed to be mostly boys. It sounds sexist, but it was mostly boys. But I'd like to get the boys into it. The ones who did had some beautiful stuff to say.

She wants to make boys more conscious of gender issues in writing and to try to use the journal as a form. At the end of the first week in Terry's class, I ask her what she feels is new. "What's new is the chance to think about it. And time. On the first day, Terry had us write questions on index cards, and the next day she said 'start answering those questions in your journal,' and low and behold, I'm already beginning to write the answers—the answers are there, I already know the answers." During the second week she tells me, "I started thinking, when I do journals with my juniors, I tell them. . . . but I never . . . show them how. I assume they know how to do it." One boy hated doing his journal, she remembers, so she suggested that he write a letter about hating his journal. "It just didn't work. This kid's not going to jump through my hoop."

Dorothy's student wouldn't jump through the journal hoop she imposed on him. In Terry's class, Dorothy looks for hoops and can't find them: "I don't even know what it is I'm sup-posed to be doing," she sighs. Like her students when she "gives them freedom," she resists Terry's class throughout the program. She is waiting for directives and not getting any. "I know Terry's leaving it perfectly vague so I can find my own topic. I know that." I ask if she's decided on a topic for her final paper. "Nothing that I would care to write about. . . . I'm perfectly willing to write a research paper, but I don't think that's what she wants."

On the day before the final class, there is much confusion buzzing about Terry's expectations for the final project. People shuffle papers and scrawl notes to one another. Terry teases them; they are exhibiting the same grade-grubbing behavior they've complained about in their students. But Dorothy doesn't think it's funny. She scowls while the others laugh, and argues with Terry:

> Terry: Being vague in assignments always goofs up the kids who want A's. (Grits her teeth, joking) Oooh, you secondary people. For those who are uptight, can someone explain?
>
> Dorothy (interrupting): I care about an A. I'm in a master's program. I feel tense. This is the first time you've seen my writing. I have no idea how you'll respond.
>
> Terry: I would hope you've self-evaluated. . . . Should I have collected it earlier? The toughest thing about the secondary group is that each of you came with a different agenda. I'm not grading the polished product . . . the purpose of learning is not grading . . . we're teaching a process and that legitimizes a grade for effort. . . .

Dorothy shifts uncomfortably in her chair and shoves her pencil eraser between her eyebrows. Terry glances over. "Dorothy, are you comfortable?" Dorothy snaps, "The chair is hard." Later, when she submits her final paper, she attaches an apology to Terry:

> Terry: I want to express my regret for what happened in class. . . . you must have felt attacked. Having been in that position myself, I'm sorry for anything I did to contribute to that effect. . . . I should have expressed my dissatisfaction sooner to you personally. . . . I feel that you should model the behaviors we'll exhibit as teachers in our classrooms.
>
> I had expected to be conferenced with about my paper; I expected an opportunity to revise and re-draft. This, after all, is the basis of writing-process teaching. I

still don't understand why we weren't given this chance. In all other regards, I've enjoyed this course very much. It has been refreshing to be with other secondary teachers, sharing ideas and techniques.

In three weeks, Dorothy adapted much of the jargon she criticized and the ideas that underlie it. Her note admits to Terry that she "expected to be conferenced with," although Terry had made it clear she believes conferences are the responsibility of the students. Others, like Therese, asked for and received frequent conferences. In her quest for modeling, Dorothy noted Terry's pedagogical strategies and adapted them. With her skepticism, her note and the final paper she writes, she actualizes Terry's dictum "There is no right way to do this."

Left alone to create an assignment for herself, Dorothy has found her own hoop and examined it. Ironically, it is an argument with her own writing; a gutsy, reflexive act. Her final paper is called "The Abuse of Journals in the Classroom," a paper in response to a paper she wrote six months earlier called "The Use of Journals in the Classroom." She reconceives her teaching as she writes about the "rosy view" she presented in January: "I provided excerpts from my students' writing that illustrated the range of possibilities. . . . I glowed about how kids loved to spend time writing in their journals . . . In short, I wrote that paper convinced that the journal was one of the most important facets of my class." She writes:

> . . . It was a researched paper, complete with detailed references to Fulwiler's *The Journal Book.* . . . However, by spring there were serious problems in our journalese. The students' fresh, imaginative entries began to dry up . . . [she describes response journals in her American Lit class]. . . . Sounds great, huh? Why did students slowly start to write only half-page entries, some pulled straight from Cliff Notes? Why did I get platitudes instead of discoveries? Worse still, why did some students stop writing journals altogether? I have a lot of questions. Some have been answered in my reading. Some have come out . . . in the process of keeping my own journal this summer. I think I'm starting to see some answers. . . .

Dorothy categorizes five "answers." Without "buying in," she has adapted what initially appeared as jargon, superficial success stories, and her personal quest for classroom "tips," and applied it to her earlier thinking. With this paper, she becomes an insider in this "process" culture, but on her own terms. She assumes a reflexive posture as she looks at her own practices, acting as both teacher and student:

1. *Instruction* What I forgot was that people forget. After the first week was over, I assumed my students knew how to do it. I realize now that I must teach, review, and illustrate good journal-keeping techniques all the year through.
2. *Sharing* The best way to teach 'journaling' is to encourage sharing among the students . . . in any number of ways.
3. *Time* I forgot that for many, the school is their haven, their quiet place. I also 'disremembered' the axiom of teaching: 'Give time in class for what you value.' If I value journal writing, I must dedicate time to it.
4. *Purpose* All too many kids see this as just another way to "Please The Teach." I can provide specific instructions, and students can learn different ways to work, to please themselves, not me.
5. *Evaluation* Sometime during the course of the year I began writing negative comments . . . such pearls of wisdom as "Try harder! "More!" or "Incomplete!" at the end of a page. . . . Pointing out the good is always more effective than condemning the bad. . . .

In response to Dorothy's paper, Terry writes "You've presented the very problems many teachers have with journals, in very real ways . . . Look for a place to publish this—it's real." Terry's class presented problems for Dorothy, and Dorothy presented problems for Terry's class. But her paper shows reflexivity and a shift in her thinking about her own teaching practices. A year ago, she was reading journals and stories of nineteenth century women. Ironically, she has reconceived what she learned from them and applied it to her twentieth century educational practice. Her resistance to Terry's pedagogy yields her own. She has questioned, and answered her thinking from six months ago. And she has met her goal—to re-examine her students' journal keeping.

## *Listening Beyond the Text*

Terry's class is not the only place Dorothy works with the goals she's set. In Ellen's class, her writing group becomes an experience in feminist learning. It offers time to write and choice of topic and genre. Its major requirement is that each person submit and read aloud several pages of revised writing at the end of each week and publish a polished piece at the end. "Submission" each week means not only a paper for Ellen's response, but responses from each class member during a Friday formal reading. "Publication" means selecting a piece not just for a printed collection, but an all-program oral reading performance on the final day.

Drafting, sharing, and revising take up most of the time—in and out of class. And inside all that work resides the content of the writing workshop: issues of genre features, writer's craft, figures of speech, rhetorical strategies, grammar and syntax, and rendering meaning for readers. Publication, sharing, and response carry stronger emphasis—and confusion—in people's experience in this class than grades or content. Ellen's class presents alternatives to the traditional models of argument and competition which form Dorothy's school history and her teaching practice. In Terry's class, she thinks "the basic student-teacher relationship is transposed. Altered." Here, in Ellen's class, she will experience it.

On the afternoon of the first day when Dorothy takes off her shoes and sits with Susan and Lenore on the thick grass outside Hamilton Smith Hall, they begin an interchange that will last for three weeks. By the second night Dorothy tells me, "I got a better idea of who people are and where they're coming from. I'm happy in that group. Very happy." She keeps a critical eye on Ellen's teaching, noting her balance between control and independence. "Ellen isn't talking all the time, she's telling us what to do, and then we go off and do it by ourselves. . . . we need both." The writing group meets twice a day, twice as long as Terry's grade level class, and its purpose for Dorothy is "to do something we've never done before. . . . It's kind of exciting to be asked to write different kinds of stuff. I've been doing mostly poetry for years and I really need to branch out a little bit. . . . I think as a writer I need to work on getting away from myself. Writing something that doesn't have anything to do with my personal past."

Her passion for language explains her personal preference for writing poetry. I ask about that. Did she write during the time she was learning languages? When did she begin to consider herself a poet? "I used to write really drippy teenage poetry. The adolescent stuff, you know, 'everyone hates me, no one understands me,' and that was really therapeutic. I've written with increased confidence over the past five years, simultaneous with starting to teach English. In forms other than college essays. Reading and teaching poetry is a part of my job. I love getting paid to do it."

Early in the week, Dorothy begins to write a piece of fiction. In her journal, she writes, "I've attempted to fictionalize a real occurrence. To do so I changed the names, setting, events, and point of view. Result? Pure shit. I hate it. It might go in some pulp mag, or under a Harlequin cover. I can't write fiction. I'll try again tomorrow using *Writing Down the Bones* for a jump start . . . I won't let failure get me down." Tuesday night, she tells me "I wrote it, but I don't like it at all. I hate the fiction I write. . . . It sounds like pulp . . . not how I intended it. . . ." She discards it for now. Two weeks later, it will serve as the core of her final piece, a short story. But for now, to be on the safe side, she's decided on an essay defining male and female relationships. She talks outside on the lawn with Susan and Lenore, trying to frame a starting sentence:

Dorothy: I'm thinking of a series of boys from my past. . . .
   Like the luck of the draw, my definitions might be different if they hadn't been in my life.
Lenore: You don't have brothers?

Dorothy: No.

Lenore: I can tell.

Dorothy: I think I'm pretty clear about what I am doing, I just don't know where to go.

Susan: You're defining your concept of maleness. [They share stories about boys in their lives: "Billy ate my shell collection," "Skipper made me take off my pants and toss them in the laundry," "Dickie impaled his sneaker on a rusty nail"]

Lenore: We remember their names when they did that stuff, don't we!

Susan: I wonder if they remember.

Dorothy: Of course.

Lenore: Alienation . . . a closeness, then a separation.

A lot of writing will come out of this short interchange, out of each woman's reading of Dorothy's ideas. Dorothy picks up on her own word, "definitions" and it becomes both title and metaphor. She takes Susan's perception that she's defining maleness to herself and Lenore's observation that women remember the names of the boys who first defined maleness for them. The talk sets Lenore thinking about her brothers: "closeness, then separation," a theme she'll use in her own writing this week about her father. By Wednesday night, Dorothy writes a plan for an essay, but it is different, more personal. Her draft is a fluid movement of thinking, a combination of her inner speech on paper, a dialogue with herself, and a text she is forming based on her conversations with Susan and Lenore:

*Draft #3: A Progression of Relationships*

A girl's life is so often determined by the males who find her attractive. Dickie Dorr lived down the street, spent his days and mine following me as I rode my tricycle until he tried to prove his gender by putting his sneaker through a rusty nail. . . . [She describes other relationships for three pages.] I married [my ex-husband] because I recognized his maleness. . . . Today I've come to re-evaluate my definition of maleness . . . I've been freed to pursue other characteristics in men. My relationship with Colin is so much better . . . STOP. 10:45 P.M. 7/10/90. Q: Where to go next? A: SUMMARIZE WORDS: male role-models, maleness, violence-power, separation-differentness, violation, alienation, "Luck of the Draw"?? It was pretty clear to me even then that to be male is to be bold, reckless, free, and sexual. The female role was . . . a victim of her own inability to get what she wanted. . . . I see that I have chosen men because they were 'masculine'. . . . To relate with that kind of male I had to negate something crucial in my soul, deny that part of me that is bold, daring, and exciting. Slowly, so slowly I've grown to enhance my own maleness or maybe find a new definition for sexual roles. It's as exciting as stepping on nails.

While she explores her thoughts in draft, Dorothy can test them on her response group. The rules are clear; Ellen has given them a way to respond. She has taught four techniques: "pointing, summarizing, telling, and questioning." It is new language to everyone, and to Dorothy it seems rather simplistic. "She's covered a little about responding, but I think there's a lot more to it than she's presented so far," she complains Tuesday night.

When I interview Ellen, I can see that she set the stage for what Dorothy experienced. Ellen likes to give very clear guidelines the first week. "It's safer for them, it allows them to feel what different responses can do." As their instructor, she begins by reading her own writing in draft, asking for specific response. But then she backs off. "I have to move in and out of the community. They're going to bond with each other, and sometimes they do it because they're mad at me. Ultimately, I have the final authority because I have to grade them." Whether she likes it or not, there will be a grade in this course, and Ellen knows that fact separates her from the others.

The guidelines for response are simple, her own adaptations from Peter Elbow's *Writing Without Teachers* (1973): "Pointing" highlights a phrase or word that has particular appeal to the responder, "summarizing" is the practice of relating back to the author what the responder has heard, "telling" suggests that the responder relate what she hears to something she knows, and "questioning" is asking for more information. By Wednesday, Dorothy and the rest of the class are using them consciously. Although she complained that Ellen covered only a little about responding, Dorothy practices these techniques again and again.

"The one question . . . thus far is how to include my own writing in the classroom without feeling vulnerable," Dorothy tells me. Ellen models just what Dorothy wants to see. "Yesterday Ellen read something she had written. That's very brave. I have a hard time doing that in my class. Something that was obviously in draft form, she read it, and she had us respond the way she had just taught us. That was very good." Dorothy never shares her writing with students, she tells me. "Frequently my writing is so personal that I don't want to share it with people in a small town. . . . I have children of school board members in most of my classes. If for nothing else than there might be a word in there that isn't pretty. . . . I feel like I have to edit everything I show them. . . ." Dorothy takes a complicated reflexive stance in Ellen's class, using double lenses as she watches both herself as a student writing and herself as a teacher of students' writing. In her compost journal, Dorothy lists comments she's heard from others:

- The response group supports quality of thought, even if writing does not yet convey that. No assignments means opportunities.
- What I'm doing now is scarier than being a teacher who writes in her spare time.
- Listening beyond the text: reason peer groups often fail is because they obsess about what is already written. Teacher can look for strengths first! Then, writer sees possibilities.

Through this class, she conducts the messy business of being at once a writer, a reader, a respondent, and a teacher of writing. By Thursday, her essay about men turns into a poem. She reads it in draft to Susan and Lenore. "I put out all the drafts . . . they pointed to the spots that were unclear. . . ." Was their help useful? I ask her. "Oh, yeah, it was. Often, when I'm done with a poem, I'll go over it six or seven times, and then I'll give it to somebody and just say 'Here, enjoy.' I'm not usually looking for response, in fact at that point I've got so much invested in it that I don't want to hear anything." Susan and Lenore have "seen it in daily pieces," she tells me, and this is new for her.

## The First Friday: A Quiet Ritual

On Friday morning in the English Department faculty lounge, each person in Ellen's class reads a completed piece; the order is determined by volunteers. Sandals clutter the carpet, toes curl around the oak chairs, legs splay against the leather chairs, ragged drafts spill out of totebags. Knees are bent, hidden under pastel cotton skirts, male and female legs exposed out of shorts. A breeze ruffles the loose papers, puffs against thin fabrics and stray hairs.

Ellen explains the procedure. Listeners will respond on slips of paper with short phrases. Dorothy interrupts to ask if their responses can be anonymous. Ellen looks at her, surprised, and then she scans the circle. No, she hopes. Ellen reminds the class that today's reading is public: "The time for change is passed. This is publication," she says, "it's not a time to be critical." She glances at Dorothy, and then adds some humor. "Be kind," she says, "it's Friday the thirteenth."

Silence falls. Muscles tense and release with each reading. When one person finishes, the others rise silently to offer their paper responses. "It's kind of like Valentine's Day," one person says. "This is a very odd feeling," another writer whispers as she gathers her slips of paper, nodding, her eyes thanking each respondent, "it's like a reading shower. Is it polite to read them when they come in?" She checks on the rules of the ritual, and smiles as she reads. Ellen had told me that this first Friday would be an emotional event.

Dorothy volunteers fifth. "I think I'm ready to read." The collar of her black cotton shirt stands guarding her neck, and she fiddles with the rope belt at her waist. Her voice quakes a little, and then she reads her poem loudly, smiling:

## Definition

Dickie Dorr raised his foot,
bragged his shoes tougher
than an upright, rusty nail.
He slammed it down and was carted off
the ambulance screams were mine.

Carl Foster, blond haired idol,
could run shouting, sweeping
muscled arms about his naked chest.
But mine were locked in a girl's
chant of watching envy.

Doug Flanders made drunk off
tenth grade liquor-mix,
made 3rd base love behind the school.
He did, I allowed;
it was, it was.

These were my boys, males, men
bold, reckless creatures
defining
friends, lovers,
a husband
became these long-forgotten names.
We could not transcend
the prescriptions for his sex.
Like a fist smashing a wall of fury,
this definition had to go.

"Will you read it over?" a classmate asks, "There's a lot of depth in there." She reads it again. They write, rise, and walk over to hand her slips of paper. Her classmates' careful listening shows in their written responses: "Word choice and juxtapositions were excellent." "It echoes a lot of "girl stuff" for me—the kind you can't usually discuss. Whew! Keep writing about this stuff." And from a man: "Dorothy, Good job. Your title was ingenious—woven into the theme of the poem, a lot of depth. May I have a copy? Keep writing poetry."

Susan and Lenore smile at each other while Dorothy reads; they share a week-long investment in Dorothy's work. Their written comments are proud and specific, based on their knowledge of Dorothy's earlier drafts. Susan points to the images that struck her, and notices that she has recrafted the first section overnight: "Dorothy: Title so effective! Images of reckless, violent males. No blame. Dickie Dorr—I will always remember with a nail in his shoe—and 'liquor mix' and 3rd base love. Such clear images. First section clearer! Good!" And Lenore writes: "Dorothy: I feel your poem is almost mine now, and I recall each of the revisions. I could tell it had its impact on the others, too."

Ellen's course requirement was to submit a minimum of two full pages of writing at the end of the week. Dorothy breaks that rule by submitting only this poem. When Ellen explains that the deadline carries with it a responsibility for a certain amount of text, Dorothy argues for the finished poem as a week's work. At the beginning of the following week, Dorothy discovers that submitting one poem "brought me up short," and she will make an appointment with director Tom Newkirk: "I'm going to argue with him tomorrow," she tells me, "that if we choose to write poetry we'd have to write five poems for it to count as one piece. . . . they're afraid we're just going to slap something together real quick and everything is going to rhyme, or it's going to sound like a Hallmark greeting card." Argument is still her first line of defense in an academic experience. Despite the week of drafting with her partners and the shower of response from her colleagues, she's conscious of the institution's requirements. Ellen will grade her, she's afraid it's "not good enough," and angry about a policy she deems disrespectful.

One week of writing in a summer writing program has not obliterated Dorothy's personal paradoxes. Writing and reading, listening and responding, traditions, rituals and a new lexicon have not transformed her into a new teacher or a new person. But the program introduces possibilities. The techniques that Dorothy complained about but practiced all week gave her new lenses for looking at her own ability to respond to others and the courage to share her writing in draft. Like all the jargon she complained about in Terry's class, what appeared at the beginning of the week as "just a little bit about response" has become a crucial idea holding an important vocabulary for working with writing. As she has learned to use the terms, she has shifted her status from skeptical outsider looking for classroom tips to an engaged participant.

In both her classes the first week, Dorothy and her colleagues have told their stories to each other in their talk, to themselves in their journals, and to the larger group through their public texts. They have chosen topics and genres in which they feel comfortable. For her first week in the writing class, Dorothy attempted and rejected both fiction and the essay. She chose poetry as a comfortable form with which to explore her personal history with men. Her first week echoed the garden she used to introduce herself at the beginning of the week. With one eye out for the "critters," she has planted "some green things," and "so far everything is growing."

With the writer's determination to construct a personal piece of writing lies the need for the others to be a safe audience of trained listeners, to explore our teaching background. Dorothy's resistant stance in the larger group has given way inside the culture of the small response group. She erects barriers around the language and the symbols of "process teaching," but the culture, the rituals, and the language surrounding the writing program have offered her the tools to write through her resistance without having to give up her critical stance. Gradually over the next two weeks, as Dorothy engages more in writing and response, her role as a learner and her involvement in the art of creating fiction overtakes her need for collecting teaching tips.

I write in my notes that this looks like a ceremony: offerings, sacrifices, rituals. This tradition of the Friday public reading is a symbol—writers enacting the creation of literature for their readers. These are different from the oral responses people practiced earlier in the week when the writing was in process. The four techniques of pointing, summarizing, questioning, and telling allowed the writer to see her writing as a reader sees it. And the ritual will be re-enacted next week.

## "It's Really Not the Topic, It's What You Do with the Topic"

During the second week, Dorothy writes a short story about deep-sea fishing. The idea began when they had the afternoon off and she took Susan to Portsmouth. Sunday, Dorothy and Colin returned to Portsmouth to go out on one of the fishing boats. She's wanted to write something entirely fictional, something that has "nothing to do with her." As the week goes by, she tinkers and examines as she revises with Lenore and Susan as guides. On Tuesday, she refuses to read the beginning of her piece to Susan and Lenore. When the group gathers in the afternoon, she knows which parts she wants to read:

Dorothy: I started writing this total garbage. And I said "I've got to get focused here. . . . I was just meandering around about fluorescent colors. . . . God, I just hated it, and I had to stop, and re-think where I was going, so I ended up crossing out stuff that I didn't like, and writing little notes in the margin . . . then I started writing from an outline. So the outline is this . . . [she gives a synopsis of the story]

Lenore: That's how fiction is born.

Susan: That's neat, giving it some structure with an outline.

Dorothy: Now I know where I'm going; it's a matter of writing it.

Using one of the strategies she's learned from Ellen, Susan summarizes what Dorothy has already read: "You've already done the physical description, they've had the little tussle about who's going to be first . . .

Dorothy answers "I've cut that whole part . . . so he's just heading out to sea. She calls her current draft "A Short Story as yet Untitled." It is five very rumpled typed pages, single-spaced, red slashes and black hand-written notes. She reads it to Lenore and Susan:

> "Do we need to show you our ticket?" asked a young tourist.
>
> "Well, you see, you don't need a ticket to ride out, but you do need one to get back," joked the captain of the *Seagazer*. George Gilmore's tanned face shone in the early morning light. His great height seemed in proportion with the size of the ship, and his hands wrapped easily around the rigging connecting him to the shore. . . . Twice he had to speak to Roger, who leaned over the stern saying fond goodbyes to his girlfriend.
>
> "Shake a leg, mate, you'll see her in a few hours!" he roared, clapping Roger on the shoulder blades. "Dan, see to the bait-buckets as soon as we are past the bridge."

Dorothy continues reading. Captain George's *Seagazer* goes out to sea, and the "fluorescent tourists" contrast with the "expert fishermen" of the crew. Old Domenico, a Puerto Rican dishwasher from the local Bell-in-Hand Pub, brings his grandson every Saturday. "The day-tourists appeared pale and ignorant beside such fishermen. They took their Dramamine tablets and applied layers of sunblock before boarding." With misplaced bait, the careless tourists attract dogfish sharks which the crew must untangle from the lines, or kill by twisting one shark's body and throwing it, bloodied, into the water to attract the other sharks. Dorothy juxtaposes this scene with one of a young child, his mother, and her boyfriend. They punish the child when he asks for a soda, and banish him to sit on a bait bucket. Captain George allows the punished boy to be his helper, lifts him up on his shoulders, and takes him to the steering wheel at the bow of the ship.

With a backdrop of New England deep-sea cod fishing and Spanish and Italian dialects, Dorothy's draft contrasts the loving Puerto Rican grandfather and grandson with the "fluorescent low-life" mother and boyfriend as they abuse their little boy. Dorothy finishes reading and apologizes: "The Italian accent I have to work on."

Susan: It feels to me like you have some momentum going now. There's some speed to it. Sort of like the boat. It has some direction.

Dorothy: Oh. I like that. This story is starting to feel like a boat speeding up.

Lenore: That's so symbolic—he lifts the boy up, and takes him to the steering wheel.

Dorothy: Yeah, and he's a tall man, so the child's going to be way up high. . . . And then the cruise is going to end. . . .

Lenore: Echo something that happened earlier?

Dorothy: Maybe something about the tickets again, I don't know. Typical essay structure, "Stop the way you begin."

Lenore: People like that, though, it's like "coming home" in music.

Dorothy: Yeah, like a coda.

Lenore: You know how you always come down? Most pieces do, it just feels good.

Ellen joins the group for a while and asks Dorothy what kind of help she wanted. Dorothy answers: "Gotta see the end in order to get to the middle. . . . I guess what I want to know is whether this is something that's only interesting to me because I like fishing. Is this interesting to an average reader?"

Lenore: Especially! I'm interested in that because I've never been deep sea fishing . . .

Susan: And I was thinking too, it really isn't so much the topic, it's what you do with the topic. It is not the fishing, but what you show us here is what we don't know all about it . . . the details.

Dorothy: Are there enough details like that to keep it interesting and not just a "Love Boat?"

Susan: The plot's enough to make it not like that.

Dorothy: The hardest part's coming up . . . that's going to be a lot of dialogue, they have to seem natural, the way people would act in such family situations. I'm making up most of it. . . .

Lenore: But you're not making up all of it.

They talk about how carelessly the fishermen handle the tangled fish, that "not worrying about the pain of animals" makes a good contrast with the captain's concern for the pain of children. Dorothy recalls, "Emerson asks the rhetorical question, 'Can't you name all the birds in the forest without a gun?'" She marks her paper in a few more places. Over her "A Story as yet Untitled," she writes "The Luck of the Draw?" On the bottom margin, she writes "make clear the theme and irony: describe captain watching both families." She fixes a few inconsistencies she noticed as she was reading, circling places where she needs to add information: unhooking the fish, clarifying the mother's relationship with the boy. Dorothy has asked for response about consistency and information, assurance that her story is interesting. She was afraid of producing "garbage," wrote an outline, and asked the group to listen for consistency. She is comforted by Susan's insight, "It really isn't the topic, it's what you do with the topic."

Dorothy's greatest fear about her story was that it would have a "Love Boat" quality, seem cheap like the tourists she created or contain boring or superficial information. Equipped with her own ideas and reassurance from the group, Dorothy heads to the computer room to create another draft, one that will be polished with dialogue and language, information, character details and irony. Tomorrow, it will have the ending she envisions today.

Wednesday, the three partners come together on the lawn. It's been a long week already, and their pieces need to be finished in two days. Their conflicts are intense today: exhaustion-elation, oppression-freedom, anxiety-concentration. They joke:

Susan: Yesterday I'd just had it. *(laughing)*

Dorothy: I went through a stage yesterday where I decided I *never* want to write ever again, and I'm not going to read, either.

Lenore: I looked at one of those photostated articles, and I said "these are hateful"—and I sat at that computer and said "Who *likes* sitting at this machine?"

Susan: Who says we have to be writers anyway? I want to be a scientist.

Lenore: I do think sometimes we're rather enamored with our own self-importance. I mean, who cares what I did yesterday? Let me quietly live my life and not litter my planet. . . . let me be like the Indians. Let me just tiptoe through and not leave such a big gash in the earth. We put an awful lot on language, we really do, particularly written language.

Susan: Now that I'm in a better mood. I'd say we might be less likely to leave such a big gash in the earth if we were more reflective.

Susan gets serious: "I would like to hear these drafts. We need to know what you want us to listen for." Dorothy has another draft of her sea story, and today she knows what she needs. "I guess now I'm most worried about significance. I'm not sure whether there's anything important about this story—any reason why anyone would want to read it, and I need some tough criticism, okay? Don't be nice!" She laughs. "I want you to tell me if this is something you'd enjoy to read if it appeared in a magazine, or if you'd just put it down after the first paragraph . . . if you hear something that really sounds dopey and dull or like *McCalls* or *Seventeen*-ish, tell me. I also need a title; I haven't got a title yet. She reads the story. It is five pages, single-spaced, and rich with the dialogue and irony she had hoped for:

> "But Capitan, you know that is the luck if she loves me today. I no can catch nothing without her." Domenico lowered his voice, "You no notice the family at the back? They bad. 'Mala gente,' we say.
>
> . . . . Sitting on an overturned bait bucket sat a little boy, maybe four or five years old. He was very pale and skinny, but his clothes seemed tight, short in the pant. . . . He wore a silver and red Medic-Alert bracelet around his wrist, which jangled as he moved his hands. He seemed engaged in some kind of fighting game with his fists. George could hear him speaking in low tones, "This is

the good guy, this is the bad guy." The fists were engaged in a heroic battle. Suddenly he looked up and addressed a woman standing nearby. She was large and red. Her unevenly bleached hair flapped around her face when she turned to face the child.

"Mommy, can I please get up?"

"Sit still, I told you!"

"I'm thirsty, I want a soda, like you and Roy."

The woman turned to her companion, who was just reeling up. "Roy, do you have any money left? Mikey wants a drink."

The man reached into his filthy jeans, all that he had on, and made a gesture of emptying out his pockets. "Tough luck, brat, I got no money left. Here, have a suck on my beer!" Roy laughed as he held out the can to the boy. "Oh, I forgot, you can't get off the bucket, so sorry." He took a dramatic gulp, and wiped his scraggly mustache with his hand. Roy turned his back, and dropped his line and the can overboard. . . . "Why don't you just throw him overboard, woman? Ha, that would be good! He weighs about as much as a chunk of clam. What do you say, Mikey, how about a drink of seawater?"

Dorothy finishes reading her story, and asks about significance. Her partners comply:

Susan: You put a lot more in since yesterday. You put the whole thing about the—what do you call them? The "low life?"

Dorothy: Oh, the "Mala gente."

Lenore: I like it that you made the old fellow Spanish. You put that Spanish in. That was good.

Dorothy: I speak Spanish, so I felt more comfortable with him putting that dialect in. . . .

Susan: It added to his character. And it's easy enough Spanish that anybody can . . .

Dorothy: Um hm, I didn't think people would have a problem following those words. "mala," and "gente."

Lenore: The fact is that you didn't make it the mother and the father, you made it the mother and the boyfriend, 'cause I see a lot of that in my own classes, you know . . .

Susan: Beautiful dialogue. I see your concern with theme. . . .

Significance? I was waiting for the end, because the end will pretty much cement it. I was wondering where you'd stop. . . . or the ticket, the ticket, you don't need a ticket to go out, but you need a ticket to get back.

Lenore: Well, if "luck of the draw" is trying to draw a parallel—that phrase—is there a parallel between luck of the draw of catching the best fish and luck of the draw of who your parents are?

Dorothy: Yeah, I think emphasizing the luck is going to have to be my job for revision. . . . and winning the pool. There's a lot of information in there.

Susan: And then emphasizing the relationship between that one family, they're so close, and then there's this other family—hardly a family at all. . . .

The discussion continues until Dorothy has a lot of options for her ending, exactly what she asked for. In her journal Wednesday night, Dorothy writes "I just finished writing the first draft of my deep-sea fishing story. I'm feeling really good. I've never completed a whole story before. . . . I balked at first, but I'm glad I've kind of been forced into it. I'm also pleased that the story has absolutely nothing to do with me!"

Although it "has nothing to do with her," it is full of her personal history, as well as a week working closely with Susan and Lenore. Dorothy's lifelong interest in language is clear in her decision to create a loving Puerto Rican grandfather and an Italian fisherman. The little boy's behavior, she tells me, is based loosely on her own son, and his mother's deference to her abusive boyfriend is a pattern with which she's familiar. The people in the fishing boat are exaggerations of those she saw on the fishing boats in Portsmouth with Susan over the past weekend. The themes and details in her story come directly from Susan and Lenore as readers—their hunger for information, the questions they've asked. In her journal on Thursday night, Dorothy writes:

> . . . . One thing I noticed is that in fiction there are endless possibilities. Changing one element of the story can result in a ripple effect. After reading my story to the response group this

morning, I felt excited. They actually like it. I actually like it. They helped me consider theme—how to create an effect with the story—how to end the story simply. I'll miss having this response group. It really helps.

## "And We're All Teachers to Each Other"

Thursday night, Dorothy invites me, Susan and Lenore to her apartment for a glass of wine. I join them after they've been there for an hour. When I arrive, they are relaxed, flopping on the chairs in Dorothy's living room. There are four piles of books on the floor, both Colin's and Dorothy's. There is a cluster in the corner of travel guides, beach towels, and tote bags. The computer is surrounded by stacks of paper print-outs, and the wastebasket is overflowing with those thin tracks of holes torn from the sides of computer paper.

Susan is delighted with the fairy tale she's written. She has been working on it for two weeks. "It's satisfying," Dorothy says of Susan's fairy tale, "like giving birth." Lenore says learning "summarizing" and "pointing" helped her with her intense discomfort. "We're all teachers to each other, for heaven's sake," she says. "I don't consider this a workshop for real writers. . . . Now, Don Murray is a real writer."

As they review their own writing processes, they talk about Murray's talk on Monday, called "Pushing the Edge" in which he took an auditorium full of teachers through a few writing exercises. "He was way over my head, completely over. All that stuff he made us do! I didn't know what he was talking about. It was like talking about the fine points of diving to someone who can only doggie paddle." She is still uncomfortable with her role as writer, and resists the implication that she should be one. Dorothy and Susan disagree; Murray's exercises helped them try new angles with the writing they were working on.

They leave the topic of writing and begin to joke about school; Susan and Dorothy complain about "the g-word" (grading) and "the other g-word (grammar)." And curriculum:

"I had my program all worked out until I got here; wait until they see what I'm going to do when I get back!" They have spent their time together creating, "pushing at their edges," and their only joking so far has been yesterday's exhausted talk about writing. This is the first school joking I've heard among them, although they've been together two full weeks. It is about school structures that muffle teacher creativity. Occupational joking is often a way for oppressed groups to relieve their anxiety, and in these jokes, they share their common fears.

But until now, they have been too busy writing to joke. I am struck by their common fear of the rules of school and curriculum despite their diversity. Dorothy is a high school teacher in rural Maine, Susan teaches junior high in suburban Philadelphia, and Lenore teaches second grade in rural Connecticut. When the wine bottle is empty, Susan, Lenore, and I drive back to the mini-dorms in the misty dark, past the lacrosse players volleying across the edges of the street, past the white lights that illuminate the lawns, around the back end of the campus. I write a memo to myself at 11:10 P.M., and finish it just as the midnight train passes my open window:

> Through the windows I see groups of people sitting on beds in their nightclothes, looking down at papers, looking up at each other. Response. Respect. Rewrite. It's not like a teacher's room here. Not time for subversive stories. No one jokes about the administration or unruly kids, houses or cars; barely anyone talks about their own children.

In the morning in Ellen's class, there is an second Friday ritual reading. Dorothy sits cross-legged, barefoot, sandals on the floor, her legs draped over the arm of the leather chair. Her black eyes are fixed on Susan when she begins to read her Australian fairy tale. Dorothy smiles, tilts her head back and closes her eyes to listen. Lenore straightens in her chair, knees together holding her notebook, her gray head cocked over to the left. She shifts nervously. Susan finishes, and the group gasps. They shower her with paper responses and requests for copies.

Dorothy looks around, searching the room to see if it's time to volunteer. Lenore and Susan beam when she begins, look at each other, then at her. Dorothy announces, "I'm glad I'm not writing about myself." Her final story is called "Winning the Pool." She reads it and performs the dialect, toward a carefully crafted new ending:

> "Here you are, mate. You've done a fine job, but now you must go back," said George, returning Mikey to his parents.
>
> "Sure you don't want to keep him, Captain? Maybe you could use a new bait-boy." Roy cracked. The mother waved a plastic bag full of cod fillets in front of George.
>
> "I won the pool. I got the biggest fish. Fifteen pounds! I won 100 dollars!" she crowed.
>
> "Come on, get going," Roy pushed Mike up the dock. The boy's eyes sought those of Captain George.
>
> "Bye Captain, and thank you," he said, waving. George waved back silently, then rubbed his hand over his eyes. He looked up to see Domenico observing him.
>
> "Catch anything, Padre?" asked George.
>
> "No bites. Today is not good to me, I think."
>
> "It's all luck, pure luck of the draw," answered George, staring down the dock.
>
> "You are 'buena gente,' Capitan. I see you next Saturday, I think maybe I go for the whole day, eh?" Domenico walked up the ramp, allowing his grandson to carry the gear. George watched the receding forms, saw Mikey standing alone in the parking lot, saw Domenico's grandson take the old man's hand.
>
> "Are you the Captain? Do we have to show you our ticket now?" asked a flaming tourist.
>
> Without turning his head, Captain George replied.

There is a hushed sigh in the room. People rise slowly to fill Dorothy's hands with slips of paper. Dorothy reads them eagerly. They summarize, they point to passages, and they explain the images her writing evoked in them:

> "Hands on the rigging, connecting him to the shore, fists having heroic battle, "mala gente" indeed—they're awful! The perfect irony of that horrible woman winning the pool. Domenico—

good voice, "flaming tourist," what a sad scene, and drawn so well"—Alison.

"Great description of tourists. . . . I got a feeling of the movement of the boat and the smell of the sea. Deep sea fishing isn't all recreation, is it? I'm thinking of the tourists and the sharks and the family. Thank goodness someone came to the child's rescue. I wonder who will rescue him next time and next time. I hope someone will. Pure luck, the kind of parents we get. Thanks."—Ellen

"Lead: "no ticket to go out" . . . good New England humor, full cycle with last line. Grandfather's dialect. Poor little Mikey! Great story. Very much enjoyed it—contrasts, vivid details"—Nick.

Ellen's and the others' responses react to the finished product. But Dorothy's response partners' papers show their investment in the entire life of her story. Susan writes, "Dorothy: Love the details about Domenico. . . . Such good dialogue: "Have a suck of my beer, How about a drink of seawater! Perfect ending! You did it! I'm so glad I got to hear your drafts!" And Lenore's note refers to the growth she's watched in Dorothy's piece over the week: "I like what you did with the ending. It really read well, Dorothy. Very entertaining. The point made in the title came across, too. You are growing every day."

Lenore waits until everyone is finished reading. "Is everybody ready to listen so we can go home? You're awfully good, all of you," she smiles stiffly at each person in the circle. This is the third time she has waited to be last in the large group. Susan thinks Lenore is afraid to recognize how smart she is. "She doesn't want to impose on anyone. . . . At supper I forgot a knife. I needed one for my pork chop and I said, "Are you using your knife?" and she said "Oh, no, here, you can use it. But I wouldn't want to impose." Her reading meets with loud howls and great enthusiasm on paper. Lenore gathers the little response slips graciously, bundles them in her long fingers, and lowers her head. That night, Lenore's journal tries not to celebrate, not to impose even on herself. It is a guilty admission of personal triumph, bolstered by the confidence she cannot ignore from her partners or her class:

> Today we had the sharing of our pieces of writing. . . . I felt no better about reading this week . . . than I did last week. I do enjoy listening to the others read. . . . Perhaps none of us appreciates our own efforts . . . the finished product does not live up to the vision we had when we began. . . . Once in a while I can step back and look with real pride on something I accomplished, and when I can, I really do savor the moment.

When Ellen made the initial decision to create this response group, she knew, as she told me then, "not to put strong personalities together. . . . Dorothy was closed, Lenore was going to need attention, and Susan was an enabler." Ellen set the environment for natural growth to happen, for relational thinking and the integration of these three women's voices. She set a stage for, in Maxine Greene's words, the "opening of spaces."

> Rather than posing dilemmas to students or presenting models of expertise, the caring teacher tries to look through students' eyes, to struggle with them as subjects in search of their own projects, their own ways of making sense of the world. Reflectiveness, even logical thinking remain important; but the point of cognitive development is. . . . to interpret from as many vantage points as possible lived experience, the ways there are of being in the world. (1988, 120)

Ellen's guidance provided not only a stage for teachers to enact writing and watch it at the same time; it also gave them a frame for an alternative style of teaching. "In order to understand our own experiences of teaching we must truly stand under them," writes Madeline Grumet (1988, 74). To learn to teach this way, to learn to help others find their own ways of making meaning in the world, teachers must have the experience themselves. It takes time and open spaces, an "intelligent audience," as Dorothy put it, and a sense of trust in the value of experience. Sharing drafts with the response group was a literary event in process, an enactment of the transaction between the writer and the reader (Rosenblatt 1938). The "intelligent audience" Dorothy found in Lenore and Susan was like the informed audience at an oral performance; the audience's response serves to help the performer construct his text as he performs (Bauman, 1975). "Historically, literature," writes David Bleich, "has been an enterprise which temporarily fixes a culture's uses of language. . . . a literary event is a pause in everyday life marked by a gathering of people with the common purpose of experiencing the event" (1988, 114). In the final week, Dorothy, Lenore, and Susan will each write a final piece. For all of them, it will be at once the most personal and the most distanced. For each of them, the final piece of writing is one she had begun and discarded at the outset.

## *Heal Thyself: Finding Fiction in Fact*

By the final class reading, everyone prepares for the ritual as they tear small slips of paper to write messages of response. Ellen checks her watch. Today's pieces are far longer than the required two to three pages: "In three weeks, everybody's writing books!" Dorothy has decided to return to the personal piece she had begun during the first week. In her journal, she kept track as she shifted a painful factual memory into fiction:

> I'm learning how to write fiction. The advice to supplant the third person for the first and then retell a personal narrative has worked for me. The story I am working on has needed to be told for a long time, but I've been fearful of writing it in the first person. . . . By turning myself into Emily, a fictional person, I've been freed up to alter the events for narrative efficiency. I was able to cut out stuff, add stuff, and outright lie, but still maintain the integrity of the feeling. P.S. I'm aware that everything I'm writing right now is pretty depressed and self-centered. I just need to get some of these things out.

She held on for two weeks until she could try again. No matter what she did with this story, it would be autobiographical; it would raise issues with which she felt uncomfortable. On Monday, she had attended fiction writer Becky Rule's reading of two short stories, and loved them. The stories swamped her with the task that she had set for herself, but they also challenged her to write more fiction. She asks for specific help from Susan and Lenore, a judgment on the theme:

> I switch time a lot in this and I need to know if it's clear . . . last night after hearing Becky Rule and getting depressed that her stories were so funny and mine is so serious, I decided I wasn't going to go for 'good,' I was just going to go for 'different.'. . . . A lot of this is autobiographical, but I have changed things. . . . I thought it would be fun to try taking the persona of the psychiatrist. . . . I want it to be a happy ending for Emily. But the fact that she can heal herself—is it there?

She's been reading about dialogue tags in fiction, she says, and in her first draft she had used the language all wrong: "I was writing 'exclaimed,' 'cried,' 'said,' everything the book said not to do, but I'm also working on character development through plot details." By now, Dorothy has objectified her story, created distance from her personal details. The narrator is not the little girl who was herself; it is the girl's psychiatrist, Dr. Williamson. This choice gave her the power and distance she needed to concentrate on the writing instead of the painful memory. Now she can concentrate on matters of craft, the very issues, as an English teacher, she wants her students to understand in literature. The piece is called "Heal Thyself," and it is told from the point of view of a psychiatrist who is treating a nine-year-old girl. An excerpt:

*Heal Thyself*
Paul Bragdon told me that his daughter had been exhibiting strange behaviors. On the phone he was concerned about Emily, for she had difficulty sleeping at night, and had acquired some unusual habits.
  "What kind of habits?" I asked
  "Well, she picks at herself."

"Picks at herself?"

"Yes," he replied, "her fingers are all raw. She has sores on her arms, legs, and face. . . . "

Emily was a small child for age nine. Her hair was brown and long, hanging over her face. . . . Emily was plump, and held her hands over her stomach as if to hide the elastic waistband on her jeans. She pulled the sleeves of her top up over her wrists. . . .

"I'm here because my father is worried about me. He thinks my problems are psychosomatic." said Emily.

"That's a pretty big word. Do you understand it?"

"Yes." she replied. "It means I'm not really sick; I'm just pretending."

"Is that true?" I asked

"No. . . . I can't sleep at night, because it itches so much." She pulled up her sleeves. . . . ."I have to press it against something cold, like a piece of metal. I walk all over the house looking for cold metal to press my skin against. . . .

The Bragdon family lived in a wealthy neighborhood . . . complete with a maid, flowering gardens, and a fragrant cherry tree in the backyard. Until her ninth year, she had been unaware of the tensions that ran under the surface of her parent's relationship . . . Most terrifying were the long silences, after the fights at night . . . Emily would rise out of bed to search for something cool against which to press her ragged skin. . . . Cold radiators worked well, too. . . . Once she came upon her mother balled up in a corner of the pantry. . . .

On the next visit, Emily brought me a picture she had drawn . . . a girl feeding a horse. Emily rolled up her sleeves and showed me her arms. . . . She was healing.

"It's about my aunt's farm in Maine. . . ." Several months after the separation, Emily was invited to her aunt's farm, where there were eight cousins to play with. . . . animals to feed, a horse to ride, a lake to swim in. . . . Emily's face shone.

"I went home at the end of August. . . . my cat had kittens while I was away. I wanted to see them . . . she had twelve, but she didn't want to be a mother. She ran away. I had to feed all twelve kittens with an eyedropper. One died because he was the runt. Mother had a new friend, Tom." . . .

"Mr. Bragdon, why doesn't Emily live with your wife?"

"Ex-wife, Doctor Williamson. She's better off with me.". . . .

Dorothy finishes her piece, again to a hushed silence. The class loves it, they want her read it in the public reading for all the program participants. She refuses. "Sorry," she says, "Everything I have is either too long or too personal." In this final piece, the one she had wanted to write during the first week, Dorothy has crafted a short story based on, as she says, "a story that has needed to be told for a long time." There are shards of the private personal history she has told me, but the story remains a fiction. Emily, a precocious nine-year old, picks her skin raw as she watches her parents' relationship deteriorate. She lives with her father, as Dorothy did; her mother had gone off with "her friend Tom," as Dorothy's mother had. With the runt's death as a reminder of real life's casualties, the little girl heals kittens whose mother had abandoned them. The psychiatrist's advice is not as strong as the child's visit to her aunt's farm.

Having spent so many hours with Dorothy, I am deeply moved by her connections between this fiction and her reality: the affection she holds for her aunt's farm in Maine as a healing place, the lake, the garden, her nurturing of the kittens. She selected the kittens deliberately: "I wanted a nice symbol, a juxtaposition," she says. Little Emily's hair hangs out of place, and she holds her hands over her elastic waistband to hide her waist. I have so often noticed that she seems so carefully "tucked in."

Dorothy is shocked when she realizes the importance of her fictional Emily's aunt. That night, she decides to call her real aunt in Maine. On the first day of Ellen's class, I reminded her, she had introduced herself with her garden, "a place to put green things and dirt," and each weekend she's gone back to check on her garden and her cat. How much of the fictional Emily is in this piece? How much of the real Dorothy? How much of Susan, how much Lenore? In her final self-evaluation for Ellen's class, Dorothy writes:

Where have I "pushed the edge?" Definitely in the area of fiction writing. I've been an avid reader all my life, and you'd think I'd find it easy. But I found it difficult to be the author. . . .

I switched pronouns. . . . I gave real people fictional names. Then I began selecting and reordering details to meet the needs of a story. My reader's eye told me what worked and what didn't. . . . And my response group. . . . revision for style, effect, language. I worked on dialogue, description, creating an effective ending. . . . How interesting it is that we have not once had to speak about mechanics or grammar usage. These things take care of themselves when the writer really cares about what she's doing. . . .

Without resonance and continuity with her response partners, I doubt that Dorothy would have reworked this personal piece during the final week. Susan and Lenore each spent the last week working on pieces that were intensely personal, grown with a distanced eye, careful control, and guidance from responses. By this week, they knew better what they needed and how to ask for it. In her self-evaluation, Dorothy writes to Ellen:

As a responder my greatest growth has been in shutting up! I've learned how important it is to listen, to wait. Before I used to jump in and give my opinion. . . . Now I see the benefit of letting the writer ask for what she needs. I can help her most by letting her read it aloud, by telling her what I hear, what I like, what confuses me.

Lenore's final piece is called "Trees I Have Known." It is a tender description of her intimate connection with the trees she planted as a child that have surrounded her home for fifty years; they serve as an autobiographical chronicle of her life. Without Susan's suggestion to identify each tree, or Dorothy's attention to detail and language, Lenore would have a mess of papers and a frame of mind that would prohibit her reading this to anyone. Like Dorothy's story, it is both intimate and literate. It reveals her family loyalty, her fierce protection of the natural world, and her commitment to a quiet life, "not wanting to impose on anyone." Lenore's last journal entry points to the strength of the community of respondents she felt in order to come to this writing:

I wish to say something here about the importance of the response group to myself as a beginning writer. I need the input of these supportive and interested people, mostly to verify my own hunches about things and to keep me on task. I question the value of my own writing. . . . I had to take the risk of exposure and failure . . . When I become emotionally involved I learn. I change. I grow. I have reached inside and labored to give birth to the writing I have produced these three weeks. . . . I wish to give the children in my care the opportunity to take charge of their learning and the time to communicate and explore their interests. I have accomplished my personal goals. . . .

Susan's final piece is a humorous essay that she did not recognize as humorous. "This Train is Bound for Glory" is a first person narrative about a midwestern town, home of an entire culture devoted to the study and elevation of the Bible. Susan takes her reader on a train ride with a narrator who sounds a bit like a mix of Garrison Keillor and Becky Rule. Her reading in class evokes yelps of recognition, tears of laughter. "Lenore and Dorothy have helped me by listening and telling me whether there is anything there, what they hear me saying," she tells me. "I work on transitions and cadence. It must have rhythm; it must flow smoothly. It must speed up where I want it to speed up and slow down where I choose." Dorothy's interest in language offered her attention to cadence and rhythm; Lenore pushed for transitions.

Susan is surprised at the class's reaction, but prepared because of Dorothy's and Lenore's responses earlier in the week. She is more surprised by her own artistry, her ability to write humor:

A high school teacher pointed out something to me that I didn't even know I did, "Tension running through the whole piece, then the humor starts to steamroll. 'How did you do that?' he said. I need to think about this one. . . . I have a skill that I didn't know I had. . . . If I need to write in order to learn what I'm doing so that I can point things out to kids, this is very valuable."

In her final evaluation, Susan writes:

I have learned that writing involves diving down deep. It was at least forty fathoms down for "This Train," and I understand now what Mark Twain means when he says "Sometimes you have to lie to tell the truth". . . . I know that writing is not as solitary an exercise as I had experienced it, that it is so helpful to have someone respond at various times in the process. . . . I know now how to leave papers alone and teach the students. . . . I thought I'd landed on the moon when I first came. Now it feels more like coming home.

It is not a surprise that after three weeks of intense writing and reflection Susan feels as if she's "come home." She has engaged in open dialogue with her fellow teachers, examining writing, assisting and receiving assistance continually, and watching herself do it. In the early part of this century, at John Dewey's lab school, there were scheduled weekly meetings in which teachers formed social and intellectual relationships. They were encouraged to reflect:

> They were both social and intellectual relationships, constantly to be reflected upon and to become the subject of discussions. . . . Dewey knew full well the kind of responsibility to interpret, even while engaging fully with the learning process itself. Today's reader cannot but be struck by the reflectiveness, the wide-awakeness for which he was asking. . . . his concern for open dialogue among the teachers becomes as striking as his interest in the school itself as a learning community for adults as well as the young. (Greene in Jackson, ed. 1989, 24-25)

In their three weeks together, Dorothy, Susan and Lenore have had social and intellectual relationships like those that John Dewey wanted for his teachers. Well over fifty years later, Tom Newkirk's program and Ellen Blackburn-Karelitz's class have offered such relationships. The "reflectiveness, the wide-awakeness, the open dialogue" has happened to this response group as they gather daily in the lounge and outside on the lawn. For each of these teachers, Ellen's class is the home of their shared literacy, that "learning community for adults" that Greene suggests was Dewey's goal. For Dorothy,

Lenore, and Susan, Ellen has not taught them; they have taught themselves in the company of one another.

Dorothy's experience has been full of paradoxes, but she has learned much about teaching, not the "tips" she came for. In her final evaluation, Dorothy writes to Ellen: "Most interesting for me has been watching you, Ellen. Your gentle, consistent orderly approach does wonders for setting this writer's mind free!" This was not the traditional course with readings and papers that Dorothy had learned to be successful in; it wasn't even the "academic" community that she had expected it to be. I ask her if she would count Ellen as one of her mentors, and what she has learned from her:

> Quietness. Unobtrusiveness. . . . I tend to be pushy with kids. . . . I'd not call her a "mentor." It would be more like a "model." I will *do my own* mentoring. What will help me is the fact that I have, in my hand, papers that I wrote. And the way I did that was by going through this process.

On the last night, Susan joins me for my visit to Dorothy's apartment. We sit at Dorothy's kitchen table, drink cokes, and talk together with the tape recorder on.

> Susan: We didn't get any negative comments at all, not once, this entire three weeks. But we have those little piles of papers. Plus the oral comments that we got in response group.
>
> Dorothy: Part of me said that those nice comments were false. They couldn't possibly be real. You know? They couldn't be sincere. . . . But they were, because they had to be specific.
>
> Susan: You can't argue when somebody remembers something in your writing. Phrases, clusters that a lot of people seem to comment on. You know that it had to be a good one if more than one person remembers it. . . .

Dorothy fills our cups. "It suddenly occurred to me today that the three weeks went by very very fast. There was a point last week when I just wanted to be home with my garden. But, even by the time one week has gone by, you're a group, and you're loyal to each other. . . . That's what kids want, too." I notice a few wisps of hair fall out of her barrette.

Susan agrees, "You know, Dorothy, it never occurred to me to do that . . . my fear was that kids wouldn't learn if I didn't teach them everything real fast . . . now I know they'll learn, more slowly, if you just *leave them alone to grow*."

"Yes, *"Heal thyself."* Dorothy smiles. "What will help me is the fact that I have, in my hand, papers that I wrote."

# To Really Cheer: Questioning Our Assumptions

During the second week, the university was host to a high school cheerleading camp. The participants looked quite different from the first week's pre-adolescent female gymnasts under the scrutiny of their male coaches. We saw the cheerleaders more than we saw the lacrosse camp boys, who volleyed their balls across the street in arcs over passing cars as they lumbered to distant playing fields. The cheerleaders were a visual presence, more than the high school instrumentalists who squeaked and strained inside the arts complex all day, made sophisticated music through the dorm windows into the night, and played an occasional game of volleyball in awkward male-female groupings.

We watched as the cheerleaders practiced their moves gliding through the cafeteria line. They traveled in packs—in the dorms, and on the lawns. They wore their school uniforms only on the last day, but on the other days, each team dressed alike. One team had hair crusted high with spray, and pony tails festooned with red fabric, another team wore long hair swept to the left side, clipped with purple barrettes. One cluster wore purple tops and socks with white shorts and sneakers, another yellow tee shirts and yellow socks with black shorts and sneakers. There were red tee shirts with names, and there were the black-and-whites, the glitter-experimenters, the green-and-pinks, and the blues. The color, volume, and identity of the teams was remarkable. They regulated policy which had not come from their schools.

The cheerleaders were the object of affectionate joking among teachers in the cafeteria : "What do you call a group of cheerleaders?" "A Gaggle?" "A Giggle?" "A Swarm?" "A Blast?" "A Burst?" The girls smiled and giggled, looking well-organized and independent despite the oppressive heat and their rigorous physical daily practice schedule. We never saw their coaches. Their cafeteria trays were full of fruit, grains, and salads, and an average of six glasses of water per girl per meal. Their food did not look like the donuts, cokes, and french fries of the pre-adolescents the week before. The girls carried large plastic water bottles that they filled each morning with gallons of water. By Wednesday morning, there was a sign outside the cafeteria requesting that they refrain from filling their water bottles. It held up the lines.

Their cluster identity was not news to teachers; teenage girls need the security a group provides, and cheerleaders are lucky to have it. Recent work of scholars in education (Gilligan 1990; Fine and MacPherson 1993) is beginning to highlight profound developmental differences in belief and identity between middle-class adolescent boys and girls. Girls in early adolescence become confused about trust and relationships and, throughout their later adolescence, they struggle to "authorize their voices" against conventions of a male-dominated society. Adolescent girls experience confusion and depression, and they form cliques to experiment with inclusion and exclusion. While boys become increasingly comfortable in institutional hierarchies, girls' discomforts and struggles increase as they get older. At this point in their lives, older adolescent girls need relationships with adult females and groups in which to experiment with the struggle between what they believe and what they think society wants them to believe. They need to express both struggle and resistance. Writing diaries, engaging in collaborative projects and performances, and entering group discussions with one another and with adult women are ways to encourage girls to articulate their developmental differences. Groups of cheerleaders enjoy such collaborative opportunities.

On Wednesday of the second week, the temperature had climbed to ninety-eight degrees, and the dew point indicated saturation. The girls bounded to the fields, giggling and gossiping in colorful clusters after breakfast to begin their morning practice. By late morning, forty cheerleaders collapsed, and were taken to a local hospital and treated for heat prostration. One teacher, who happened to be writing a poem on a nearby lawn, reported, "I remember them being carried out, poor things. Their heads were lolling, their eyeballs were rolling. They looked so unfocused. They were limp. They had to be dragged away, and the other ones had their legs dangling over the stretchers." Ambulances shuttled back and forth to campus, the local newspaper announced the incident. Several of the girls spent the night in the hospital. Jokes among the teachers erupted. "Did they drop in a gaggle, in a squad, in a pile?" "Didn't anyone notice when the first one fell?" "They looked so much alike, how could they tell how many fell?" "Why didn't the coaches stop them?" "Why didn't they drink more water?" "Did they go down screaming?"

Inside Hamilton Smith Hall, Alison becomes angry when she hears the ambulances. At forty-two, she is an aerobics instructor and an ex-cheerleading coach as well as a teacher-administrator. She was a cheerleader herself. Over the next week, she writes seventeen drafts of a personal essay that begins with a sad comment: "Today forty cheerleaders had to be carried off the field. . . ."

On the afternoon before she crafts her final draft, she shares it with a group of four women. "I really need some response from you guys on this. I'm almost done, but I need you to hear it:"

### To Really Cheer
Knee-jerk reactions make me want to punch the jerk in the knee. Some words seem to hold the power of those little, hard, rubber hammers doctors use to test reflexes. You say the word, you get an automatic response. "English teacher" produces nervous comments about watching grammar. "Cheerleader" evokes a grimace of distaste. These reactions, I contend, illustrate a human unwillingness to question assumptions.

English teachers are not grammar police. They have more interesting things to do than carp at split infinitives. A cheerleader's focus is not the focus many assume: look good and yell loud. In fact, cheerleaders are multitalented. Like athletes, they need aerobic fitness for two hours of practice daily, then a three-hour sequence of leaping, clapping, and using their lungs. Like musicians, they need a sense of rhythm; crowds won't respond to an arrhythmic cheer. Like dancers, they need balance and flexibility to stand atop a peer's shoulders or somersault into a supple split. Like artists, they need creativity to determine patterns for at least fifteen floor and fifty sideline cheers. Like teachers, they need patience and diligence, working for hours to achieve both unison and unity. Like any team member, they need cooperation. You can't have jealousy of the one who's in front or on top because he's the shortest or she's the light-est. Like entertainers, they need to be continually pleasant and smil-ing; nobody pays attention to a scowl or pout. And like drill sergeants, they need to be loud.

When Alison finishes reading this section, she talks, experi-ments and reconceptualizes in the company of her responding peers:

Pam: Are you saying that just anybody can be a cheerleader? . . . I think you're right, it is hard work—the picture is wrong. So I think there's some confusion there.

Alison: I'm saying anybody has to work hard. But you're right. It's confusing.

Susan: I didn't know whether we were going to be hearing about whether teachers are cheerleaders, or cheerleaders are teachers.

Alison: I'll just take the English teacher stuff out.

*(In unison, like cheerleaders, the four women yell "No!")*

Alison: So somehow I need to move from "cheerleaders are special" to "one quality they have is a universal support"— I think that's what I'm trying to say—they're not just flashy show-offs who jump around in short skirts.

Dorothy: Just like English teachers are not just people who go around slashing papers.

Susan: Exactly.

Alison: Maybe what I should try to do is in . . . this transition . . . use that power, or that spirit, or that joy, as an exam-ple . . . then try to carry it on. . . .

Pam: Yeah, that's good.

Susan: Mmmm. Exactly, because not all principals—not all of those people you list are cheerleaders. . . . sometimes they're just playing their own game.

Alison: When I finished last night, I thought, "I'm not done," but I really didn't know where I was going. . . . I don't want my audience to be just English teachers. I want my audience to be every person in this profession. . . . I get so angry when people say, "Oh cheerleaders, show-offs," because they're so much more than that. And I have an English teacher's perspective, because that's who I am.

Dorothy: It would be funny to use split infinitives through the paper.

Alison: Well, the title is "To Really Cheer."

*(They laugh)*

Alison: If I try to convey the universal quality in that third paragraph, and then I might end up with a different beginning, and just clean up the ending a bit.

Pam: Or talk more about our assumptions.

Alison: *AH HAH*, I need to go back to assumptions at the end.

Susan: Right, because that's what you're really talking about.

Alison: Okay, thanks everyone, that helped a lot. *(She makes a triumphant flourish with her pencil and closes her stuffed folder)*

Pam: Good stuff!

Alison: Well, it bugs me enough, it ought to be good. I was a cheerleader for eight years, and a coach for ten years, and I know whereof I speak. It pisses me off when people start criticizing.

As teacher, student, and athlete, Alison crafts her idea into a passionate personal essay with the help of a support group—four women, two of whom have been cheerleaders themselves, all of whom are students and teachers of adolescent girls. First, the discussion centers on distinguishing between cheerleader and teacher, that both involve hard work and spirit and little understanding, and Alison's confusion rests on "whether cheerleaders are teachers or teachers are cheerleaders." Their common frame as teachers makes them joke about using split infinitives. But

Pam's attention to "our assumptions" signals a switch in the conversation. The boundaries blur between teacher and cheerleader, Alison recognizes that the term "our" is her key to the assumptions they share as a group of teachers. She is writing about team spirit and connectedness as they practice it in the group. With a flourish of her pencil, she completes the connection. The following day, she has reworked the final sections:

> We can learn something from these girls in matching school colors. The discipline, the physical exertion, the uniform may pertain to the sport of cheerleading. But the energy, the unity and the joy are universal. There is something about the spirit of a cheerleader which ought to translate into the larger arena of school and community. Perhaps it is the desire to urge a group toward a common goal.
>
> Think of the particularly joyous, spirited fan whose energy at a game raises a riotous yell at the crucial moment. Picture the faculty member whose very presence spurs sharper play, or the principal who offers words of advice and encouragement to an excitable crowd of students before the annual game against the cross-town rival. And what about the coach who can revitalize flagging energies at half-time? Or the player whose entry into a game ensures a spurt of superb play from teammates? These, too, are leaders of cheers.
>
> Do we grimace at them? We usually applaud. We support the spirit, joy, and pride. Cheerleaders do not deserve their customary scoffing, any more than English teachers warrant grammar-bashing. Assumptions are thoughtless reflexes; they do us no honor. We must always remember what it is to really think.

Belenky, et al. (1986) found that women learn best in a state of "connected knowing," which comes from collaborations like these. And they describe "connected teaching," as a state of "disciplined subjectivity." Alison and her colleagues were doing both:

> . . . educators can help women develop their own authentic voices if they emphasize connection over separation, understanding and acceptance over assessment, and collaboration over debate; if they accord respect to and allow time for the knowledge that emerges from firsthand experience . . . These are the lessons we have learned in listening to women's voices. (1986, 229)

The cheerleader topic and Alison's theme is an apt metaphor for this encounter. Here, these women examine their assumptions about girls, talk, learning and teaching. With the same "team spirit" she evokes in the cheerleaders she writes about, Alison has engaged with her colleagues as they practice "connected teaching." As she reconceives her writing, she confirms the major themes of her argument and crafts the rhetorical and syntactic strategies she'll use to do it. With their help, her piece links the work of a cheerleader with the work of an English teacher.

# Four

## Joyce Choate:
## The Matter of Head-Watching

*All the arts need to be supplemented by philosophical chatter and
daring speculation about the nature of things: from this source
appear to come the sublimity of thought and all-round com-
pleteness . . .*

—Plato, *Phaedrus*

$T$om Romano's high school class in the Institute for
Reading and Writing meets on the second floor of Hamilton
Smith Hall, near Room 218. The lights are off and the yel-
lowed window shades are pulled down. A bright strip of alu-
minum roofing glows from outside one crooked shade; a
pine bough drips over it. It is the second day, and Tom
Newkirk has revised the coffee decision. We can smell it
brewing down the hall.

Romano is wearing leather sandals, khaki shorts, and a
faded red tee shirt. He chats with his teacher/students as they
come in. As high school teachers who have had previous experience in writing programs, they are ready to consider the
addition of "reading" to their approaches to teaching writing.
Many of the fourteen were here in previous summers, and
close groups have formed after a single day. In the dorms, in
the cafeteria, and in Durham's eateries, there has already been
much sharing. By today, Tom knows everyone's name, and
each person is writing quietly. "You guys are gettin' tough,"
Tom compliments them as he walks around the room. His
neck stretches over his clipboard as he inspects drafts. The

161

pocket in his tee shirt holds a single index card and he pulls it out periodically to jot down reminders. Tom and I are fellow students and colleagues; we've taught classes, taken courses, studied together, and presented at formal conferences. I have never seen him without an index card in his pocket.

His syllabus is clear and complete. There are two books and a packet of other readings: Craig Lesley's *Winterkill*, a novel Tom has wanted to read, and William Stafford's *You Must Revise Your Life*, a book about writing. His syllabus invites more reading and writing, and it offers a few requirements and a few options. The syllabus reads:

*Reading* First order of literacy: We'll dig into Lesley's *Winterkill* for reading and talk. . . . We shall also read various articles out of the Kinkos packet and Stafford book. . . . The remainder of your reading is your choice. You know the personal and professional reading you want to do. Dive into it, write about it, talk about it. . . .

*Writing* Writing is not a sketch, but a big-world mural. Poems. Personal essays. Fiction (historical, contemporary, for children, adolescents, or adults). Letters. Professional articles. Columns. Satire. Myth. Fable. So many genres and combinations of genres.

Each morning there will be time to read, write, and confer informally, and after the break, from 10:30 until 12:00, time for small and large group discussions of reading, writing, and teaching. Tom's syllabus explains his requirements: a completed written piece each Friday, a personal literacy portfolio, including a one-page letter duplicated for the class, and an optional journal. The two page syllabus ends with a quote from Henry David Thoreau, a *Peanuts* cartoon, and a quote from Rainer Maria Rilke: "I know no advice for you save this: to go into yourself and test the depths in which your life takes rise."

"It's an awful big world of writing there. . . . If you're going to write, write about what you're passionate about," he says. Today, Tom is conferring with one writer at a time. As each person asks for a conference, he sits down with his clipboard, recording notes. His attention is on the writer. He leans in, concentrating, furrows his brow, and asks questions. In a conference with Frank, Tom talks for fifteen seconds, and then Frank talks for two full minutes about his plans for a piece about his nephews and baseball. Tom agrees, "God, I know what you mean," confirming Frank's decisions, "try one genre, then try another." The piece might lend itself better to a story or an essay than a poem once he gets the details, but Frank might not want to decide that quite yet.

Tom pads on to Lila, moves a chair to face her, leans in, and listens. She reads for twenty-five seconds. Tom responds, "I'll be interested to see what this looks like if you choose to work this out." She talks longer, about her plans for a short character sketch. Tom smiles, looks into her eyes, blocking out the rest of the room, "That sounds really good, Lila." He moves his head in affirmation as she talks. Like the famous Marx brothers' mirror routine, a conference with Tom Romano is an act of reflexivity, writer to writer. "Well, I'll let you go," and he moves on to another writer.

The people in this group are comfortable with the shared rules, vocabularies, and rituals of the New Hampshire Writing Program. Already, by the second morning, people have chosen topics, they know that only a writer can know when it's time for a conference, that not everyone works at the same pace, that a piece of writing can "work" or "not work" for a person, that choosing a genre can be restrictive at the beginning of a "piece." The writer has the option of "working out" a piece or rejecting it. It is called a "piece" precisely because the genre isn't chosen yet. It is clear that this group shares the program's language and behaviors. Tom's conferencing style is smooth, collegial, unintrusive. He confers only with the people who are ready to talk, and the group understands that. In his syllabus, he describes choices. The basic ideas of time, choice, community, and response associated with the UNH program are built into the culture of his class, both inside and outside the classroom. "I teach all year long and now this is *my* time," Ronald, a man from Pennsylvania tells me. After last summer's workshop he bought a word processor and began to write daily. He corresponded all year with Lila, a colleague from last summer, and now they are together in class again.

## A Professional Kick in the Pants

I spot Joyce Choate sitting in a corner during break. She looks flushed and somewhat uncomfortable, a marked contrast with the other teachers in the room. Yesterday she almost went home, she says, but last night she changed her mind after spending time with Ronald and Lila. Lila tells me Joyce's confidence is low, "she's with the big guys," and Joyce thinks she should have signed up for the New Hampshire Writing Program instead of this Advanced Institute. When she decided to sign up for this summer's Institute on Reading, Writing, and Learning, it had been ten years since her last summer writing workshop. She knew from the brochure that this was not a course for beginners. She admits:

> I needed a professional kick in the pants—I did expect, after I read the brochure, that we would be moving on, and I'm looking forward to making the connections between reading and writing . . . if there's anything I do well in my classroom it is the sharing of literature, and speaking together. But, if I feel a failure, it's my own floundering in the field of writing. I'm not writing. I'm not writing. Except sometimes if I'm mentally filled up. . . . So I come here and I think, okay, they're going to give me another shot in the arm, and I'm going to go back and I'm going to be better. . . . I said that professionally I'm weary . . . one lady thought that it took a lot of courage to say that . . . I needed it to be known that I'm not feeling like Ms. Professional. Don't think I am, folks, 'cause I'm not. That gave me a sense of release to be able to say that.

Her purpose for being here is clear and focused. She is here for a "shot in the arm," a "professional kick in the pants," in her words. She does not need to solve any personal problems through writing. She has done that quite successfully for herself in other ways. She is a seasoned English teacher who lacks confidence in one of the requirements for teaching English. She has never been comfortable personally or professionally with writing. Joyce simply wants help incorporating writing into her teaching and into her own literacy.

Yesterday she wanted to leave and today she's decided to stay. I wonder what happened last night. Late into the evening, she talked and read with Lila and Ronald for two hours, and the camaraderie she felt quelled her fears:

> By the end of the day, by seven at night in my hot sweltering room—sticking to my chair, my brain just will not work, the tears are beginning to come and I thought, GET OUT! Go out into the world and touch somebody. Get out there, you're like an ingrown toenail, you're so frustrated and sore! So I put on my running shoes, I put on my short shorts and my tee shirt, and I started to walk, briskly, because I was so tense.

Joyce talks for ten full minutes in eloquent detail about her walk around the campus, "I thought, Joyce," she says, "you have the talent, you ask very good questions, you bring people out, you have to try to pay attention to that and remember that's a gift you have." Then, she explained, the wave of fear came back as she ran closer to the dorm. "I really was thinking, Joyce, let this tell you that you want to leave teaching . . . don't be afraid, let the truth come out." So she walked into her room and closed her door:

> I heard my name in the hallway and I thought well, there are other Joyces in the program, and I wasn't sure I wanted to hear my name . . . and then the knock . . . there's Lila and Ronald, a team from last year . . . they had their *Winterkill* in their hands and smiles on their faces. . . . We're going to get some ice cream, sit in some air conditioning, and read this, you want to come? And one side of me said "No, you must work. And the other side said "Yes, and if you go, this isn't work, but you want to go . . . I said, "Yes."
> . . . . We stepped through the doors into the evening, sitting at this little latter-twentieth century Grover's Corners ice cream

table. Gathered around it, we were very close. . . . Two hours, we didn't stop talking about that book. . . . I was very grateful. . . . Then we read aloud, in the ice cream parlor, for an hour and a half . . . and then I realized, "Oh, for heaven's sakes, I'm watching myself here. I'm watching Ronald, I'm watching Lila. . . . I have something I can write about. What is happening to me? What is happening as I perceive it to the others? How are we working together? What would I like to do with this in my classroom?

There is a transformation quality to Joyce's story. She tells a therapeutic narrative; the sense of community she felt with Lila and Ronald brought her through her fear and toward a re-definition of herself as writer and teacher. I will come to see that Joyce weaves her three-week story here with oral eloquence and her love of drama, fear of writing and surprise at the value of community and self-reflection. Already she is entranced with the notion of "watching herself." In the ice cream parlor on the first night, she begins the powerful thoughts that will inform her writing. Her three weeks will end in triumph, at the public reading, with a personal essay she will call "Watch Your Head."

Joyce is an eloquent talker, a superb dramatic reader, and she enjoys direct contact with people. A classmate phrases it well: "Joyce, you speak in final drafts!" Her first love is drama; she is both singer and performer, and along with her personal passion for reading, she has loved being able to share her dramatic skills in the classroom. "I've always enjoyed being able to take a text in class, to read it out. I love to read. I am a good reader. And they eat it up. Like it was frozen yogurt. Just eat it up."

But she worries that her students are not getting enough, that they need more writing. "As excited as I can get the students from talking about literature and reading literature, enjoying it myself, I'm letting an entire area of teaching go, because I am anxious about it. Very anxious about it, in my own life, and in the life of my students." Loving them, "the children" she calls her fourteen year old ninth graders, is not enough, she has decided, "professionally speaking, I am concerned for more than just my relationship with the students. . . . I hope I haven't done anybody a terrible harm over the last ten years, but I have not done them a great service either."

That second night, we eat dinner together and continue our talk, finishing our frozen yogurt cones as we walk down the hill, through the woods to the dorm. She is slender, athletic looking. I calculate she's in her early to mid-forties. She has that preppy look that evokes clothing catalogues for the casually elegant. Her hair is short, curly, and sensible, and tonight she wears a pink mesh cotton shirt, pink and green madras shorts and tennis shoes. Her tiny gold hoop earrings touch her ruddy cheeks. Her looks might suggest that we are discussing the country club or the swimming pool, but we're talking about school and home. Isn't it nice, we marvel, that we don't have to cook or clean while we're here. "It's not only nice," she says, "it's very important not to have to use any creative energy in thinking about the running of the household because you've got to have it all for the writing." She returns to her fear of writing in almost every subject we treat.

She admitted this morning that she did not feel like "Ms. Professional," that she is terrified of writing, and she is "professionally weary." I asked her if she would say the same to her colleagues in an English Department meeting. "I think I'd frighten them if I told them. They would be concerned. . . ." She shares an office with colleagues in other departments: "It's a real fraternity/sorority," she tells me. Although they don't share philosophical concerns about reading and writing, they share what she calls "professional concerns." "We work in a large room together, we have six desks on one side of the room and six on the other. . . . In the eleven years I've worked with these people, we've become pretty darn close."

Joyce teaches at a small high school in upstate New York, a "lovely place to teach." After seven years of single parenthood in several southern states, she settled in with her teenage son and second husband Gordon, a gun engraver. Her in-laws, now deceased, were farmers from families of schoolteachers and writers, "intelligent people who would much rather have been professors at the university, but fate would have it that they live on this little rural farm."

Joyce recognizes that her teaching-self-esteem has had a slow leak over a long period of time. "I've been having real concerns about myself as a teacher. I love the kids, but I'm not sure I like my teaching." Here, on the second night, as we walk through the woods to the open forum, she begins telling a series of stories in which she examines her past as a teacher and a student. "Just two incidents does not a confident person make . . . because we're looking at thirteen to eighteen years' worth of something else that happened in my life. What do I bring to my teaching that comes from my first day in kindergarten?" This is a theme that will recur for her and appear in a poem.

Although her goal is to learn to work with writing in the classroom, Joyce will use much of her time here to examine her personal learning history and then connect it to her teaching. "Somewhere along the line in my growth and development, my speaking was reinforced. I know that my mother and I spent a lot of time together in my early years. . . . Wouldn't it have been wonderful if somebody had asked me, 'What do you like about school?' And I would have said 'Music.'" By remembering her own learning, Joyce will gradually notice that her comfort with music and talk gave way to her discomfort with writing as she continued through school. The subtle, steady pressure of remembering our past, "the rememberer's interlocutor," as Jerome Bruner calls it, helps us reconstruct our experience with narrative and reconceive our ideas about our cultural institutions. "Experience in and memory of the social world are powerfully structured not only by deeply internalized and narrativized conceptions . . . but also by the historically rooted institutions that a culture elaborates to support and enforce them" (1990, 57). Our own stories of schools reinforce how we produce school stories in others. Our memories can serve a dialogic function as we begin to question and interpret our narratives.

As Joyce tells me about her past, she begins a three-week investigation of her own verbal literacy—speaking and listening, reading and writing, and how schools support it, and how they do not. Joyce began teaching twenty-some years ago, for a year in a small town in Connecticut, married, moved to Florida and had a son.

## Depending on a Voice out of Heaven

She returned to teaching full time in Kentucky six years later, when her son entered first grade. By then, she was divorced. "I had a hell of a year that first year. I was a damn yankee schoolteacher and the kids and I . . . The blacks and whites were two separate cultures and me—trying to get along. They did beautifully but there was always that coldness there in the classroom. There was the obvious disparity in their backgrounds and what they brought to this white man's cultural education. Oh, golly!" It remained a struggle for a while:

> I finally said to the principal after a troubled day, "Mr. Row, I *do not* have control of this class," and he simply said "Oh." And I thought, the man isn't hearing me. I can't cry about it anymore. I can't have a nervous breakdown about it. I have to have this job, I want this job, I want to teach these children. . . . If you wanted to learn, you pulled your chair and just got to the front of the room. If you didn't, and you stayed back there I wasn't going to ask you. So I was teaching these few kids at the front of the classroom. . . . I was not going to make them join the group, but I was going to hold them responsible for what the group was doing. The kids at the back of the room pelted chalk at me, every time I turned to write on the board, I'd feel chalk on my back. It was a real Gettysburg. North and South, again. But the kids who were near me could hear me because I was talking with them, as you can tell, in a very direct voice. *This voice* is to my advantage in teaching. Can you tell?

Joyce's speaking voice is, in fact, controlled, dramatic, and expressive. She chooses her words and her metaphors slowly and carefully. I laugh at her Civil War metaphor, and I can picture the lines of battle, the chalk bullets, and Joyce sitting, brave and straight-backed, in the middle. Eventually, she continues, "It was noisy that day and suddenly I heard this voice from the speaker on the wall. . . ." Her principal sent for the troublemakers, paddled and suspended them. "We had peace in the classroom for a week. . . . They knew if I wasn't gonna do it, 'The Lawd' was on my side, and he was right up there on the wall listening all the time, a voice out of Heaven. And when we had that kind of enforced peace, we were then able to begin to love each other. . . . I had a lovely, lovely senior year with the same kids."

All those years ago, Joyce talked herself out of her trouble, invoking the principal's intervention. She saw the battle lines drawn between her students and wanted to create peace in her classroom. She perceived the classroom as a battleground then and uses a war and peace metaphor now to tell the story. The reality of school as she saw it as a young teacher was, in fact, a matter of taking sides. Lakoff and Johnson suggest that our own metaphors guide our future action, become self-fulfilling prophecies (1980, 156), and metaphors when applied to schools (Tomlinson 1988) can be inexorably mixed with the way we see curriculum. Joyce's stories of her past will bear this out for her.

Early in her career, Joyce knew that classroom literacy was her responsibility, but to carry it out she needed some divine intervention. The "voice out of Heaven" suspended the militants for a while, confirmed her decisions, and "enforced" the peace she needed to cover the prescribed curriculum. But even then, she worked her way through the problem by using silent talk for herself and carefully crafted talk with her students. She is sensitive to voices, hers and others: "This voice is to my advantage in teaching. Can you tell?" she highlights her voice to me. And it was her memory of Mr. Row's voice on the wall, the "voice out of Heaven" that saved her.

Throughout her literate life, Joyce has built her personal knowledge through talk, and she will use these three weeks to examine how. Her oral, narrative style serves her in the same way prewriting exercises serve others. James Britton and James Moffett have taught us that it is in talk that students learn. "The quality of our words in the head, inner speech, must be closely tied to our experience of talking with others which gives us resources for thinking and learning, for self-prompting and intellectual adventure" (Britton 1982, 126). Joyce produces compelling oral commentary, and she knows it, and she wants to discover how it ties in with her fear of writing. "Some children need to discover their voices, find their tongues, and some teachers need to rediscover theirs. When pupils are free to talk, teachers are free to observe and to understand what kind of learning is going on. For in the end, the teacher can only make sense of his pupils making sense" (1982, 127). For Joyce as she functions as both student and teacher, and reflexively as both observer and observed, she will begin a powerful dialogue with her own self in the act of making sense.

## *Writing from Talk:*
## *"The English Language Should be Heard"*

Talking to herself and with others on tape is Joyce's way of organizing her thinking, and she uses it like others use journals. On the seven-hour drive to UNH, she tells me, she spoke to her tape recorder about her expectations for the program. All the way she talked about her comfort with speaking and her discomfort with writing. "Well, from the moment I got here, I loved being with the people. Never for a moment did I not love being with the people . . . if it was reading and talking about what we were reading and learning, I would have absolutely thought I'd died and gone to heaven."

She worries on Tuesday about the writing she must produce by Friday, and decides she might write the story of her first night's walk around campus. She hadn't minded my tape recorder, but so far she hasn't written a word. "I started to walk, briskly, because I was so tense." Because she was tense, she imagined tension in each of the clusters of people she passed. A group of young couples was having a cookout in the married student apartments: "How the hell were those mothers going to manage their work with the toddlers running around, and when were they going to get in and get started?" She walked by a group of teenage girls: "They were in that slow walk, walking backwards, animated kind of conversation, one girl, very alive in her face, caught my attention when she said 'Oh yes, the first thing I'm going to do is get out of New Hampshire.' I thought 'I'd like to get out of *the world* right now. Get out of New Hampshire. Honey, I can relate to that.'" Then she ran into a young man playing on the lawn with a Beagle puppy:

> So he flopped in the grass and I got down low, because that puppy is only nine or ten inches long, but doing all the things a girl dog would do. I enjoyed talking with him, I listened to myself. For a few moments I felt a release, that my mind was empty, but then the wave of fear came back. It came back because I was getting closer to the dorm . . . to the task at hand. I really was thinking, 'Joyce, let this tell you that you want to leave teaching'. . . . So I blasted through the door, and two young women looked at me, I don't know what the look was in their faces. . . . My son says 'Mom your eyes get wild and your hair gets frizzy when you're crazy,' and I knew I was crazy, temporarily.

She had just entered her room when Lila and Ronald, "my ministering angels," invited her to join them for reading together in the air-conditioned ice cream parlor. She had felt overwhelmed with the prospect of writing, and even the bulk of reading responsibilities began to bother her. "Tom Romano said, at the end of class. . . . 'I want you to read a big chunk of this tonight, because I want you to finish it by Friday.' It's three-hundred-thirty pages! And that threw me for a loop because for me, reading a novel together is . . . sitting and experiencing that story and that language out loud, to me the English language in many cases should be heard." I ask if she does that with her students. "Yes, it's a spiritual experience!

Which I wouldn't miss for the world, and if there's anything *I do well* in my classroom it is the sharing of literature and speaking together."

Ending her first day with the "spiritual experience" reading aloud with Lila and Ronald enabled Joyce to decide to stay. Not only does this "spiritual experience" serve her in her writing this week; it foreshadows a triumph that will come for her as she reads aloud her own writing three weeks later.

Tonight she is under pressure to write. She must share a draft in the morning in a small group, and so far she has written very little. I offer the tape of her story, and suggest that maybe it will help her to shape a piece of writing. She takes it. Her writing agony lasts until Thursday, through drafts and small group conferences, tapes, and transcriptions. Her drafts are handwritten in large, feathery script, double-spaced, and they use every inch of her notebook paper. The margins are full of angled notes to herself ("I could write all day, no problem, if I didn't have to share it with the group.") Her doodles are sequences of budding plants and flowers, arrested in their growth. Chunks of words reside in little boxes. There are straight cross-outs and wavy deletions. Each page is dated and numbered. Of the drafts remaining outside her wastebasket, I count nine separate starts for three days' work. She calls the drafts "heavy" and "out of control."

Although she is wracked with insecurity about her writing this first week, Joyce is equally secure about her strengths in reading and responding. On Thursday, she is still upset about her own piece and she defers to others: "By then my piece, the first one, had grown to gigantic proportions, heavy duty, go-nowhere. Frank needed a conference. We gave it to him. I kept saying, 'Joyce, one of your joys is helping the other guy and seeing his or her writing grow. Remember that. Remember that. Get away from yourself and work with Frank and enjoy it.'"

She returned to the dorm alone, in tears. "I thought 'Joyce, you CAN go home. It's only money. And if you go, you don't feel like a failure. You just say, 'This wasn't for you at this time.'" When she reached the dorm, her husband Gordon called on the phone. He asked if she had been running, and she told him no, that she was crying and she wanted to come home. "He said, 'Well, that is a choice. I hope you don't. I hope you stick it out. I want you to do it.' And then he went on to give me a pep talk as only Gordon can. . . . He wasn't pompous, but he was focused," she tells me:

> "Remember Abraham Lincoln," Gordon said, "when he finished reading that Gettysburg Address, as far as he was concerned, he was a failure". . . . In my head I remembered it, my eleventh graders had just done *The Gettysburg Address* as a musical piece, and what a gem of simplicity it was. . . . He reminded me of his brother, who takes piano lessons and plays in recitals when his playing isn't as competent as others. . . . I was listening but I wasn't hearing. . . . But all of that information must have stuck in my head, because when I went to my desk I realized that keeping it simple was, for me, a solution . . . that will be my message to my students. . . . Quantity is meaningless if there is no quality, and very often you have to chip away at the hunk of coal before you get to the diamond.

After Gordon's call, she settled in her room, read what she had written all week and looked for the parts with which she was pleased. She began to transcribe the tapes of our conversations. She wrote, she listened, she transcribed. She blended Gordon's pep talk, her taped stories, her memory of the Gettysburg Address. And suddenly, she stopped. "I got to the point where I could stop transcribing. And I realized, 'The reason you can stop here, Joyce, is because it's finished! You've said what you need to say. Eureka! I was flying. And I thought, 'It's only Thursday night!'" She flew down the hall to one colleague's room and then across the lawn to another in her writing class. "At least I'll know. They'll tell me the truth. And so I read it to them:"

> Cindy said 'You've said what you need to say.' And David was positive. We remembered one of our classmates talking about the book *Writing Down the Bones*, that a writer is simply someone who writes, and writes, and writes. I realized that that is what I

had to do all week to get my piece, and I had to have the faith, which I didn't, that something would come out of all that writing, and it did. . . . I went off in euphoria on Friday morning, to breakfast and to class and to the rest of the day. So I went into Friday going 'Phew.' Feeling light-hearted. Feeling that I could read it.

Cindy and David in the dorm, like Lila and Ronald at the ice cream shop, listened to her writing. Here, Joyce was able to present it orally, in the form that gave her comfort. She recognized that they were available respondents, and she used them. "It's the forced proximity that was so helpful," she told me. Joyce was conscious, even during her agonies, of herself as a student and her experience's implications for her as a teacher. Her final piece, written in her black feathery script, is a letter to her students detailing her week's discomfort:

Woodruff Hall, Room 120

UNH, Durham: July 13, 1990

Dear Kids,

Remember in *Great Expectations* how Matthew Pocket pulls himself right up out of his chair by the roots of his own hair when his wife's craziness drives him mad? Well, I pulled a Matthew Pocket last night, going crazy with anxiety about my writing for the group I'm in.

You remember I told you I'd be a student this summer at UNH, and some of you smiled at the thought of me out there where you've been all year? So, you can feel satisfied because your misery is now mine. . . . one similarity you can definitely relate to is all the work . . . my teacher must think we've got clones of ourselves here helping us do some of this. . . .

I was fighting with my writing mind, forcing it to grow up . . . now! But my mind is more stubborn that I am, and it was winning the fight. The more I pounded, the less it produced. The less it produced, the more panic stricken I got. Even though brainstorms covered my desk, none worked. I'd shuffle through all those papers hoping one of the ideas I'd started would befriend me and take me further, but each brainstorm was nothing more than an acquaintance on the way to someplace else.

That's when I pulled my Matthew Pocket routine, jumped out of the chair, yanked on shorts and sneakers, and marched out of my stifling dorm room, down the hall, and into the night air. I figured I could walk my fear away, but I'd have to push it. So I forced my body just like I'd been forcing my mind. . . .

Joyce's letter describes the people she saw on her walk, much of it an embellishment of her story as she told it on tape, and it ends simply saying "I'm still here and thinking of you." She closes with an old-fashioned handcrafted, feathery scroll, and a very traditional "Mrs. Choate."

She reads the piece in class on Friday morning with dramatic intensity and flair in her voice. The class listens intently, and after she has finished, they sigh and mumble, shuffle and smile, bend over the file cards Romano uses for responses, and write notes to her. They walk their cards across the circle to her, placing them on Joyce's desk. She reads each one, smiling. The class is silent for a few minutes while she reads. As in Ellen's class, the written response accompanied by silence is an important Friday ritual, and although this is the first Friday, the members of this class have participated in this ritual before. Tom does not need to explain it. Class members have assisted in crafting this piece all week long. The Friday response ritual marks the writer's finished contribution and the audience's investment in it.

The cards are thick with specifics; Joyce's audience of high school teachers responds to her piece with comments about style, diction, and effect. Some point to imagery, genre, and word choice: "Comparison to *Great E*—good lead!" "'Clones of ourselves'—great line!" " 'Walked backwards!' Great idea—a letter—and it works." "The eloquent descriptions of your turmoil, the mother slumped over, the teenager who wants out . . . very effective! Keep on writing." "I like the genre you chose—who else to write to when you're struggling with writing but the people you teach?" "The line 'would befriend me and take me further'—love it."

Other responses mention its emotional impact, and recognize Joyce's week-long agony: "Well, Joyce, you gave us you and ourselves. The truth screams back 'the writer is an observer.' You did and we reflected with you. Come hold my hand." "You convey well the turmoil. Will you show it to the kids?" "The humor and the anxiety were very real," "A trip to find yourself—I shared your experience last summer—I have never been so frustrated, homesick, and lonely in my life. Would love to talk."

And in others, there is a shared philosophical connection with the theme of Joyce's piece: "Our students don't realize that we struggle many times just like they do. I think your students will enjoy and identify with your letter." "It ties in the reasons why we're here—kids, writing, and self." "A fine projection of a teacher as student." "Bravo! I'm sure glad you're still here. You made some excellent choices both personally and in your writing." "I don't feel so alone now."

## *Bringing the Talk to School, The Challenge to Create a Receptive Spirit*

Joyce is fascinated with the Friday reading ritual: "It's fascinating on Friday to see what happens to pieces that you were part of conferencing. I would very much like my students, perhaps with a paper or two a week, have a volunteer early in the week, read a rough draft and then get to hear that paper again on Friday, being conscious of what stage that writing was in—let's say Tuesday or Wednesday. And I'd like to see my students capture the spirit of cooperative learning, in helping each other with their writing and improving the voice, clarifying the information, etc."

"Cindy and I helped Frank on Thursday, and he was all excited. . . . But then to hear his piece and to see what he did with what we expressed were problems, and suggestions we made, to help him clarify what I thought was a very difficult job he was trying to do. He was recapturing a moment in a stickball game, and he was juggling dialogue to reveal character . . . he was

177

juggling the fact that readers might not know the rules of a stickball game, and he was juggling the actual development of the game itself." Joyce found herself engaged in Frank's creative process. She noticed his "juggling," his week-long manipulations of words around the writing problems he had set for himself—between character development, attention to audience, and the actual information he needed to include about stickball itself. Her investment in Frank's piece is strong, and she is pleased with the finished product—for the collaborative effort, and for the writing itself. Her pride in the collective work of the class mirrors her surprise in her own success. Having experienced it herself, she needs to think about how she'll work with this experience in her classroom.

After Friday, Joyce decides to spend the weekend alone, reading and thinking. I can see that she needs to separate herself from everyone. She offers to talk to me on tape. And during the weekend like she did in her final piece, she folds her weeks' experiences as an insecure student into her life as a secure teacher. In the quiet of her reflection, she is able to think about the physical dimensions of her own classroom and about herself as a classroom designer. "We sit in rows, the teacher's desk is at the front of the room, you've seen it a million times. That's okay for some things, and I won't change it except when we read aloud pieces to the group . . . I think I will invite us to sit on the floor and to create a circle where we just celebrate the writing . . . let that create a more receptive spirit . . . a circle of friends rather than rows of competitors."

Joyce postulates some larger projects for her colleagues and her students: "I'd like to think that there will be some kind of support group that we teachers will get together. I would prefer to keep it very small, maybe even just women . . . maybe four of us. I'd also like to get a network in which we get in touch with more student publications and help students to prepare pieces to send in for possible publication." She stops, listens to the tape she's just made, and then she adds a reflection at the end:

I heard two things that made me think how lingering old thought patterns and habits are. One of them is I've been referring to MY classroom, MY curriculum, etc. I hope that I will go in this year in the spirit that this is OUR classroom, this is YOUR ninth-grade year of English, and I am here to help you accomplish that which you feel is important . . . to look at the options to decide what you might like to do with your ninth grade year.

Also, I realize how traditional I am in thinking of myself as a *student* in Tom Romano's class. I thought more about *his collecting* a piece than *my reading* it to a group of peers. I might be willing to take more risks if I knew that this was not going to be evaluated so to speak by my peers, but simply listened to and perhaps conferenced or responded to . . . I might have done something more imaginative than I did, still put as much thinking time in. But I was very academic. I put physical and organizational time into it, thinking I was putting it into the hands of a teacher who wouldn't have me there reading it aloud for him.

Joyce's first week was exhausting; she observes and recognizes it in others. "I noticed the weariness of participants at the end of the week. It's a challenge to be helpful to each other. We got very tired—five hours of sleep for many of us Monday through Thursday. There's also just so much sympathy we can give. People were very good to me, but that's that. That's enough now, Joyce is here, she will stick the program through, and we can laugh about it and we're not going to discuss the stress anymore. You just have to get in there and swim to keep your head above water." For the remainder of the weekend, Joyce catches up on her sleep and her reading:

I found it a great relief just to be here pretty much by myself. I cherished the fact that I was alone and I was not surrounded by talk of the Institute. I needed a rest from that intensity. . . . I read two hundred pages on Saturday, I outlined the draft to my response to the novel, and I felt a big relief at having done that. Today, I've been reading toward my Friday writing, and that's a little slower, that's a little bit more sluggish . . . like the humid weather we're having today, the work is dragging a little long, about the pace that the people's bodies are.

When I listen to the tape, I realize, as she does, that she is far more comfortable with the academic tasks of reading and outlining for her teacher. She anticipates another week of writing. She chooses to do the more academic tasks, and despite her success this past Friday, is still feeling "sluggish" about her writing. She has used the weekend to collect herself and prepare academically for the coming week. But her second week will yield more than she expects: an even richer mix of talk, events, books, and eventually writing. And she will concoct the mix. Like the past week, much of her thinking will come outside of class in informal talk with colleagues.

## Filling in the Blanks

Although she doesn't know it, Joyce is thinking about themes that came to her during the first week: competition as it clashes with community in schools, personal learning histories, and writing apprehension. Friday is still four days away. Donald Murray's morning talk, "Pushing the Edge," had both set the week's writing in motion and cut down on class time. His message? Writing means finding tension. "The edge," Murray said, "is the outer limit of our confidence and experience, when we attempt more than has been possible for us before . . . to learn, we need certain conditions: an experiment, an instructive failure, and a sense of humor." Joyce was moved by Murray's emphasis on exploring and experimenting, the essential element to move forward in a piece of writing. "It's the irony of the thing," Joyce told me after Murray's talk. "And yet, what will make a story is going to be, as Donald Murray says, the tension. That's really what I did, isn't it? *I signed up for a little tension.* . . . It's 'Get your ass out there and flex your buttocks, baby!'" She laughs.

It is just before twilight on Monday. I join her with Bob, whom she calls one of her "support people," a colleague in her writing group. The rock is flat enough and large enough for all three of us to sit. It is the one at the edge of the circular drive, from which we can survey our crescent of mini-dorms.

A few people shuffle in and out of the doorways, swapping papers and books. Bob is wearing a tank top and shorts, about to take his evening run. Joyce is relaxed, having refreshed herself over the weekend.

She has just finished reading Mike Rose's *Lives on the Boundary*, and Bob has read John Mayher's *Uncommon Sense*. Both books investigate the structure of public schools, the implicit values of "the system." Joyce and Bob discuss both books, but they also tell stories of personal failure and competition. Bob explains:

> John Mayher is helping me to see why (the system) operates the way it does on us. Well, you know, common sense education is "We are paying those teachers. . . . they've got the knowledge, they've got the answers. You sit and shut up and they'll impart that to you". . . . we've got to have students sit there and be consumers of education. We can't have them visiting among themselves because that will waste time. That's inefficient. On the other hand, the research would say that in order for students to become articulate users of language, they've got to use language. One cancels out the other . . . every page is loaded with ideas I'm connecting with my own education.

Although Bob is both teacher and administrator, he thinks first about his own education as he talks with Joyce. Their reading recalls their own school histories before they investigate their teaching. Joyce begins to talk about her school memories. They are sparse, but they fall into the two categories: learning in groups to create, and learning alone to compete. She remembers the joy of making butter with her class in kindergarten, and then gradually learning "the challenge to be first."

> In fifth grade I was shamed by my reading teacher into the knowledge that I was not reading. . . . I did a report on a little bunny rabbit . . . a book probably for first or second graders. I didn't want to do a book report. My teacher asked us all to stand in front of the room . . . when I gave mine, there was a silence, palpable. And the teacher just looked at me . . . deadpan . . . I read from his face, 'If this is where you want to stay all your life, help

yourself, but you've got to realize you are not growing up . . . from the look on his face, the blame was on me."

She has no other memory of that year. She "read his face." The following year, by sixth grade, Joyce says, she had mastered "the system:"

> In that class I learned that getting 100 on a spelling test meant I could give the next week's test from the front of the room. And now I see where I enjoy that aspect of teaching—being at the front of the room. I learned to organize, I learned to study and memorize. In January and June we had exams just like they did in the high schools . . . if you had a 90 or better, you were exempt. And I worked every fall into the winter so I could be exempt from exams, and the same from the spring . . . I was very proud. . . . That was my elementary school education. . . . What was I learning to do? Be proud of memorizing . . . I was learning the system.

Bob replies, "Learning the very thing that imprisons us. Learning how to put the bars around ourselves." His voice is strangely soothing, ironic. He stares out toward the minidorms, where doors open and close, groups of people trade papers and others read together on the lawn.

"Yes. Yes, absolutely." Joyce answers quietly. "I nailed in my own coffin nails, you know."

"All of us. We victimize the victim. We blame the victim for his or her learning problems. . . . I failed first grade"

"And what impression do you think that made on you? On your life and your education?"

"Well, I think fortunately . . . given how young I was . . . I don't think it hurt . . . Although, who knows? I still bring it up, don't I?" Three times already, he's mentioned his "failure" in first grade. Bob has taught at every grade level, raised two grown sons, and is now a language arts coordinator for a large state agency in the midwest. But he is determined to return to the classroom. He has just received a sabbatical from his administrative work so that he can teach third grade for a year.

Joyce finished *Lives on the Boundary* over the weekend, and she tells Bob she was moved especially by Rose's problems in elementary school. His high school experiences were unusual, and he was lucky. "As Rose goes on into high school, although it's still powerful, I think I become jealous. All of a sudden a very influential mentor, Jack McFarland, comes into his life. There was no Jack MacFarland in my life. . . . I don't know that my teachers were necessarily that interested in me . . . for those of us who were girls and most of our teachers who might have mattered, the Jack McFarlands in our lives were men."

Bob stiffens, moves back and forth on the rock, his arms grasping his knees, and looks up at the sunset. "Oooh, yeah, that kind of relationship couldn't have happened . . . the high school male teacher, going out of his way . . . to help her come into the temple . . . couldn't do that. . . . Boy, Joyce, that's powerful."

She continues thinking about women in her past. Joyce's years in junior high shaped her gender identity, she remembers, but not her knowledge. Women taught her to "be a good girl." Miss Bell, "who was neat and proper and young and clean and short-cropped hair . . . again I was rewarded for my neatness and my good-girl behavior. . . . I do not remember anything I read with her in seventh grade, I don't remember writing anything. I remember filling in some blanks." But she remembers clearly an eighth-grade science class: "While I was listening, the kid to my right leaned back in his chair and without my realizing it, he put his left arm behind my back, and in an instant grabbed and snapped my bra strap. And I could cry now . . . Because the teacher laughed at him."

"Male teacher?" Bob asks.

"Male teacher!" answers Joyce.

"Your memories of junior high are *not* nonacademic. They have the aura of what happened and what didn't happen," Bob observes.

"It spoke about school and what happens in schools. . . . It broke my heart. It made me feel foolish to be a girl. . . . Like I was being used. And I was an object. Donald Murray talked today about having a sense of humor. *Tell that to an eighth-grade girl.*"

Joyce's high school memories, too, are gender-bound, she discovers: "being in love with my English teacher, Mr. Ford," and starring in the play "Girl Crazy." "I have a singing voice. And I learned my lines. I had no soul in my lines, but when I sang my songs, I wowed them. Again, non-academic. . . . From tenth through twelfth grade, I hated school. . . . It was totally competitive. And that was it for me. I paid my dues, I got my fees . . . I became anonymous. . . . They called me 'Kron,' my last name. They called us by our last names. And if you didn't answer the question in about five seconds, they went on to the next."

"Why did they do that to us?" Bob asks.

"I have no idea. Was it post-World War II? Was it post-Korean? Was it male-military system?" Joyce snaps her fingers and swings her arm in a marching cadence. "We put 'em in rows. We march 'em out. We produce 'em. . . . Okay. Kron, when was the American Revolution? When did it start and what were three causes? You didn't get it? Okay. We'll go on to Welch."

"Assembly line. Performance. Produce. Product." Bob volleys words like a machine gun, echoing Joyce's military rhythm and the industrial metaphor she evokes. In the book *Counterpoint and Beyond*, the National Council of Teachers of English's (NCTE) response to the 1985 U.S. Government national report called *Becoming a Nation of Readers*, an examination of the metaphors in the report points to the very paradigms that Joyce and Bob use as they talk. These are the metaphors that entrapped them as students: "research as debate, winners and losers in the teaching of reading," learning to read as industrial training, and educational policy as quality control (Bloome, et al., in Davidson, ed. 1988).

Joyce resists being measured on a hierarchical scale rather than according to her success in group-centered learning (the butter making, the music, her dramatic successes). She resents that her self-image in high school was shaped by the males with whom she interacted. The recent work of feminist scholars such as Flynn and Heilbrun supports Joyce's informal

observations of herself as a student. None of her male teachers could have provided a mentor like Jack Mc Farland was to
Mike Rose, and in her adolescence she "felt foolish to be a
girl." Even her dramatic success was tied to loving a male
teacher and speaking "lines that had no soul."

Together on the rock, Joyce and Bob begin to speculate on
their roles as teachers. Bob uncrosses his legs, shifts position,
and points. "How the hell did you end up wanting to be a
teacher?"

Joyce laughs. "That's what my students ask me. I tell them
I really can't answer that question. I say 'I don't think it's to
inflict pain' . . . they laugh . . . I think, though, although it is
lovingly administered, there's an element of pain . . . I think
I'm searching through my teaching to find the love of learning."

As they finish their talk, Bob observes that their own pain
will insure that they will make it better for their own students.
"I think we have a double-edged advantage if we reflect and
use our experiences." Their collective past shapes the histories
they create for their students.

Later in the week, this talk is the nucleus for Joyce's final
writing:

> . . . Bob helped me out of the rough there. . . . I went to my room
> and I wrote my 'I remember' piece. I remember kindergarten, I
> remember first grade, I remember second grade, and I went on
> and on and on. And I was remembering very well. . . . I may not
> have been putting down writing that was artistically done, but I
> thought, 'I *do not* want to write. I don't know why. I don't want
> to do this.' So I flipped my paper over and I wrote 'What do I
> want to do? I want to show that the system has betrayed me, that
> it probably blotted out whatever creativity was starting by the
> time I was four or five years old.' I wrote two or three more
> things on the side of the paper, then I drew a line down the cen-
> ter and on the right side I tried to crystallize all that, in images. I
> realized that if I had anything, I had a form. All I could do was try
> to crystallize it into one great expression of what I was feeling the
> first week . . .

The talk with Bob had offered Joyce a chance to examine her past and rethink her teaching. So had reading *Lives on the Boundary*. In her journal, Joyce wrote some notes: "Rose as a writer, student educator. . . . Amazed at the contrast between Rose's desolate environment but his obvious alertness to all its details—the people, their jobs, their fatal flaws, his poor education. . . . Implication of the book for me: the need to review the patterns of my own learning—literacy—home and school to have my students do the same, evaluate their literacy past."

By the end of the week, Joyce writes another letter, this time to her class of colleagues: "Mr. Rose reveals the status of students in the latter twentieth century. Horrified and hopeful, I read: 'Harold was made stupid by his longing, and his folder full of tests could never reveal that' (127). The writer of II Kings tells how a lost axe head floats to the surface of the Jordan River, and I believe I've seen the miracle repeated several times this past week."

Joyce's own writing "miracle" takes shape during the week from reading, writing, reflecting, and collegial talk that helped her dig into her past. She writes: "My response to reading Rose boiled down to a single reflection on my own elementary school education. What had begun on Monday night as her "I Remember" piece, by Friday has become this poem:

### Winthrop Ave. Elementary, 1951

After kindergarten,
they took the brassy, flashy cymbals,
the silver, tinkling triangles,
the rolling, swaying, pounding piano music and locked them away.

They handed me the scissors,
   sticky with old paste,
   stubborn like cold fingers
   fumbling with a key.
Struggling for smooth, I cut ragged edges.

Then they took the scissors
And pushed a pencil in my hand,

a fat, leaden, pokey pencil.
My sprawling letters,
   wayward and willful,
Strayed from the straight-lined path.
My mind did, too.
So they tied me
   to the words
      on the page      of a book.

Like a chain gang detainee,
I sounded off, in turn,
   around the stumbling circle,
   shackled with the words
   they forced on me,
      the links
      chaining my thoughts
      to theirs.

## *Attesting to Arrested Writing*

Joyce's poem is full of alliteration, sound images, and a cacophony of silent shrieks against a system that valued words on a page over making sounds, a system that taught her early to "sound off in turn" and "shackled her" to words she didn't choose. Her poem receives enthusiastic responses from her colleagues in class on Friday, but Joyce's fear of writing has not disappeared. "Have I improved in my writing? Slightly," she tells me at the end of the week. "But that's going to take years, because if my theory is correct, somewhere in that part of my mind, my growth is arrested. . . . Much more than I have had any time in my life. I've written papers in college, but they were always responses to what I was reading . . . what so-and-so said about something . . . I did enjoy those papers. I can remember the hysteria of writing for twenty-four hours with books literally piled all around me, and the adrenaline was pumping, and I guess I did pretty well." She enjoyed those papers in college; she had mastered the system's formula for writing, and she saw it as a challenge.

But this summer, she is having to construct her own assignments, conceive her topics, choose her genres. For Romano's class, she compiles a portfolio to represent her reading and writing choices with an explanatory letter to her classmates. She is reading *You Must Revise Your Life* by William Stafford, and in her portfolio letter to the class she writes: "Mr. Stafford speaks and I listen reverently." She quotes Stafford's poetry:

> And you discover where music begins
> before it makes any sound, far in the mountains where canyons go
> still as the always-falling,
> ever-new flakes of snow.
>
> —"You and Art" (27)

Joyce's chosen quote shows her lifelong interest in sound. She conceives Stafford as "speaker" and herself as "listener." As she reads, she participates in his writing struggles and thinks about her own. She writes nineteen quotations in her journal and chooses this page of it for her portfolio. On the edges of her notes, she scratches: "write, write, write, boil, boil, boil. Writing is not speaking for me. Music. Voices. Rumbling bass harmonies." From very early in her life, Joyce's engagement with words is through their sounds. At the end of her note to the class, she quotes Stafford again: "Maybe your stumbling saves you, and that sound in the night is more than the wind." Her poem "Bill Writes," a tribute to Stafford, reflects her own writing struggles and her fascination with his. She describes it as a "study in spontaneity:"

## Bill Writes

Bill bashes his brain
As he thrashes his paper,
Whipping it with his pen.

Bill snorts as he sorts
The words which flow
For awhile then
Stop short.

Bill suffers from brain fever,
Mind malaria,
His psyche convulsing
From the bite of an idea
So small
He never saw it coming,
Hardly felt the sting.

Joyce adds a note to her poem: "I'd rather get rid of the rhythm and try to maintain the sound in a freer form. I'll set the poem aside, and when—if I go to revise, I'll begin in my head—use words spoken aloud in some lonely spot, then I'll return to paper." In his response to her writing of that week, Romano writes: "Joyce, I was there at the genesis of 'Bill Writes.' I'm not so much pulled by the rhyme as I am pulled by the rhythm and meaning in the last stanza. . . . In reading through your notes, Joyce, I can see what a big impact Stafford and Rose had on you . . . You're reflecting carefully and letting go bit by bit. I can see it."

Reading Leslie, Stafford, and Rose, producing several pieces of writing, and assembling a portfolio in two weeks has been a major task for Joyce, but she is not alone. Romano knows he's asked a lot of his class. This week, there has been an undercurrent or resistance in many of the Reading/Writing Institute participants. I've heard complaints in the cafeteria, in the dorms, and in the hallways, and I've recorded them in my fieldnotes. "Is the second year in this program a disappointment? I wonder. How far can 'reflection' go? Can any experience evoke a feeling of 'transformation' twice?" Reading time is cheating writing time, they say. They returned this year because they wanted to write as they had done last year. "We've all felt that we have not had the time that we needed to get into our writing, to conference the way we wanted to, to talk about our pieces, and to write, and to revise. That's a six to eight hour a day job if you're going to produce a piece by Friday," Joyce tells me. She complains that they have not had "enough time to bond," and the weight of the reading assignments is keeping them from writing more. Like Joyce, many of the participants are confused and tired, unclear about what they need to be doing.

"Ronald was saying last week that he felt it was too soon to come back. But today he changed his tune. He realizes now he needed to come back this soon because the steam was working its way out of his engine. He needed another jet propulsion here, to make him go back this year with more spirit, more information, more goals." I write in my fieldnotes that people rely on the program itself to give them what Joyce calls "jet propulsion." This week, this program is giving mixed messages.

"Yeah, there's been some frustration. There was a real directive that came down on us at the beginning of the week. And that when we chose pieces for Friday's big read-in, that we would try to choose responses to reading, and then everybody said, 'Waaait a minute. This is against the very philosophy that we're supposed to be working with'. . . . So we're puzzled." Because this group has lived with the program's rituals and pedagogies, because they've carried their own versions to their own classrooms, they look to the program to confirm the rituals and behaviors they remember, not to add new ones. In Joyce's group at the beginning of the third week I hear jests and dissatisfactions:

"Are we written out by this time?"

"I could go home right now, I pushed myself to where I want to be. I'm happy, for heaven's sake."

After Joyce reads her Bill Stafford poem, her classmate Elaine says, "I felt that Tom had sort of given us a 'prompt,' when he said he would like us to write a response to our reading, and I thought "I don't wanna respond to reading—I don't *have* to do this, so I thought, well, I'm *just not* going to do this. I want to write another piece of fiction, but I just realized when I listened to you that I *am* responding to a piece of reading. The writing *has come* from my reading—my listening to my son's reading over the phone." She continues talking about her son:

I thought, I think he's trying to emulate what I'm doing—while I'm writing here, and so he's writing this week, too. I was proud of myself. I didn't play mother at all . . . I did some nice teacher questioning . . . and he called and read me his piece. Well, of course it was a long fourteen-year-old robo-suit story . . . someone cuts off someone's head. . . . I love him so dearly, he works so hard to be cool, to be accepted, and he's just not. . . . he's going to be a four-eyed loser for a while. So what I wrote about was him. My first line was "He stood off to one side of the cafeteria, contemplating his strategy, like a stray dog."

Elaine's story illustrates that the addition of "reading" has invited her to question what "reading" means, and the interconnection of writing and reading. Joyce's reading of Rose and Stafford triggered her memories and eventually her writing. Elaine's phone conversation with her fourteen year old helped her expand her definition of reading and triggered a piece of writing. It took time and reflection for both to document those connections.

Like Dorothy's complaints about Terry Moher's class, these participants direct their frustration toward Tom Romano and the program itself. They view the problem with their two pairs of eyes: as teachers and as students. In their attempt to follow what they perceive as Tom's directives, their very resistance helps to solidify their beliefs. And they begin to think about their own teaching, their own classroom directives. Joyce reports, "Where else might there be balking? It could be just the nature of us high school teachers. . . . Lila is doing a reading response. And she is not enjoying it one little bit. Ronald is liking the books he is reading. I don't think Tom meant to be directive. One little misrepresentation can fire a class." Joyce starts to make plans, toying with what she's seen as teacher directives and student resistance.

I'm going to start my school year . . . I'm just going to treat it as if we'd been together since the whole summer, and 'Hi, come on in. Sit down. I have something to share with you.' And then we're in, and that's it. Just begin. . . . There's a lot I have to do next year, but I think I'm going to have to simplify. I think my kids are just going to read and write next year . . . I have decided we're going to have some real quiet time in the classroom, where everybody can write. . . . We're going to have time when everybody can either write or talk. We're going to have time when we can read alone, their own choice. We're going to have time when we can read together and hear and enjoy the language together. See the words on the page and feel them.

Joyce's plans incorporate what she's learning about reading and writing with the language and listening she already loves. By questioning and resisting Tom's plan for them, Joyce's classmates handle their frustration by looking backward at their personal reading and writing and forward toward their teaching. In their resistance to Tom's curricular directives, they re-envision their own. The portfolio is a place to document these choices for their classmates and teacher, exactly what Tom's syllabus had suggested that they do.

## *Prelude: The Way I Knew Not Of*

Despite their collective resistance, Joyce's group continually talks and swaps books. For the coming weekend, Joyce borrowed Joseph Langland's *Twelve Poems With Preludes and Postludes* from Tony, and Peter Elbow's *Writing Without Teachers* from Elaine. Both have inspired her:

> This morning in my room I was reading my little devotional book and it begins with a verse from Isaiah where the Lord says "I will lead the blind in a way they know not of . . . and I just mused on that, thinking of myself as the blind, wanting to know the way . . . realizing I just have to be faithful and walk on, even though I can not see. . . . And then Tony begins the session telling us about this book of poems he found in his house, the author talks about reading and memorizing his own poetry, and then when he's alone, setting it to music, so I asked Tony if I could see the book, and as soon as I started, there it was—"The way I knew not of!"

Each poem is followed by a postlude, a story about what happened to the poem since it was written, and in many cases, the poems have been set to music. "I'm finding out how creativity, writing, poetry, all of this has got to spring from the freedom to find out what's inside of yourself. Although these poems are inspired by something external". . . . She is intrigued by one poem written by a soldier during World War II after his brother has died in combat. Since its writing, the poem has had a long history and a world-wide readership. "And so here this man writes this poem in his grieving, although it was many years after his brother was killed. Little did he know it would be translated for the very people who were his enemies, the very people against whom his brother was fighting, the Japanese mother who herself lost sons, and how it helped her through her grief."

On Monday she reads the poem aloud, "And that is what we want writing to do—to go out into the world and be of some help to someone else, and I appreciated that because that's what I needed to hear." To get too attached to my own writing and to only write for myself is imprisoning, it's just awful, it's worse than what I think dying might be. But to think that I might be writing something, that even though I don't send it out into the world, it would go, in some way, and it frees me up." Joyce's interest was piqued, once again, by her engagement with oral texts—where they come from and where they go.

By now she considers the "freeing" quality of writing, and reading Elbow on freewriting frees her more: "I decided I had a few minutes, and I would push my pen. And let my mind flow through. So I found that if I did not pick up my pen, didn't ever separate my pen from the paper except to go to the next line, that I could keep writing. But then last night when I came back to it, writing in the conventional style of separating words from one another, it took me five and a half hours to put something down on paper that isn't flowing along at all. Would you listen to one little thing I wrote about that?" She asks her group to listen to a paragraph she's written, which was inspired by a different poem from the Langland book. Inspired by a story of some divers who swam into a grotto in the Mediterranean Sea, she sees the grotto as a metaphor:

> They swam down . . . not knowing the way, not knowing what they would find, and into the cave in which light filtered both down to the sea and up into the cave and reflected from its walls and roof. My cave, my grotto is yet unknown to me. My fears are as a diver, fears of close places, fears of surprises, of the unexpected, searching, finding my own cave is difficult, but ever beckoning me on, and that I'm really a fearful person—I have no idea how far back we could go—[Joyce breaks into a nasal voice, mimicking a psychiatrist] 'Into the womb, you know, perhaps we should go through the birth experience.'
>
> And that's what's happening these three weeks for me. . . . I'm rediscovering an opportunity to just push through and keep going. And if it weren't for Fridays, I wouldn't do it. Fridays help create the fear, but because it's there, and I'm supposed to produce something, it makes me keep going into that cave. I'm not very deep into it. The fear of being wrong is the fear that dominates my life. Getting me out of my fear has to do with my community. I cannot do this unless I am with my friends.

Joyce's metaphor helps her see what she needs to do. She links her immersion in the program with the divers' immersion in the grotto. She notices that it is her colleagues, being "with my friends" that move her out of her cave-like fears of doing something "wrong" and having to share it. The community that will receive her Friday productions is the community that she needs to quell her fear. She recognizes that the purpose of this community is not to judge "wrongness," but, like the divers in the grotto, to assist her in finding whatever might be there. And one small moment with her community will spark the piece she'll produce for the last Friday.

## Metacognition: An Act of Head Watching

At the beginning of the third week, Joyce writes an equation on the margin of her notebook, "(meta)cognitive = thinking about thinking." She circles the word "metacognitive." Her freewriting already proved that her reading and writing about reading and writing immerses her with thoughts about thinking as she learns about learning. She has watched her own process of writing as it takes shape inside a community designed to support it. She has examined her ability to express herself orally and her lifelong love of reading, as it contrasts with her fears of expressing herself in writing. By re-examining her educational past, Joyce has had a peek at her own literate processes. By the end of the three weeks, she labels it "a phenomenon:"

> I don't know how I speak, because I do it spontaneously, pretty much. The human response, you're looking at me when I'm speaking, and I can tell by the look on your face what's happening. . . . And then I go to write! It's back to first grade again, afraid of making mistakes; when I put something on paper, it seems permanent.

"The human response," as she describes it, is what's always made speaking easy for her. But writing is still tied to fear of making mistakes. But what she will learn in her writing this final week is that "the human response" is one writers have, too, when they use opportunities for reflection and create communities for human response like the one she's had here. She completes her time at UNH writing a personal essay borne of her three week obsessions, which she titles "Watch Your Head."

With her characteristic mix of fear, curiosity, and thoroughness, she tells me she began the piece, inspired by Elbow, by conducting "three-minute experiments" with herself in free writing, "where I just wrote on, on both sides of a sheet of paper, until I filled the paper, I didn't stop, I didn't lift my pen until the paper was filled. . . . at least I have an idea in my head." This week she feels better because she's had an idea since Thursday in the cafeteria: "I was putting my dishes away, and I heard back here "Watch your head." And Lila said "Joyce! Watch your head!" When I turned, the lady is passing me right by with this big wad of glasses on a tray and she's trying to put them up on a shelf past me. I said, "Lila, isn't that fascinating? 'Watch your head,' I mean, *where are you* if you can watch your head?" I thought, that interests me. I'd like to see if I can play with that. So that's what I did, and I realized *that's what we'd been doing for three weeks*. We've been watching our heads."

By Monday, she laughs when she tells her group "I don't know what it is. It's called 'Watch Your Head,' it sounds like I'm taking drugs." Although she won't read it today, she knows she will read it to her colleagues tomorrow in its early stages and finish it somehow by the end of the week. Joyce may believe that the idea for this piece began in the cafeteria last Thursday, but she's been toying with its themes since she arrived here. I see it in my notes. I've recorded it in her talk, in my tapes, and she's recorded it in the writing she's produced so far. On the first night during her reading session in the ice cream store, she looked at herself and Lila and Ronald, and told me: "It was the joy I needed, and then I realized, 'Oh for heaven's sakes, I'm watching myself here. I'm watching Ronald, I'm watching Lila. I have an observation to make here. I have something to write about." From the very beginning, Joyce has worked hard to take a reflexive position in order to understand herself as a literate person. "You could say, so *tell* me something new, Joyce, and I can see you don't have any trouble. . . . But, send me back to the dorm, and put me at my writing desk. That's an entirely different story."

This final week she faces her writing with a sense of experimentation, swimming around in her "grotto" she wrote about last week, looking for the unexpected in filtered light. Her essay begins with an aural incident in the cafeteria: someone shouts "Watch your head." In its early stages, the essay exists on seven slips of paper stuffed into her notebook. One piece has three comments scratched on it:

1. Lighten up, cut your hair, lose three pounds. Get a life— got a life. Freedom for mind to do when and how. Letting go of categorical thinking.

2. At best, watching your head is both science and art, method and madness, and is probably best done both critically and fancifully.
3. Free-flow writing helped me escape self-consciousness. It moved me where I could watch my head and surprised me that I could break away for a moment from my 'clothes closet' thinking, that organized style which puts my brains behind bars and forbids any foolishness. Now I look forward to practicing foolishness, interested in where it will take me.

These comments on the margins of the first draft of "Watch Your Head" illustrate her reflexive posture, even as she is working on it, and she knows it. "The crossed out sections, the margin writing, writing on the backs of pages, showing my thinking, my honing process. I've lightened up— ideas flow—taken one idea through entire piece." By Wednesday, she reads a draft to her small group: "Whatever the circumstances, you've got to be somewhere outside yourself to get an objective look. . . . At first all I heard was the jeering crowd, the voice of my own guilt at not having practiced what I know to be good." On the margins of this one, she writes "What do I hope to convey? The value of writing as headwatching, the value of head watching." She scratches "Peter Elbow, *Writing Without Teachers.*"

After she reads the draft, Joyce tells me "my people now know where I'm coming from. . . . That is, for them it is a terrific piece. For me, it's a nice little thing; it's fine. . . . I have another side of my mind that can look at my writing and see that it is rather . . . immature. . . ." She demands a lot of her writing, she knows it, more even than her peers. But she is grateful for their positive response and it pushes her from that side of her mind that she labels "immature" toward her final version. In her final portfolio letter to the class, she thanks them for helping to shape it:

July 25, 1990

Mis Amigas y Amigos,

The writing is . . . my most recent and, in my opinion, reveals my growth during these three weeks with you: "Watch Your Head." Thank you, all! Either directly or by your example as expressed in your writing and discussion, you've given me what I needed, what I came for, and that is a kick in my professional pants. Thank you, too, for giving me what I'd hoped for—your genuine encouragement and support. Your kindness will be passed on through me to my students. I've gone the distance, grown in confidence and ability, and rejuvenated my enthusiasm for my own and my students' literacy development. Your friend,

—Joyce Choate

Joyce's final essay summarizes her three-week story better than I ever could. It details the reflection she agonized to record in writing, and it records the very themes she read about and talked about. I include here the complete text of her final version:

*Watch Your Head*

The other day while standing in the cafeteria line putting my dirty dishes away, I heard faintly from somewhere behind me, "Watch your head." Since I still had mine, I paid no attention. Then again, I heard more forcefully spoken, *"Watch your head!"* and before I could consider, my friend ordered into my left ear, "Joyce, watch your head!" just as the cafeteria worker three inches from my right lifted a rack of drinking glasses to the shelf above.

Watch your head, I thought. It's an interesting imperative, don't you think? Where are you if you can watch your own head? What's your vantage point? Are you somewhere in the jeering crowd as the gleaming guillotine blade falls to sever your exposed neck? Or on the shore with the other frightened spectators watching as you sink the second time because you swam out over your head? Perhaps you're sitting in the neurosurgeon's office studying the X-ray of your skull as the doctor points out the shadow behind your right eye socket. Whatever the circumstances, you've got to be *somewhere outside yourself* to clearly see your own head.

And how do you get out? Do you bolt as if from a burning building or slip away as you would from the back of the sanctuary on Sunday morning when you'd rather not face the minister? In order to watch your own head, detachment is a must; movement outward gets you to the vantage point.

Once you're out there and ready, how do you watch, in what stance, and attitude? With amazement as you would view the finger flight from over the concert pianist's shoulder or with critical concern as when your son takes off in your new car for his first solo drive? At its best, watching your head is both science and art, method and madness, and is probably best done both critically and fancifully.

Here at UNH for the past three weeks we have immersed ourselves in a means of head watching called writing, which, until recently, has been a practice reserved for the gifted and educational elite. But, here at UNH the doors are flung wide and all who would are encouraged to enter, challenged to write their way ever closer to consciousness. Not having written and read the mentors regularly, I entered the program a backslider and found the lack of practice made writing painful for me. But, in the fellowship of other writers, I've endured the jeering crowd—the voice of my own guilt—and I've stood with the spectators watching my head bob to the surface, albeit blubbering and sputtering, as I begin to write again.

Watching my head emerge on paper, I discover the angry, fearful child within and by giving it voice, cut the cord of inhibition that threatens to destroy the life I hope to nurture. But inhibition clings fiercely and restrains writing's free flow. The only release comes in the doing: writing freely, fancifully, even madly if we must to break from the gripping fear, "Am I making mistakes? Does this sound stupid?"

Tonight, I wrote non-stop on a single sheet of paper until I filled it, giving no care to sense or convention. Here is some of what came from my head.

. . . as the trumpets and the flutes and the trombones practice in the dorms nearby I'm going to practice free flow letting my fingers fly watching the words eat up the page and wondering what's next. My friends will smile to see the mess but will be happy with my success because of them I've got the guts to try. . . .

Free-flow writing helped me escape self-consciousness. It moved me out where I could watch my head and surprised me that I could break away for a moment from my "clothes-closet" thinking, that organized style that puts my brains behind bars and forbids any foolishness. Now I look forward to practicing foolishness, interested to watch where it will take me.

Free-flow writing showed how important the writing community is to me, another surprise, because I've allowed the community only selected opportunities to help me with my writing. Fear of facing and working on all the problems I think they'd find in the week's time frame has kept my requests very limited. I've looked to them to cheer me on, and they have, enthusiastically. But, in a real sense, they are the neurosurgeons I referred to earlier. Eventually, I will give them my writing and we will step back together to view my head with both amazement and concern. Their object is not to alter my thinking, but to help me remove the shadows from my writing that hide my thinking from the reader. Brain surgery couldn't be a more delicate process than this.

My free-flow writing might help here to show the relationship of the writer to her community, the value of watching your head in the company of other writers.

> Together we write and read together we discover what's in our heads we watch each other's minds float out around the room and light where they will on chair or window sill they say what they want instead of what they must I trust my friends to accept my place so far for I've not come so far as they but I am moving ahead away from anger and fear and on toward creativity in which I discover my own soul and mind and heart.

So here's to head watching. If I see yours in a crowd, I'll be sure to point it out to you.

When Joyce finishes, her class cheers. They laugh, they clap, and they vote her to represent them at the final reading. The room quiets, and they go about the ritual of writing responses. Not only do they confirm her piece as a clever and well-honed essay, but they celebrate Joyce's personal triumph lurking inside her metaphor. Tom Romano writes: "Joyce, am I exaggerating if I say that you've had a monumental three weeks? The probing you've done, the writing, the reading . . . the thinking. You became one with your voice. This last piece, 'Watch Your Head,' is a synthesis. The metaphor works, and for so many of us, watching our head is exactly what we are doing. Talk about metacognitive!"

A member of her small group who has heard it in several stages, writes about its growth: "Joyce, when I heard the beginning of this on Monday, I had no idea where it would lead. Your way with words astounds me, your ideas always intriguing. Thanks!" Several classmates note her use of figures of speech: "Your comparisons are lovely. My favorite part is the neurosurgeon—examine head with amazement." " . . . brain surgery, great analogy. Great piece! Joyce, you are a wonder. Many thanks for your humor and encouragement— and your writing. May I have a copy?" "You capture the writer's vulnerability and insecurity. Thank you for reassuring me in your empathy. The interweaving of images and metaphors is wonderful."

Others' responses recognize her personal growth: "Free up—you did it nicely—I'm sure you'll continue to write, watch, and grow." "Your perceptions of tiny details that I miss because of my blindness add poeticness to your writing . . . three weeks ago, you could not have made such a statement. Don't let the profession lose you."

It is fitting that Joyce's final triumph is oral and dramatic. On the final Friday of the program, in the summer heat, she stands crisply at the podium, dressed like a teacher in a skirt and a neat white blouse. She glances at her writing as she reads it into the microphone, but mostly looks out at the crowd of over a hundred faces from the Reading and Writing Institute. She punctuates her strong, clear voice with flourishes of hand gestures. Her reading is slow and expressive. The audience laughs every few sentences, and explodes in applause when she finishes.

I remember our first interview, when she told me that she loves to read aloud to her classes, "I've always enjoyed being able to take a text in class, to read it out. I love to read. I am a good reader. And they eat it up. Like it was frozen yogurt. Just eat it up." Today Joyce is reading a text she's authored. We can hear that she is a good reader, that she loves to read aloud. And, watching our heads while she invites us to watch hers, we eat it up like frozen yogurt.

# Of Fathers, Sons, and Special Education: Making Meaning Is the Test

Frank Maselli's age belies his physique. He writes about baseball and his suntan suggests that he's spent a lot of time outdoors. His dark hair grays at the temples. His tee shirts look like they've enjoyed many years of intense activity. Stories hide behind their ragged edges and blotches, probably more interesting than the written texts on the front. His eyes dart and his hands fidget. Every few minutes when he gets an idea, he scratches it down in his notebook. Frank carries his books, his writing paper, and his lunch in a faded backpack, zippers partly detached. He writes in a furrowed blue notebook with bent, stretched metal spirals. Each day he breakfasts with his son as his wife sleeps off her night shift. He delivers Jimmy to day camp, and then commutes ninety minutes from the lakes region of New Hampshire.

It is here that Frank has learned to work with writing. This is his fourth summer writing program. Over three other summers, he has written about his status as a stepfather, collaborated with another teacher, crafted a few poems, and written a research essay from data he gathered at a local nudist camp. This summer in Tom Romano's class, he writes about playing baseball with his son and nephews, and he reconsiders his definition of literacy again. He sleeps with his son in a tent in the backyard and they read together with a flashlight. While Frank reads John Irving's *A Prayer for Owen Meany*, Jimmy reads a large composite *Superheroes* comic book. Frank has written a note to Jimmy every day of his eight years, and now that Jimmy writes, he leaves notes for Frank. Frank keeps one of their exchanges in his portfolio: "This note to my son reflects meaningful print. I have been writing and reading with Jimmy since before he could read or write. He's doing just fine. There's a little bit of both of us in this one."

Frank was born in Brooklyn and raised for nine years in a home for boys in Connecticut. His older sister lived "up the hill" in the corresponding home for girls. "I was a happy kid," he assures me, "it was small, comforting; not traumatic at all." His parents divorced when he was a baby. His father disappeared and his mother worked odd hours as a waitress. And when Frank was ready for high school, his mother was ready for him. He left the security of the small boys' home to join his mother and attended three different high schools and four different colleges—flunking out, moving, or just not completing requirements. He was a "white American history major by default," he says. "I didn't have a passion for anything except baseball, and that's still true. . . . playing, not watching. I'm tactile, kinesthetic." In Tom Romano's class, Frank moves while he talks. His first week's piece is about playing baseball with his son and nephews.

Frank comes to most of his life decisions, he remarks, "through the back door." He flunked Spanish at his fourth college just before graduation. He joined the Peace Corps in Colombia, South America, and spoke Spanish, "to work on my fear of taking risks." But he always knew he would work with kids. Eventually, he passed college Spanish, got his degree, and became a houseparent at a home for boys like the home he grew up in. Although he "grew up a lot" in that job, he left it to move to New Hampshire with a few Peace Corps buddies, sharing a house and doing construction jobs and truck gardening.

It wasn't long before he dropped good wages and satisfying physical labor to teach in a summer vocational program for dropouts. One winter of administering and teaching led to a longer string of government-funded education teaching jobs with "alternative kinds of kids." Frank's jobs have been tentative, marginal, and always in jeopardy, just like his students. He admits that he's had the same struggles he sees in his students: an inability to focus: "too many frigging stimuli around." He whispers loudly into my tape recorder as I interview him: "Here's a secret. I don't have the strategies myself."

"I feel I can't function in a regular classroom; there are too many variables and expectations I can't deal with. These kinds of schools are appropriate places for certain kids. Somebody's got to work there. It may as well be me. . . . I almost hate to use the word 'literate' with me. . . . I don't conceive of myself as a font of knowledge. . . . I'm good at pulling stuff out of kids; I'm not very good at putting stuff in . . . *I teach from the hip.* . . ." He sees the circle as a natural shape for a class with five or six kids, "where we're just plain facing each other."

Frank objects to students' personal writing ("self-pitying" he calls it), but he encourages written exploration as a way to write about ideas. Although he is a journal keeper himself, he notes the problems with school journals. For a while, he says, the journals in his classes became long letters that "got too far off on the psychological. . . . Lookit, this is not *'share your insides with Mr. Maselli,'* you know?" Frank uses his journal for exploration— to record his ideas and the ideas he reads in books, not to "share his insides."

His tee shirt collection intrigues me. Like our students' tee shirts, collectively they define his passions and chronicle his history. One day during the second week, I notice a black one, with white words in various typestyles, set in a geometric square. When I read closely, I see a string of phrases: "Fuck piña coladas, fuck unnatural acts, fuck scrod, fuck the fleet, fuck cocoa butter, fuck Monday." Neither the coarse language disguised in fancy type nor the cultural irony is a surprise; it is consistent with what I know about Frank. "I got it in Provincetown, Cape Cod, for very special occasions." He is wearing it, he says, for the poem he's writing.

"I'm not a poet. But a teacher's supposed to write this stuff at some point. . . ." Frank's poem has a lot of history even before it is written. During the first week he reacted strongly to a poem written by a classmate: "I think out of it came this piece. There was one phrase at the end of her poem that said something like 'Santa Claus, slash God,' or something. I decided 'I don't care what she meant right now. It's fun thinking what she might have meant.'" For Frank, her poem connected with a recent trip he had taken with his wife to Cape Cod. They visited a Unitarian-Universalist church where they were camping. A female minister talked about alternative God concepts. She invited people to respond. Frank remembers:

> Well, God, I never heard of this. . . . I raised my hand and she didn't see it . . . so I stood up and I said 'I don't believe in God.' . . . And I went on to talk briefly about how Jesus was a hero of mine, I certainly don't have a lock on truth. . . . I shared it . . . because someone invited me to share it. . . . And my wife's sitting next to me, she's heard my rap before. And it's very different from hers. And so I said, "Damn, maybe now it's time to write about it and get it behind me" . . . and driving down to school, I heard an author interviewed who said that the Navajos' God is just feeling at peace with themselves. We had just finished reading *Winterkill,* and I said "Jesus, I feel at peace with myself, but I don't believe in God. So it's time to write the thing."

His poem is wrought from a rich amalgam: his encounter with his colleague's poem, the minister on Cape Cod, his wife's theology, his own counter-theology, the radio piece about Navajo theology, his recent reading of *Owen Meany* and *Winterkill,* and responses in class. He chooses the tee shirt for inspiration. As he begins writing, Frank asks for a conference with his instructor Tom Romano. "I have no sense of poetic form or structure or anything; I kept talking, he kept listening." He returns to two phrases in his notebook from *Owen Meany*: "Rituals are comforting; rituals combat loneliness" (280) and "Faith takes practice" (334). He revises with a response group. At the end of the week, Frank hands me his finished draft, attached to six earlier versions. There is a note on top. "I walked out on the porch and made more revisions. I think this is it. It's 11:30. I began these revisions on the computer at 6:00. Good Night."

## coming out in provincetown

i don't believe in God . . . never did

i have asked Jesus to enter my heart
he comes and goes
the Golden Rule . . . do unto others . . .
the Bible is the best book on my "How To" shelf
i am a christian
yet . . . i don't believe in God . . . never did

the stepchildren were her concern
now it's my son we're talking about
i used to worry
that i would never find Him
i do know the power of faith
but . . . i don't believe in God . . . never did

who created whom?
isn't it easier to believe that God is
than is not?
if no God, then what?
what is Buddhism?
live it for thirty years . . . then you'll know
myths help explain ourselves to ourselves
so . . . i don't believe in God . . . never did

perceptions that find The Spirit
in the rock . . . in the leaf . . . in the wind
the wonders of birth . . . of love . . . of metamorphosis
desire for balance . . . for harmony . . . for peace
what's wrong with these?
isn't heaven a place
where dreams come true?
no . . . i don't believe in God . . . never did

"you are confused
I've been there"
i may be wrong
but i'm not confused
we are stuck with our pasts
yes . . . you believed in God. . . . i never did

it was thoughtful sermon on the Nature of God

in that house of man
a God personally experienced and studied
she asked if there were any responses
eventually. . . . i stood up and said
"i don't believe in God"
gently, comfortably.

God, that felt good to say.

Frank did not actually intend to spend this summer reading *Owen Meany* or *Winterkill*, or writing about God or baseball or his son Jimmy. He set out to finish a practicum for his master's degree in Special Education at another college. He needs the certification to keep his job. He owes the college a long paper on curriculum development and testing. But like other moments in his personal history, Frank has chosen action. Instead of finishing his master's degree at the other school, Frank is back here for a fourth time, writing and reading to find out what he's thinking, to know what he wants to know. He felt this would be best for his students:

> So much of writing for school and trying to put together exposition about learning disabilities, the sort of writing that makes an argument . . . is so fucking hard. . . . I didn't finish two of my three courses. It's a pattern with me since day one. . . . I have incompletes all over my transcript. It's disgusting . . . I still identify so much with my students. . . . why should I keep trying all these other things if I'm still struggling to write what I think? . . . I see myself at the gaining fluency stage. I worked my butt off to produce everything you see here.
>
> . . . . I like six hours of one course for three weeks. This is so focused that it's liberating. . . . I love it. This is the way I learn. . . . I don't know if I could ever teach that way, but I know I can learn that way. . . . This is a vacation, when you're allowed to do what you want. There are no tests. The test is figuring out what the hell you mean. . . . Making meaning is the test.

In a portfolio letter to his classmates, he suggests humor as an alternative kind of test. The remark evokes the shock value of his tee shirt: "These [jokes and humor] are examples of language uses that are at least as valid a measure of intelligence and insight, despite their crudeness . . . perhaps we should use these as part of our intelligence tests in our official evaluation documents. . . . Those fragmented individualized curriculum plans we call IEPs, driven by the tests take away their options," he writes.

In his last chapter of *Lives on the Boundary*, Mike Rose's words echo Frank's story and, ironically, the curriculum project Frank didn't write: " . . . the longer I stay in education, the clearer it becomes to me that some of our basic orientations toward the teaching and testing of literacy contribute to our inability to see. To truly educate in America, then, to reach the full sweep of our citizenry, we need to question received perception, shift continually from the standard lens. . ." (205).

As Frank's poem says, "we are stuck with our pasts." But the past is a signal for action, for growth. Whether he considers school failure, plays ball, reads with his son, goes to church with his wife, or teaches a school dropout, Frank is in continual shift from the standard lens. In his own words, "making meaning *is* the test."

# Five

## Back to School: Summer Revisions

*The docile teacher is a comfortable instrument for the designs of others. But students, and through them most of the rest of us, can only profit from critically conscious, informed, and self-directed teachers whose knowledge of the making of knowledge lies at the heart of learning and therefore the heart of our growth as a literate society.*

—C.H. Knobloch and L. Brannon,
"Knowing Our Knowledge," in *Audits of Meaning*

### The Lobsterfest

Two long brick walls flank the foyer of Philbrook Dining Hall. Each wall holds an open grid of small wooden boxes. This afternoon they don't hold the student backpacks, baseball gloves or lab equipment they were designed for. Tote bags of straw, plastic, and canvas spill out of the boxes and cover a corner of the floor. The bags are stuffed with books, journals, and stacks of drafts; the work of the summer writing program is far from over. It is midday of the final Thursday, the afternoon of the annual lobsterfest.

Tomorrow morning, one teacher from each of twenty-two writing groups will read into a microphone to two large audiences in two auditoriums. The writing they read will be their own. Tonight in the dorms as the train rumbles across the field marking each of the small hours of the night, they will draft, listen, revise, encourage, rewrite, suggest, and prepare. By tomorrow afternoon, two hundred thirty-three people will be packed into cars and planes and on their way home.

But today we fill our paper plates from trays piled with lobsters, corn on the cob, fried chicken, and a giant stainless steel pot of steamed clams. We scoop from bowls of salad, pots of baked beans, buckets of drawn butter and clam juice. The room looks less like a school cafeteria than usual; there are red and white checked tablecloths, silverware, napkins, salt and pepper shakers, and lobster-eating instruments.

Teachers amble from table to table, stopping to chat. We are neither patrolling the room nor gulping food. Here, there are more than eighteen minutes for lunch. We chat about writing and reading, graduate programs and school policies. And I am noticing tee shirts. I've been looking at teachers in tee shirts for three weeks, intrigued with their value as readable texts. Their messages fall into categories. Some offer subversive jokes:

"All stressed out . . . and no one to choke"
"Harvard Forensics Tournament: Crush the Weak"
"I Don't Do Mornings"
"I Think I Can"
"Read a Book: It's Educational."
"Love a Teacher: It's Educational"

And some announce political messages:

"Women Hold up Half the Sky"
"There's Something in My Library to Offend Everyone"
"Deaf People Can Do Everything . . . Except Hear."
"Alaska Teachers Strive for Excellence."

Still other shirts picture authors and playwrights: Hemingway's house, Mark Twain's house, four Shakespeare theaters—Stratford, England; Stratford, Connecticut; Stratford, Ontario; and the Folger in Washington. There are faces of Samuel Beckett, Virginia Woolf, Humphrey Bogart. Some tee shirts mark special identities: a map of Casco Bay in Maine, Florida Oranges, Pottsville Basketball, California Angels, Indiana University, Cable News Network, the London theater production of *Starlight Express*. And there are

*211*

tee shirts from other years of the New Hampshire Writing Program: '85, '86, '87, '88, '89.

Instructors, professors, and participants sit at tables for four and six. Some are authors of published books, others are first-time writers. We share techniques of lobster and steamed-clam eating while we talk about reading and writing. I fill my plate and sit with Susan Landon (Dorothy's writing partner) and instructor Tom Romano.

After three weeks of intense research, I am beginning to think of all artifacts and behaviors as readable texts, and I notice that Tom and Susan's lobster-eating discussion seems a metaphor for the shared beliefs about learning which are now so important to this group. She's never eaten a lobster, and he offers his metal cracking device and wooden pick. He doesn't open the lobster for her. He coaches her from across the table as she learns to open the shell and get the meat for herself. She dips it into her cup of butter and enjoys the first bite.

"Hey, you're a good teacher," she laughs. They talk about places to publish poetry, mandated testing policies in several states, and the use of first-person narration in fiction. Before Susan took her first bite, Tom lent her the tools and coached her from across the table until she found her own way to crack the shell. She stopped long enough to recognize his action as good teaching. I listen, eat, and take notes. There is much to read in this room, and there is much I know I'll write about. For these teachers in tee shirts feasting leisurely together, reading writing and teaching writing is a social drama very different from the one in which we usually meet our colleagues.

I spot Therese standing alone in line looking hurt and confused. Ahead of her, three women in line are laughing. She is afraid the older teachers are laughing at the writing she has shared with them that morning, she tells me later. She writes about it in her journal after she discovers they were laughing at something else. But writing about it in her journal makes her think about her students. How many times has a high school student had this experience? She asks herself. How might she arrange conditions for them to be able to encounter one another as she did with those teachers? Why hasn't she thought about this before?

For Therese, Susan, Tom, me, and the others in this room, our notions about schooling are loosely wrapped in long threads of personal autobiography, personal history, professional knowledge and experiences, literacy habits, mentorships, and rich stories of home, workplaces, administrators and colleagues. There are threads of success and threads of failure, of power and oppression, theories and beliefs that are at once acceptable and unacceptable. Wrapping those threads around a professional lifetime, then unwrapping to expose them open, is something a teacher cannot do in the flurry of an academic year. Repatterning our own threads and helping others to repattern theirs requires knowledge, reflection, and time. The summer program has offered three weeks of knowledge, reflection, and time, complete with its own tradition-bound set of beliefs, behaviors, elders, rituals, and language. What each person will do, like Susan as she learns to crack her lobster shell, will be each person's design.

## *"A Good Movie," Creative Reconstruction*

So what has happened? What will these teachers do with their summer experience? Was this an experience in teacher education? Teacher literacy? Transformation? If so, where does it show? There's no time at school in September to write private thoughts for a public audience of peers, tinker with genre, languish in book talk, put into consciousness ideas for a possible curriculum in a perfect school. The days and nights to revise subjective realities into objective fictions will disappear with the tee shirts and lobsters. In September Susan writes to me:

> My first thoughts upon arriving home. . . . "Did I dream New Hampshire? Am I the person who wrote those pieces? Did I think those revolutionary thoughts?" It's a good thing my writing notebook and all my new books were spilling out of my suitcase. I might otherwise have thought I had made it all up, seen a good movie. . . .

213

Like Susan, Therese, Dorothy, Lenore, Joyce, Alison, Frank, Lee, and the others, each "saw a good movie," but not the same movie. There were two-hundred thirty-three "movies" during the summer of 1990. Now each teacher will produce her own movie. She will create a classroom culture different from the one she had last year—partly because of her experience this summer; partly because it is another year. Maybe as she makes curriculum choices for her classroom, she'll have more confidence. Maybe she'll write or phone or visit another teacher from another place who's made a similar choice. Maybe she'll move the classroom furniture out of rows and into a circle, or keep the grammar books as references on her shelves. Maybe she'll join a curriculum committee, or organize a writing group. Maybe she'll be politically subversive.

But each teacher will choose in her own way. On the first day, at his welcoming session Newkirk said, "I hope we present a divided front." His joke encapsulated his program's philosophy: not to affect curriculum change directly, but to affect each teacher's literacy—"to help participants discover (or rediscover) their own voices and develop their skills . . ." and to understand "the relationship between language and learning and to the special contributions that writing can make to the learning process" (1979). She may have entered expecting to learn how to "do writing process," or to "add reading to writing," but she left having examined the multiple processes of her literacy and the processes of others. Looking closely at "the divided front," Newkirk's program would hope that she saw *difference*: that writers select from options, readers select from interpretations, and so do learners and teachers. How she does it depends on who she is.

When she arrives in her classroom in the fall, what each teacher will offer her students is far too complex to label "change," too subtle to label "transformation." The summer was an encounter in a culture designed to be different from school, and out of it—two-hundred thirty-three times—came a single teacher in revision. The program's goals attempt to make her critically conscious, in Knobloch and Brannon's words at the beginning of this chapter, more a person "whose knowledge of the making of knowledge lies at the heart of learning."

Who we are one year is not who we are the next. Our differences—in language and experience—make us each represent and interpret our environment creatively. We recognize our expectations and intentions gradually as we let them grow. We revise continually as we add more experiences to our world view (Kelly, 1963). Language, written and spoken, establishes us *to ourselves*, as thinkers able to act. It is not a new idea that teachers need opportunities to see themselves using words. "Language," said George Herbert Mead at the turn of the century, "put the intelligence of the individual at his own disposal" (Britton, et al. 1975, 126). Twenty-five years ago, Harold Rosen argued that teachers should develop their content knowledge through language:

> The quality of our words in the head, inner speech, must be closely tied to the experience of talking with others which gives us resources for thinking and learning, for self-prompting and intellectual adventure. (1969, 126)

The summer experience enabled Therese, Dorothy, Joyce, and the others to pinpoint their processes of creative reconstruction through language, to reinvent their literate histories. It was, in Rosen's words, the stuff of self-prompting and intellectual adventure. For each in her own way, participating for three weeks gently disrupted her view of school long enough and safely enough for her to raise some questions about teaching, language, and learning she hadn't raised before. The experience itself placed each teacher in "a strange coexistence of solitude and dependence," as one participant called it, and allowed her to rethink that stance for her students.

I wanted to stay in contact with each person I'd followed. How did she answer the questions she'd raised? What connections did she make or didn't she make, consciously or subconsciously, back to the summer? How did each person meet the demands of her school? Did she work toward students' differences in literacy? Was she more conscious of conflicts between the curriculum and her students' needs? Did she have a community with which to share her reading and writing? Did she create one? I wanted to see her school, her work with students in reading and writing, her connections to summer colleagues, and whatever else she felt was important. But I let each person choose how she'd maintain that contact for that year. I knew they'd each meet my request differently. I knew they'd each return to school differently. And I expected I'd learn much by seeing what choices each person made.

It is not a surprise that my contact with Therese, Dorothy, and Joyce reflected them as I knew them in the summer. Therese wanted to stay in touch by phone and mail; she wanted direction and mentorship from me as she had from her instructors and colleagues. Dorothy asked me to spend a day with her to see for myself; she wasn't sure what I wanted to know, nor did she feel that she was doing much that was different. And Joyce talked to me via her tape recorder as she had done during the summer. She preferred talk.

## Therese: "It's Not Just a Job Anymore; It's a Commitment"

Therese was on the west coast and I was on the east, so we had long phone conversations after midnight in the east. She sent me three greeting cards, thanking me for "paying attention" to her and wishing me good luck. She called often to talk about her teaching and to ask advice about the master's degree program in which she was enrolled. Her thesis topic, she had decided, would be theories of writing as self-discovery—an idea that she got from Don Murray's "writing as therapy" in *Expecting the Unexpected*. I wasn't surprised. "It's not just a job anymore," she told me one night, "it's a commitment."

Because I couldn't visit, I asked her to send photographs of her school and classroom, and she followed my directions precisely. She mailed six snapshots of her classroom, desks in straight rows, shelves stacked neatly, six numbered computers surrounding the perimeter of the room, and posters of landscapes arranged by size were stapled to the bulletin boards. There were neither students nor students' work in sight. Like her arrangement in the dorms, Therese's desk gleamed clean with only a paperback dictionary on its surface.

Five more snapshots showed the school itself: an early-seventies vintage high school, vertical glass and concrete, stretched on flat sun-parched land with dim hints of green and surrounded by the dry brown bush of California winter. There were no students on the outside of the building, either. I hadn't specifically asked for pictures of students; I simply assumed they'd be part of her view of school. But she had sent what I'd asked for, quite literally. She added a snapshot of herself, smiling, away from school, on a weekend trip to a resort town. So Therese's physical image of "the school" as she portrayed it in her photos not only didn't include her students; it didn't even include herself.

Although no students entered her snapshots, they spoke through the photocopies of the papers she sent. For Therese, mentoring had triggered her self-reflection. She needed mentors, and she was able to get them in her instructors, the live authors of the books she loved, the women in her writing group, and even me. The culture she created for her students was like the one she experienced: one in which an individual can meet her mentor, follow new rules, examine old rules, and even possibly break them.

Therese's mentoring of students echoed the mentoring she had sought, and her assignment sheets echoed that. Students chose which papers to submit for a grade and with each one they wrote a detailed "Reflection Sheet." She required "at least five sentences" evaluating the usefulness of five features of the writing itself: writing workshop procedures, writing activities, mini-lessons, weekly writing assignments. Her final exam for the semester was to "write an evaluation of yourself as a writer and your progress this semester based on the comments you made in the five areas mentioned on your

Reflection Sheets." Layers of metacognition. Five of them. Rules lined up like the shoes in her closet. Therese set the stage for her students to engage in the self-discovery she experienced during the summer, and she did it her own way.

She and her students wrote daily. "It's like a drug," she told me on the phone, "I can't stop writing." She reads her writing to her students in order to get them to share theirs: "I take a deep breath and I share it with the kids. This is hard for me, but it invites them." In one class, it was November before anyone else volunteered to read. Persistence, discipline. It reminded me of her climb up Mount Chocorua. She is exhausted after a day of school. "Now I believe in it emotionally as well as intellectually," she wrote, and she described the students whose writing she sent. Each writing sample was a complete set of three: a student piece, her comments to the student, and a letter to me about that student's writing. All five student pieces were personal essays of self-disclosure, writing-as-therapy, her thesis topic, much like the ones she had written herself in the summer. Here are three excerpts:

1. *Therese's letter:* Talia is in my fifth-period Intermediate Comp/Grammar class. Her attitude is often one of sarcastic hostility, but she is always revealing a deeper side through her writing.
   *Talia's writing:* When you are in love, you are usually in danger of making decisions that you normally would not make. . . . you must first be sure of what the person you are in love with will want you to decide. . . . This may be good or bad, it all depends on the two people.
2. *Therese's letter:* Danny is no longer in my seventh period English Skills II class. He is no longer at Whitfield High, having encountered problems both social and academic. One day, the boy, in Tom Romano's words, "cut loose." I include what he wrote.
   *Danny's writing:* My mom is sick, real sick. I have been ditching school to see her in the hospital. . . . Why does it

happen when you are doing good before you know it something bad happens? If it takes me to fail school to help my mom I will do it!!! Why does love hurt so bad!

3. *Therese's letter:* José was a triumph of human achievement. I taught him last year, and he failed the first semester. Last semester, he repeated my class with a great deal of success. His writing speaks for itself.

   *José's writing:* (excerpts from final reflective essay) Conferencing may have been good for me and not so good for others. . . . It helped me explain my thoughts more clearly and freely . . . read-around groups helped me. In a way I felt uncomfortable because I didn't know whether or not to trust the group . . . At first I would keep what I really felt inside . . . the final drafts on the computers helped . . . It takes a lot of work but it is also fun . . .

Therese received a Christmas card from a colleague in her writing group, the woman in this book's Intertext who wrote the poem "Sanctuary." It contained a picture of her with her husband and two little boys, the family she wore on the buttons of her backpack. "How are your classes going?" she asked. "My freshmen have really responded to my changes, just like Terry predicted. I'm still having problems breaking away from my traditional methods with juniors and seniors, though. Would love to hear how you are doing."

Therese isn't transformed, although she says it was the most important experience of her life. She is affirmed, though, and more courageous in the classroom. She writes and shares, she responds to her students more personally. But she struggles as she did before with following rules and making them for her students. Her classroom is arranged as neatly as her "Response Sheet." Her metaphors, "not a job but a commitment," that writing is a "drug," still imply that the control for all of this lies somewhere outside herself. But her obsession with personal writing, "writing as therapy" is where she is beginning—with more study for herself and more opportunities for her students. When she looks at her students' writing, she sees beyond the mechanical, past the assignment, and into a person putting a piece of a self on a page. Just what her mentors and colleagues did for her this summer.

## Dorothy: Writing with Students, Detentions with Counseling

I visited Dorothy one frosty October morning just at the end of New England's foliage season. Her high school looked small, sleek, and contemporary, hidden from the main road, nestled in a pine grove inside mountain foothills. A few lingering leaves echoed the brick-red of the building and the bricks of her apartment at UNH.

Dorothy's room displayed her interest in feminism, writing, and language. The bulletin board titled "An American Album" held two posters: "The Early Romantics," tiny oval portraits of male writers and a large portrait of Susan B. Anthony. Student writing in many genres hung next to the portrait display: analyses, critiques, poems, fictions, and journal projects about American literature, including a poem of Dorothy's. At the bottom of the bulletin board were five drawings labeled "Mom," signed "Paul," her four-year-old son, and a piece of writing by her daughter in second grade. Including her students, herself, and her children on the American literature bulletin board, along with an array of small historical portraits of men and a large historical portrait of a woman, Dorothy suggests the very shifts of power and privilege that she has spent much time thinking and reading about.

A large computer banner on another wall announced "Writing at its Best." It displayed sixteen student pieces, including the journal paper Dorothy had written last summer in Terry's class. Dorothy uses the word "best," suggesting that someone must make decisions about quality, but she told me what goes on the bulletin board is everyone's decision. And she mixed her sense of humor and her interest in language in a banner at the far wall—a purple-leaf Victorian border quips:

"Some are born to greatness, Some achieve greatness, Some grate cheese."

Her desks were arranged in a circle in her classroom. I remembered Dorothy telling me her work was "never good enough" to share with her students, that she didn't like to get personal, but her writing, her reading, her mothering, her intellectual history, and her sense of humor were all on display in her classroom for her students. Last spring she never shared her writing with her students. This spring she will arrange a three-day weekend with two of her students, writing at a workshop in Bread Loaf, Vermont.

Dorothy met her students with the same paradoxes she had explored in herself. Next to her classroom door, there were four blank calendars, one for each class, on which students signed their names. One young man stood up just as the late bell buzzed, tugging on his faded red shirt as he read the poem "The Horse Chestnut Tree" by Richard Eberhart. Dorothy smiled, thanked him, and made a mark in her rank book. He had signed his name to the calendar that day. Dorothy began class with a poem—no response, no interpretation—just one poem of one student's choosing, each day. "Just to hear the language," she told me, "but it's their responsibility to sign up, and they get no credit if they don't."

During late morning, she left a class of juniors watching a video of *The Scarlet Letter* to transport her son from daycare to kindergarten. They lay on the floor, chins on stacks of books, hands sprawling responses in notebooks. They talked, comparing the book with the video as they read from their journals. When she returned, they had refined their questions and answered some. She was eager to hear their answers, and asked questions of them. I remembered her dream of the perfect classroom—the students marching with their Annie Dillard books to the rhythm of the *1812 Overture*. I remembered her questions about students controlling the class.

At the end of the day, she kept a student after school for detention. The girl hadn't turned in any writing, and showed no signs of keeping the drafts she had written in class. Dorothy pulled up a chair next to her, and spoke quietly:

> I want to support you in your writing, not make you feel badly about it . . . I try to save all drafts of my writing, especially poems . . . shall we set up a plan? Can you pass in two poems on Monday? Two poems will count as 'one piece.'

The student told Dorothy that she couldn't write in class, and she couldn't write at home. Dorothy suggested that she bring music to class, and earphones. "It's okay with me if it helps you relax. I won't tell the administration. If anybody asks, just say you need them. . . . I hope things work out for you."

"She's an enigma," Dorothy told me later. The girl's mother was in jail for shooting a state trooper, and she was living with a foster family. "They're slime balls," she said of the foster family, "Six or seven junk cars in the yard, and noise in the house. No place to work quietly." Dorothy offered her a solution that runs counter to school rules, and encouraged her to continue writing at all costs. She gave her student a workable and satisfactory assignment, one that recalled her own discussion with Ellen last summer about drafts and poems and "what to count as a poem."

Dorothy and I ended the day in a local coffeeshop, talking with the tape recorder on the table, as we had each night of the summer program. Dorothy wondered as she reviewed the day: "Why do my detentions always turn into counseling sessions now? Last year, they straightened out the shelves and erased the boards." Her view of herself as an English teacher had shifted, as had her picture of her students.

Her view of herself as a writer shifted, too. Not only did she share her writing with her students, but she was willing to share it by mail with someone else's students. She exchanged letters with Alison, the subject of this book's Intertext "To Really Cheer." Before the summer program was over, Alison had asked Dorothy's permission to photocopy her final piece "Heal Thyself" for her students to read. The following April,

Alison sent an envelope of fifteen student letters, some typed on their private school stationary, some on personal letter-heads. Alison wrote:

Dear Dorothy:

I asked my students to read "Heal Thyself" in my Short Story course. . . . So . . . enclosed are the letters I asked them to write to you, and I hope you'll find them both interesting and help-ful. . . . These kids are . . . from a variety of socio-economic lev-els, but primarily upper-middle-class. . . . Many of them have divorced parents. . . . the kids make some interesting assump-tions—that you used a "case study" format, that you are the doc-tor, that the doctor is male, that the doctor is female, that this is a draft . . . but *they all assume you're a writer.* Have fun!

The students' letters noticed the very goals that Dorothy had worked so hard to achieve. One commented on Dorothy's use of language: "This story reminds me of a case report done by a doctor because of the simple use of language. Was this your intent?" Others related their personal reactions to her rhetorical choices:

*Letter:* I enjoyed the way in which you presented the troubles that Emily had to endure—through the report of the psychologist. . . . it seemed to me that the parents were more like children than Emily was.

*Letter:* Right now my parents are divorcing and the story was uncomfortable to read at times. I saw myself as that girl in many areas of the story. Instead of eczema, I slept all the time. . . . you used that well by having the girl physically affected by the tor-ment.

*Letter:* I liked the metaphor you created between eczema and "the tensions that ran under the surface of her parents' relation-ship.". . . . The external fighting of the parents created a volatile stew of emotion that was suppressed inside Emily. . . . The burn-ing in her heart seemed to be surfacing on her skin.

One letter writer assumed that the character Emily was Dorothy: "Did things get better for you? Did you have a choice of which parent you wanted to live with? Was it your intention to make parents more aware of their children? I think you did accomplish that." Six letters commented on the detail of the summers at Emily's aunt's house in Maine: "The summer was a wonderful idea to have the child's problems almost escape from her. I thought that was discreet and effective." "The summer at the farm helped me to understand the great conflict it had on her normal life." Some letters gave suggestions for changes: "I've read your story through four times and each time I seem to be looking for something more. . . . I'm dying to hear, as a reader, the feelings of the doctor. . . . Please consider my comments for your next draft . . . the story has a lot of potential." "As a whole, at the end of the story I was angry at the parents of Emily. . . . stories are supposed to evoke emotions. The only real problem I had was . . . it ended too abruptly. I wanted to hear more about what the doctor would say to Emily. . . ."

Dorothy loved receiving the letters; it "gave her a real boost," she said, and after writing a note to Alison, she went back to the story to revise it. She told me she felt "immensely flattered," that Alison's students had "no ulterior motive to say nice things." The students, as readers, "picked up the things I was trying to say without anyone having to hammer it into their heads." The "biggest thrill was to be taken as a professional writer. . . . Their comments were serious."

Alison's students' view of her as a writer inspired Dorothy to revise her piece, and she found time to do it. Her goal for the summer, as she told me the first night, had been to find "time boxes" for writing. Although she had resisted sharing her writing with students, her experience with Susan and Lenore in Ellen's class shifted that resistance. On her bulletin boards, in her classes, and through the mail, she made her personal writing more public. From Terry's class she had wanted "tips" for her teaching, particularly with journals, but she's yielded to a far more complex understanding of teaching. More than using tips, Dorothy was blending her personal self into her teaching self: she trusted her students to choose poems, to use journals for a literary discussion when she wasn't even there, she supported a student's writing against the domination of both home and administration, she noticed that her "detentions have turned into counseling sessions." Although Dorothy remained the same skeptical, paradoxical person, she enacted her role as a teacher with echoes of her summer.

## Joyce: "I Just Stood There and Served Them"

I had very few phone conversations with Joyce. Each time we scheduled a visit, she canceled because of schedule conflicts. It didn't matter. She sent three audio tapes, and they covered more than I could have observed. She talked on a single tape over five or six morning car trips to school. It was much the same relationship we'd established during the summer; she was best at talking out her most intimate thoughts. On the tapes she spoke in eloquent detail—as her colleagues had joked last summer, "in final drafts." She explained her classroom and workshop procedures, profiled students and their interactions, asked and answered her own questions. She offered me descriptions of her New York state countryside, complete with literary references, as she drove. Here is an example from early spring:

> Good morning, Bonnie. You can probably tell from the background noise that I'm in the car again. . . . I can hear in my voice the lethargy of the day. It's a very gray morning. Sometimes the sun is so dazzling. . . . I like the muted colors. Right now I'm going through a flat section and the balsam trees are plentiful. This morning they are almost black-green. They stand out against the gray sky. The mountains are still brown, and yet the raspberry bushes in the lowlands are a deep rosy red. They're stalks. The Indians called them "purple swords," I think I remember that from reading Conrad Richter's *Light in the Forest.*

Joyce sent lots of papers. She wrote a letter to her students in September, much like Tom Romano's syllabus, explaining her curriculum and expectations. She mailed samples of student writing, reading logs, and portfolio letters. But it was not a surprise to me that the tapes of her spoken words held the most interesting clues to her classroom's culture; her tapes had always offered me Joyce's most interesting clues.

Unlike Therese who needed her teachers as mentors, or Dorothy, who found her peers as mentors as they focused on her writing, during the summer Joyce had enjoyed mentorships with her colleagues outside of class. Her talk with Bob about school had triggered a personal memory that led to a poem, her readings with Lila and Ronald had led to reflective talk about writing and eventually to her "Watch Your Head" essay. In the tapes, her oral reflections showed some complex shifts in her view of herself as a mentor, and recalled the relationships she experienced during the summer. It seemed that she began to loosen her definition of what a teacher needs to do in a writing class in order to "teach" writing. Here are a few snippets about one writing workshop:

> One word I'd like to use to describe it is "loose." Not that my expectations were loose . . . I just let them go. I simply stood there as a resource. I would leave them alone, be available to them. They found that they wanted to speak to me quite a bit. They simply got in line. . . . there were times that they discussed with each other the problems they had, and I would watch them drop out of line. I assume their peers helped them. In this loose fashion, they did hard work. . . .
>
> It gave me freedom to serve my children, *completely serve* them. I didn't need to lead them, I didn't need to control them, it was lovely. I just stood there and served them. And they came to me because they wanted it, not because they had to have me, and that was pure pleasure. . . .
>
> There was a lot of instruction going on. "What do you call this?" "See what I've done here, what do you call this?" I'd say, "An introductory participial phrase." Well . . . never in my wildest dreams would I throw that out to these children at this point. . . . whether they remember that or not doesn't matter to me. They wanted to know. But what they did learn was *how to*

*make* this thing. You could call it a rose, a pig if you wanted to, it doesn't matter. . . . they were interested to see how you subordinate an independent clause, attach it at the beginning of another independent clause for variety or condensation, or to tighten up. They wanted to know what you call a sentence that has one subject and more than one verb, and I was very pleased with that.

One boy's writing was sparse—it was all "telling," making statements, but it lacked life. This kid is a very tall, skinny kid . . . he could stand to have a lot more flesh and muscle on his bones. And his writing fit him—it was *skinny writing*—it's one thing to tighten it up, it's another thing to starve it to death.

Joyce repositioned herself in this classroom workshop; she was there to "serve" her students, waiting to see each one while she also "let them go." They lined up to see her, but they helped each other in line. They saved the questions about grammatical construction and subtleties of exposition, and she was delighted at how they learned to apply her answers. But the work was hard and, like her writing during the summer, she was deeply serious about it. She singled out one boy with his "skinny" writing, adding details of "flesh and muscle in order not to starve it to death." She found herself singling out all of her students, and was overwhelmed with her ability to help them, but also with the immensity of the task. The workshops discourage her sometimes, she told me, "because this way every child becomes an individual. My temptation is to stay in control . . . I like my chickens under my wing." Now they are confronted with the fact, she said, that education is their responsibility, and "I say, okay, get out of the way and watch them go."

While Joyce examined her own school history last summer, she discovered that in her life like most of her students', education had *not* been her responsibility. The design for Joyce belonged to someone else. It was not, as her poem about kindergarten or her writings about reflection, even related to her life. Learning to connect school with real life requires, as Joyce describes, placing them in their own control.

The support from her colleagues continued through the year as it had begun on the first night in the ice cream store. In October, Lila wrote:

> It's nice weather for a dip in the pool, but unfortunately during sixth period, I'm gasping for air. I don't think I'll ever enjoy a relaxing swim. . . . sophomores who have failed English 9. . . . I want to create literate young people, but it ain't gonna be easy. Don't you usually sink before you can swim? . . . I'm making time for pleasurable reading. I still have to force myself to write regularly. I do keep a reading log just like my freshmen. . . . It would probably be better with an oral reading and a trip to the yogurt store with you.

Her school was not interested in her professional activities, Lila told Joyce, but she still felt bolstered by colleagues from the summer. She'd received a letter from Ronald that week and two reprints of an article she published in a national journal. Shortly afterward Lila had received a note from Tom Romano, her instructor, saying he'd read it. Remarking on a metaphor she got from Joyce and used through several letters, she wrote:

> I'll keep the swimming metaphor going. . . . This week, I feel as though I've done a perfect ten from the high board. . . . I gloated near the people who fail to realize I know what I'm talking about. . . . Thursday I received a postcard from Tom Romano. . . . The next day I got a call from a school district five hours away. They needed someone to do a "Writing Across the Curriculum" workshop on Friday. . . . I had one ready and my principal said it was okay. . . .

Lila and Joyce maintain mail contact throughout the year. The swimming and sinking metaphor runs through their letters. They gloat together over the knowledge that her colleagues "don't even know" about Lila's article or her workshop. Only the principal knows because he had to grant permission. They remark about reading logs and workshops in which students read and interpret their readings together. In her letters to Joyce, Lila reaches back to the readings in the yogurt store and credits it for the improvements she's making in reading with her students. And they've both made more time for pleasure reading.

## Summer Revisions

Neither Therese, Dorothy, nor Joyce entered the summer experience thinking of herself as a very literate teacher. In fact, writing and reading were either personal luxuries or obligations on their lists of priorities. Therese's need for simple answers to complex questions turned into unconventional poetry and a scholarly investigation into the principles of writing as therapy. Dorothy's search for "time boxes" and "tips" yielded carefully crafted personal writing, and her "jangling horsecart" quieted down. Joyce's desperate run around the campus the first night and the collegial reading ended in her beginning to understand her ability to construct knowledge and writing through talk. And those yields enriched their classrooms. Each person began the summer with an expectation, ended with something different from what she expected, learned something about herself, and applied it to school in her own way.

Despite any mandate with which teachers may have been sent by their schools, curriculum reform was neither part of this program's overt nor part of its implied agenda. To claim an explicit need for curriculum reform would be to disclaim a teacher's personal value, and that was not the purpose. She was there first to listen to her own voice and to hear the voices of her colleagues. The application to school depended on her.

None of the teachers in this book is particularly "empowered." No one is really "transformed." They will not return necessarily to affect curriculum change. The shift is far more subtle, more internal. It is not a shift toward an externally induced curriculum. Rather, because it is a deep, internal shifting, change becomes possible inside each teacher's classroom no matter what her school requires.

The summer writing program's time is short, but it is concentrated time, hot and dense. Teachers form close bonds without much competition, but their internal realities compete like electrical activity in a summer thunderstorm. To reconceive writing and reading means bumping up against a personal definition of literacy, and against a school's definition of curriculum and evaluation. To reconceive teaching means crashing against a personal autobiography, often one that holds old stories of literacy failure. To reconceive learning means wandering around in time and space, colliding with personal stories of learning that happen in places outside of school. Those stories need to be told and heard. They need to be written and read. And it is in the telling and hearing, the writing and reading, that the summer revisions begin to take place.

# *Afterword*

*O chestnut-tree, great-rooted blossomer,*
*Are you the leaf, the blossom, or the bole?*
*O body swayed to music, O brightening glance,*
*How can we know the dancer from the dance?*
—William Butler Yeats, *Among Schoolchildren*

*W*hen Therese, Dorothy, and Joyce returned, there was no change at school. Neither their classrooms nor their curricula were new in September. Indeed, on the surfaces, not much at school is ever very different. For most teachers who attended the summer program, they will walk the polished hallways in late August, unpack the cartons sitting where they left them in June, unroll the posters and dust off the cardboard Globe Theaters for another year. They will place new names in red rank books and on seating charts, and there will be new files in their metal drawers. Colleagues will tease them about spending three weeks writing; a few will be jealous, and a few will want to hear a little about it. They will listen to their superintendents' welcoming speeches on the first day. Last year's scuff marks will be gone from the floors and the pencil graffiti scrubbed off the desktops. In the next ten months, there will be new scuff marks and more penciled messages. There will be no new curriculum, no change in administrative support. Hardly anyone will care that they spent three weeks reading, writing, and thinking about teaching.

## Remarks on the Unremarkable

I was surprised by the differences inside the summer community and all that I'd lived and seen over many years in teach-ers' everyday workplaces. When I began this study, I expected to follow storytelling like that I heard in my teaching life and my research studies in teachers' rooms and gatherings of English teachers. Stories in school involve quips and jokes about responses to literature, student success and failure sto-ries, stories of subverting the administration, stories of losing papers, stories of being out of control (Sunstein, 1994, 1989).

The stories in summer fell into very different categories: personal school failures, personal writing failures, teaching failures, classroom bumbling. There were far more questions than there were stories; people engaged in inquiry because they were encouraged to do so. But as they shared stories, asked questions, and began to disrupt their own views of schooling, the teachers in summer formed a temporary ver-sion of what Jerome Bruner calls a "folk psychology," which "summarizes not simply how things are but (often implicitly) how they should be. When things are 'as they should be,'" writes Bruner, "the narratives of folk psychology are unneces-sary" (1990, 40).

But no one telling stories knew she was constructing narra-tives within a folk psychology. Stories would crumble if tellers were conscious of such lofty intents. No one noticed that the stories were a necessary feature in the revision of a literate teaching self. And certainly no one noticed their stories fusing into a larger story about curriculum and literacy education—testing, as Bruner says, not simply how things are, but how they should be. They were too busy doing it. "The most remarkable feature," anthropologist Don Handelman writes of such events, "is just how unremarkable, noncommittal, and innocuous they are. They really tell us almost nothing, apart from some vague sort of instruction, perhaps akin to "PAY ATTENTION: SOMETHING SPECIAL IS GOING ON HERE AND NOW" (1990, 11).

Away from the oppression of the school day and in the context of the literate community, teachers may indeed have a transformative illusion. They may think, as Susan said, they are in "a little bit of a cult," and they return with the learned rituals and written artifacts to prove it. During the event itself, they perform the rituals, enact the symbols, create the artifacts, tell and write the stories. The three weeks serve as a liminal state, betwixt and between—no home, no school—just time and a community to reinvent the self. It is "a flash of *communitas*," as Victor Turner describes it, three weeks inside "the subjunctive mood of culture" (1982). It is in these liminal states that human cultures enact the social dramas which mark important passages in our lives. In them, we are not transformed; we are more deeply and reflectively ourselves.

The summer program, in Tom Newkirk's words on the first day, simply "honors the teacher." It allows for personal reading and writing; it offers simply time. The culture in school does not. Teachers can tell the stories here that they can't tell in a school culture that oppresses them. They can revise themselves as writers, readers, and as teachers. The program does not transform. Rather, it affirms.

## Teacher Education and the Context of School

Research on high school teaching writing practices is sparse, but it is arid in teacher education for high school writing teachers. In his survey of 1,557 studies over five years, Russell Durst (1990) observes that although composition studies are abundant, studies in teacher education represent only 4 percent, especially concerning literacy in high schools. Durst suggests that studies try not so much to resolve questions, but to ask new questions and learn from the pendulum shifts in writing pedagogy, like the shift in attention from process to context.

The teachers in this book have the high school as their daily context, a culture that holds goals of completion and mastery, not the processes of revision, response, or collaboration. In this book, I have tried to detail processes inside a context, teachers writing in a culture quite different from school.

Education inside the culture of the high school, for teachers and their students, is not the same. Joyce told me:

> By the time they come to me in ninth grade, my students are hardened, prejudicial, cynical about teachers. . . . I hold them partially responsible for not giving me a chance, but on the other hand, I also realize that probably a lot of the reasons they are hardened against school and teachers is because school and teachers have wronged them more than one way, more than one time.

During the winter, one of her students broke into a local liquor store on a Saturday night and was shot by the owner. The boy bled to death as his friends waited for the ambulance. Joyce heard about it the following morning:

> . . . I have spent many many days thinking about that boy's death, why and how these young people became involved in breaking and entering in the first place. . . . I daresay I was closer to him because he and I wrote together. . . . Once that writing is shared, more of that person is shared . . . I guess I just found myself very angry with . . . school as an institution for doing not enough for helping children learn quickly and decisively the consequences of their actions. . . . I wonder how writing might enhance the teaching of consequences. We're not doing that early enough in children's lives.
>
> . . . I think children should be protected. They are very dear and they are very tender. . . . perhaps reading and writing workshops, if we truly hold our children responsible, will be to help them take responsibility. When they fail they will not be able to say, "I failed because the teacher gave me a bad grade."

In her thoughtful grief, Joyce is angry at the institution, and sensitive to the ironies it suggests about freedom and responsibility; she offers a quiet plea for students to consider themselves as agents for their consequences. Joyce spent the summer reviewing her own consequences, her own responsibilities. Freedom and responsibility for teachers isn't much better than it is for students. Social pressures assume that an English teacher comes to school complete, finished, certified.

Arthur Applebee writes, "School programs have an inertia which can create a surprisingly large gap between educational thought, as expressed at conferences and in the professional literature, and educational practice as it actually transpires in schools" (1974, 29). One participant observed that paradox when she told me, "I'm sorry to say that I just don't trust all teachers to use these approaches. This assumes that a teacher is a wellspring of life and love and literature and information about writing. There are several in my building who died a while back."

"Those who died a while back" died in a hard squeeze between approaches to literacy and approaches to measuring schools. The general public—those who make the decisions for high school teachers' working environments—frame their idea of "school" on authority, control, replication, and reproduction. And this frame is the base for curriculum and textbooks (Apple 1986, Shannon 1988). Our high schools, teachers and students, curriculum choices, and time allotments are set by standards from commercial curricula, college entrance examinations, and national and state measurements. One participant told me:

> The writing curriculum where I am . . . has a philosophical core they call "process," but we are supposed to teach spelling, we have vocabulary from a workbook . . . and grammar chapters out of Warriner's. . . . We have to pass our plan books in once a week, and the administration reads them . . . I don't give the vocab from the stupid exercises, the kids work them into their writing, but in the plan book *it looks like* I'm doing what I'm supposed to. . . .

The teacher who wants to focus on "the process" feels subversive. She must plan, as this teacher does, to "make it look like I'm doing what I'm supposed to do." At one point, Joyce mused, "I wonder if the taxpayers would continue to pay me if they realized what I believe. . . . I am using writing and reading to encourage young people to get in touch with their minds and their hearts and their social consciousness." Joyce is confident about what she believes, but she's not as confident in the institution that employs her.

The summer writing program put the systems in place for the teacher to experiment, to act as her own agent for change as she wrote and read and reexamined what she was doing. It encouraged her to determine new ways to enable her students to confirm and revise their knowledge and changes, no matter what her institution expects. Without realizing it, by choosing her own literacy as a way to engage her students, she chose to subvert the system.

## Toward a High School English Curriculum

If there is a villain in this story, it is the American high school. It is an aging, silent villain, barely a hundred years old. The villain is benign, classically educated, and oblivious to history. The high school began homogenizing the English curriculum when English as a subject was in its infancy. The eastern U.S. colleges issued their Uniform Booklists in 1894, based on nineteenth century ideas of literacy and privilege (Applebee 1974, 49). The dissenting voices were there then as they are now. At the turn of the century, John Dewey, Jane Addams and others argued for more experience-based and socially equitable models of teaching. But most of the public, then as now, wasn't listening to the calls for reform. The American high school was sorting out its "best and brightest," and packing them off to college (Cremin 1961, Shannon 1990).

The high school hasn't changed much in its hundred year history. James Conant's 1958 report *The American High School Today: A First Report to Interested Citizens*, was designed to address the needs of the growing post-Sputnik population, midwestern farmers, city factory-workers and others in high schools who were not headed for college. After a thorough study of fifty-five of the best high schools he could find, Conant made twenty-one recommendations for a comprehensive high school that would train all of our citizens in separately tracked programs. Among his guidelines, he high-lighted English composition:

> The time devoted to English composition . . . should occupy half the time devoted to the study of English. Each student should be required to write an average of one theme a week . . . no English teacher should be responsible for more than one hundred pupils. . . . Obviously, adequate instruction in English composition requires that teachers not be overloaded. (1958, 50)

Conant acknowledged that writing ought to be important enough to make up one-half of the English curriculum, and that overloaded teachers cannot teach writing. Time has taught us a few alternatives to his tracking system and the concept of corrected "themes." But it is close to forty years later and most of today's high schools are still struggling to meet his recommendations. Now, too, the postindustrial American high school population is quite different from the one Conant studied. Most of today's English teachers not only attended high schools just like the ones Conant described; now they hold tenure as employees. If anything has happened, it is that our Silent Villain has outlived itself.

Since Conant's report there have been more attempts to redefine the English curriculum and describe the teacher's role in it. Most recently, the English Coalition Conference gathered for three weeks in the summer of 1987. Sixty school and university teachers from eight professional organizations created another report that would redefine "English studies" and "Language Arts." For high school teachers, the coalition agreed on the following principles (Lunsford and Lloyd-Jones 1989, 17):

1. Learning is the process of actively constructing meaning from experiences, including encounters with a broad range of print and nonprint texts.
2. Others—parents, teachers, and peers—help learners construct meanings by serving as supportive models, providing frames and materials for inquiry, helping create and modify hypotheses, and confirming the worth of the venture.

3. Learners at different ages and stages of development may well learn in different ways.

The conference itself was an event like the summer writing program in this book. It lasted three weeks. People left their families, their homes, and their schools—for no pay, just room and board—and gathered at Wye Plantation in Maryland. "It is not my notion of the ideal use of summertime to spend three weeks conferring about anything with anybody," Wayne Booth begins his foreword to the official report. But with an edge of surprise, Booth calls it the most profitable "conferring time" he's ever spent, that the experience was close to inde- scribable even for a rhetorician: "The heart of any prolonged and unique experience escapes reporter's language." The con- ference recommendations, he observes, emerged from partic- ipants' talk. As he and the other participants shaped goals for students, they discovered what they needed for themselves:

> . . . what was new was our having enough time together—three weeks soon began to look too short—to get beyond our stereo- types, to listen to each other, to try to understand and fail to understand and then try again . . . we found that our own "learn- ing problems" resembled those of our students back home . . . our own learning illustrated just why our students show so much resistance to learning: like theirs, it was inevitable "recursive," spiraling, requiring repetition after repetition. . . . After all, it is only when we teachers engage in reflection on what we want to learn and why, only when we "take responsibility for our own meanings," that we become models of what we want our students to become. Only if we lead our students to take such active responsibility will they become full participants in the political and cultural life they will meet after they leave our care." (Booth, in Lunsford and Lloyd-Jones 1989, x–xiii)

Like the summer program in this book, it was the partici- pation, the processes, the shared behaviors, and the time they had to reflect on what they were doing that taught the Coalition participants what goals they valued for themselves and for their students. Peter Elbow was another Coalition participant. His book, *What is English?*, is a personal account of the conference. The three week encounter between knowledgeable people, Elbow observes, was more important than the core of knowledge we call "English:" "Perhaps English can end up being a discipline that is, above all, about making knowledge rather than about studying already existing knowledge" (1990, 118). The rich literate exchange among English teachers was the most valuable source of knowledge there; talking, listening, swapping books and reading writing, and a "fierce commitment to process rather than product" (7).

Both Elbow's and Booth's experiences at the Coalition Conference, like the teachers in this book, led them to reflect on their own histories. Booth, a professor of English, pokes fun at his own resistance to spending time with "pre-higher education" teachers, and admits, " . . . of course, I love elementary and high school teachers. My grandfather was one, my mother was one, my daughter has been one. . . . Two cousins, one niece, and one nephew now are schoolteachers" (vii). Elbow writes, "I wanted to grow up to be a tweedy pipe-smoking professor just like the teachers I admired. . . . I write very much as an academic, having almost always either studied or taught; yet also with a deep sense of detachment, perhaps even alienation, having failed and quit" (261). Both suggest that their careers as teachers, like most of ours, are complex tangles of mentors and fantasies, family expectations and personal disappointments, professional successes and failures, and much reading and writing.

## It's Not About Literature, It's What Literature is About

Most English teachers didn't become teachers to make new knowledge or to work with teenagers. They are often people whose love of reading—not usually writing—led them to choose English as a major in college. One participant told me:

My theory is that English teachers are so afraid they are going to be found out . . . to be non-writers, and not terribly good writing teachers. They're so afraid that the jig is going to be up . . . that someone will discover that they masked it all with "I really don't need to know anything else. I have my way and it works for me.

. . . . People can be English teachers because they like to read good stuff. And they don't feel their forte is really writing. . . . I think you can blame the models. In college, they were The Answer Men. They were the people who had memorized all the footnotes, knew all the allusions and T.S. Eliot and Ezra Pound, and could tell you what James Joyce was talking about. And I just stood in awe of them. . . . I figured never in a million years would I pick that up, without reading reams of stuff. And we grew out of that tradition.

All over the country, English teachers are emulating their models: stuffing their students with the stuff of "The Answer Men:" curriculum-prescribed literature, state-mandated literacy "requirements," school-mandated "skills," and a test-inspired illusion of what colleges want them to be (Sizer 1984, Goodlad 1984, Powell et al. 1985) Without reflection or appropriate preparation, we know that teachers teach according to the models with which they were taught (Britzman 1988). Teachers with a traditional English literature major as their primary background, without much work in either composition or pedagogy, duplicate their own teachers (Grossman 1989). And new teachers in public high schools are often discouraged from working in new ways.

High school teachers fare no better than their students in terms of support for academic growth. They are isolated from their colleagues (Lortie 1975, Lightfoot 1983), they feel flattened and powerless (Goodlad 1984, Johnson, 1990); the curriculum and the school day are more fragmented and distracting than they were when Conant recommended them (Lightfoot 1983, Sizer 1984, Powell, et al. 1985).

The public demands high test scores, textbook companies design "teacher-proof" curriculum materials, forcing teachers to work mechanically (Apple 1986, Shannon 1988). In high school English classes, student writing is more content-based, less personally expressive than in elementary or middle schools (Britton 1975, Applebee 1984). The older the students are, the less time their teachers have them spend writing in class (Applebee 1981, Simmons 1991). And teachers don't have the time, the support, or the self-confidence to change. One participant described a friend who teaches across the hall at her school:

> She's an awesome lit teacher, she just has a real passion, and the kids sense that. . . . I've heard them say "She's the best literature teacher I've ever had," but she's a terrible writing teacher. Her idea of responding to a piece is to read the whole piece and on the last page she writes a grade and "Thanks for sharing." So they might write ten pages . . . the kids have no idea how they might revise. . . . She wanted to take a class this summer and all the lit classes were booked. So I said "Why don't you take a writing class?" "No. I've been teaching writing for fifteen years," she said, "and I know how to do it."

Like this woman, most high school teachers are not encouraged to expand their teaching methods or philosophy; they are only expected to enlarge their content knowledge. Public school teachers who attend conferences or hold office in professional organizations usually go at their own expense. To take time off without pay for scholarship often means risking or losing jobs. Inservice programs, according to Susan Moore Johnson, are not effective when they are mandated, and they are usually mandated and in-house. Most funded support is "payoff-centered" these days, tied to in-house, inservice groups and not individuals. Schools willing to invest in summer opportunities, "learning and restoration" for single teachers, have more committed teachers who consider themselves professionals. But such support is neither cost effective nor evenly distributed, so most public schools reject it. The summer writing program offers what Johnson's study identified as the crucial piece of teacher development—"investment centered support" for individual teachers to evoke "restorative powers" (1990, 261). In short, schools must invest in the teacher herself.

In order to understand teachers' classrooms, we must look away from the classrooms and look toward the teachers. In order to respect teachers, we must understand the complexity of what it is to be a teacher—who she is and how she got there. Each point of contact between a teacher and a student involves two personal histories: the teacher's and the student's. When both can tap into the depth and breadth of that history, into their own literate behaviors, then the exchange between teacher and student we call education can begin to take place.

For English teachers in high schools, curriculum change will be superficial without attention to the teacher's growth. Preservice and inservice education ought to be "investment-centered," as Johnson calls it, ought to focus on the teacher herself. It ought to include opportunities for personal inquiry in a collegial context. Teacher writing and reading groups held after school, meaningful collaborations with other academic communities or with writers, actors, publishers, support for participation in professional conferences, on-site teacher-research projects in and out of school, literacy autobiography projects that question and disrupt personal patterns of learning and teaching and offer time to reconstruct those patterns—are opportunities for reflection and collegiality like those the summer program offers.

There is rich teacher education inside the culture of a summer writing program. In the talk and the sharing, in the reading and the writing, each person reinvents herself. She develops the personal principles she will put into place in her own classroom. There is storytelling and performance in this culture—what folklorists call verbal art (Baumann, 1975). Each time someone renders a draft and shares it, each time someone interprets a reading, a literate re-invention takes place in the group and the process of personal and professional revision continues. Teachers learn responses and develop language to enable the others' continuing verbal creation.

In short, by reading and responding to their own spoken and written texts, they enact the very literature they create.

This is not just about learning literature; it's enacting what literature is about. For many high school English teachers, this part of the literate experience is new. And they read the culture they have composed. Participants learn specific beliefs about the program's community of writers, and when they return, they apply it in their own ways to their own students.

"In the teaching of literature," writes Louise Rosenblatt, "we are basically helping our students to learn to perform in response to a text. . . . The reader performs the poem or the novel, as the violinist performs the sonata. But the instrument on which the reader plays, and from which he evokes the work, is—himself." (1938/1983, 279) In the text that is the summer writing program, the instruments are teachers who perform what they write, and who "play" what their colleagues read and write by performing in response. They read the culture, too. It acts as their accompaniment.

# Appendix A: Organizing Questions

The main question framing this study was: What kind of culture does a summer writing program provide for a high school teacher? What does a high school teacher do to carry this culture back to her classroom in a public high school? Inspired by Denny Taylor and Catherine Dorsey Gaines' "organizing questions" shown at the end of their book *Growing Up Literate*, I used these questions as guidelines during my data gathering:

- What are the differences between the stories high school writing teachers tell in a summer program and the stories they tell in their schools?
- What is the relationship between a high school teacher's own writing and her beliefs about teaching writing?
- What is a high school teacher's attitude toward her own writing? Does it change over three weeks?
- What do high school teachers choose to write about? Are their writing choices influenced by the conversations they have?
- How do high school writing teachers shape a social context in three weeks with their colleagues in order to reconsider and reconstruct their professional knowledge about writing and teaching writing?
- How do high school teachers interact with teachers from other grade levels in their writing groups? In the dorms? Does this change as the time goes on?
- What dissonances show among high school writing teachers during a summer writing program? What do they complain about? What do they joke about? What do they express conflict about? What do they challenge? What annoys them?

- What are the cultural features—verbal art, artifacts, rituals, behaviors—in a summer writing program that enable people to create a community in such a short time?
- How do those cultural features differ from the cultural features of a high school?
- How does one teacher react to these cultural features, and what is her relationship to her colleagues in the culture of a summer writing program? How does she view herself as a writer in this context?
- How do seven teachers differ in their relationships to the culture of a summer writing program? In their knowledge about themselves as teachers and writers?
- What are the differences between beginners and repeaters? Why do people need to return to a summer program?
- How do teachers absorb and synthesize the influences of a summer writing program, reflect and re-write it for their classrooms? For themselves as teachers in a traditional system? For themselves as literate, creative people?

# Appendix B: Data Collection

During the three week summer program, I balanced participation/observation time among my selected informants. What was in it for them? An opportunity to document their own reflection, to have some extra attention, to share their writing with me; to "slow down" their thinking and learning enough to look more carefully at themselves as members of the community. Of the people I invited to participate in my study, not one declined.

## Informants:

1. Periodic interviews
2. Daily classroom observation
3. Multiple verbal data sources: drafts, completed copies of writing, journals, notes, letters, tapes, written responses from others
4. Tapes of conversations
5. Follow-up in classrooms and school collegial contexts (department offices, teachers' rooms) of each informant

## Other sources of data:

1. Fieldnotes from observations written in class: condensed and expanded accounts
2. Nightly self-memos in journal: my perspective as participant and observer
3. Taped interviews with informants
4. Complete collected writings of informants, selected writings of their peers
5. Collected artifacts from 1990 New Hampshire Summer Writing Programs and instructors

6. Photographs
7. Photographic observation
8. Collected artifacts and interviews with instructors and administrative staff

# Appendix C: Guidelines for Interviews

## Week I

- Draw up an "academic history" map and a "mentor model."
- What do you expect from these weeks? professional? personal? for students?
- In what ways do you feel like an "outsider" this week? What problems have you had?
- Have you had personal difficulties managing getting here for three weeks? Getting away from home?
- Do you have collegial relationships at school? Dissonance at school?
- How does writing fit into your high school curriculum?
- What is your school's expectation of you as a writing teacher?

## Week II

- What is surprising you?
- What difficulties are you encountering?
- In what ways do you feel like an outsider this week? Like an insider?
- What are you writing about?
- Any new relationships with people? How have they responded to your writing?
- What have you learned about other high schools?
- What's new for your classroom?
- What's new for you as a writer?

## *Week III*

- What have you learned about writing?
- What have you learned about yourself as a writer?
- In what ways do you feel like an insider/outsider this week?
- Have you had some personal victories?
- What has helped you learn?
- How will writing fit into your curriculum?
- What will you try that's new in your classroom?
- What will remain the same in your classroom?
- Rework the "academic history" map and "mentor model:" How has it shifted?

## *For returnees:*

- Why did you return to the New Hampshire Summer Writing Program?
- What do you expect from this summer's program?
- In what ways do you feel like an insider? An outsider?
- What personal writing habits have changed for you since the first writing program?
- What were some of the important experiences from the first writing program?
- In what ways are you thinking about the connection writing has with reading?

# Appendix D: Overview Schedule for All 1990 New Hampshire Summer Writing Programs

## Daily Schedule

| NHWP | IRWL | Explorations in Genre |
|---|---|---|
| *8:00–8:30* Video showings, browse in lending library in 218, pick up newsletter | | |
| *8:45–10:00* writing groups | *8:30–11:45* grade level groups | writing time |
| *Morning break:* pick up newsletter, coffee, and browse in room 218 | | |
| *10:15–11:45* grade level groups | grade level groups continued | writing time continued |
| *11:45–1:00* lunchtime: brown bag lunch talks, staff meetings, social time | | |
| Wednesday picnics followed by P.M. classes, Lobster Fest on final Thursday | | |
| *1:00–3:00* writing group | *1:00–3:00* writing group | *1:30–4:30* M–Th, class |

## *Special Programs*

### Morning Presentations

Professor Donald Murray, "Pushing the Edges"
Children's book author and illustrator Barbara Cooney
Entire writing program staff: "Mini-Conference"
Selected participants: final reading programs (separate for
    NHWP and IRWL; Murray's class attends one of their
    choice)

### Brown Bag Lunch Talks

Prof. Sarah Sherman, "Sarah Orne Jewett: An American
    Persephone"
Prof. Patricia Sullivan, "Feminism and Composition Studies"

### 7:30-9:30 evening programs

Open Forum
Charles Simic poetry reading
Rebecca Rule fiction reading

# Appendix E: Major Pieces of Writing by Informants

|  | Week 1 | Week 2 | Week 3 |
|---|---|---|---|
| **Therese Deni** | Essay: Fragments of Fear | Crash Poems: Course in Reality<br><br>Looking from Chocorua | Letter: Lest I Forget |
| **Dorothy Spofford** | Poem: Definition | Fiction: Winning the Pool<br><br>Essay: The Abuse of Journals in the Classroom | Fiction: Heal Thyself<br><br>Essay: The Abuse of Journals in the Classroom |
| Dorothy's Response Group<br><br>*Susan* |  | Bidgie and the Bunyip (Australian Fairy Tale) | This Train Is Bound for Glory |
| *Lenore* | My Father's Stories | The Sisters | Trees |
| **Joyce Choate** | Letter: Letter to Students | Poems: Winthrop Ave. Elem., 1951<br><br>Bill Writes | Essay: Watch Your Head |

## Other Writings

- journals for grade level groups and writing groups (NHWP)
- portfolio letters in classes (IRWL)
- commentaries in Explorations in Genre
- reading response log to personal readings in fiction, nonfiction, and poetry as well as professional readings
- writing exercises done in classes, at Murray's presentation, and at miniconference
- response slips and notes on others' writings as they read it in small and large group
- personal course evaluations and formal course evaluations

# Appendix F:
## 1990 Schedule of Special Events, Including Activities of Informants

## Week One

| Sunday 8 | Monday 9 | Tuesday 10 | Wednesday 11 | Thursday 12 | Friday 13 | Saturday 14 |
|---|---|---|---|---|---|---|
| • Check in at dorms<br><br>3:00 P.M.<br>• Register | 8:30–8:45 A.M.<br>• Opening welcome meetings<br><br>• Brown bag talk: Sarah Sherman: "Sarah Orne Jewett: An American Persephone" | 7:30 P.M.<br>• Open forum | • (newsletter announces it is "hump day" and coffee is restored to room 218)<br><br>12:00 P.M.<br>• Picnic<br><br>• No afternoon classes<br><br>• (Dorothy goes to Portsmouth with Susan) | 8:30 A.M.<br>• Charles Simic meets with Murray Classes<br><br>• (newsletter announces first tee shirt committee meeting)<br><br>7:30 P.M.<br>• Charles Simic, poetry reading | • Formal readings in classes<br><br>• (newsletter mentions options for weekend: open poetry in Portsmouth, swimming at UNH Mendum's pond, restaurant recommendations, outlet shopping on coast, etc.) | • Therese goes to Boston<br><br>• Dorothy and Colin go fishing and to beach<br><br>• Susan drives coastal route to Maine<br><br>• Lenore writes and reads in library<br><br>• Joyce stays on campus |

## Week Two

| Sunday 15 | Monday 16 | Tuesday 17 | Wednesday 18 | Thursday 19 | Friday 20 | Saturday 21 |
|---|---|---|---|---|---|---|
| | | *8:00 A.M.*<br>• video: Roald Dahl | *8:00 A.M.*<br>• video: Katherine Patterson | *8:00 A.M.*<br>• video: "One Child's View of the Classroom" | *8:00 A.M.*<br>• video: "Collaboration"<br><br>*8:30 A.M.*<br>• Classes as usual | • Dorothy and Colin go home to cat and garden, return and go deep sea fishing<br><br>• Therese climbs Chocorua<br><br>• Joyce goes home to New York State |
| | *10:30–12:00 P.M.*<br>• Don Murray: "Pushing the Edge"<br><br>• (newsletter notes: four videos to be shown this week beginning tomorrow | *10:30–12:00 P.M.*<br>• Barbara Cooney lecture "Hattie and the Wild Waves" Cooney meets with IRWL writing groups 45 min. each | *10:30–12:00 P.M.*<br>• miniconference | *10:30–12:00 P.M.*<br>• miniconference | • (newsletter announces tee shirt update | |
| | second tee shirt announcement: meeting at 3:00 P.M. today) | • Third tee shirt announcement: meeting at 3:00 P.M. Design must be at printers Wed. | *12:30 P.M.*<br>• Picnic<br><br>• No afternoon writing groups | *12:00 P.M.*<br>• Brown bag talk: Professor Patricia Sullivan "Feminism and Composition Studies" | *12:30 P.M.*<br>• Formal class readings | |

## Week Three

| Sunday 22 | Monday 23 | Tuesday 24 | Wednesday 25 | Thursday 26 | Friday 27 | Saturday 28 |
|---|---|---|---|---|---|---|
| | • (newsletter announces: videos for this week and UNH October conference) | *8:00 A.M.* • video: "A World of Difference" | *8:00 A.M.* • video: "Toni Morrison" | *8:00 A.M.* • video: "Reading Recovery" | *7:00–8:00 A.M.* • Check out of dorm<br><br>• Formal reading sessions | |
| | *8:30 A.M.* • Classes as usual | *8:30 A.M.* • Classes as usual<br><br>• (newsletter has final reminders about check-out times) | *8:30 A.M.* • Classes as usual | *8:30 A.M.* • Classes as usual<br><br>*1:15 P.M. and 3:00 P.M.* • Lobster Clambake | *12:00–3:00 P.M.* • Check out of dorm | |
| | *7:30 P.M.* Rebecca Rule fiction reading | | | | | |

# Bibliography

Apple, Michael. 1986. *Teachers and Texts: A Political Economy of Class and Gender Relations in Education.* New York: Routledge.

Applebee, Arthur N. 1974. *Tradition and Reform in the Teaching of English: A History.* Urbana, IL: National Council of Teachers of English.

———. 1981. *Writing in the Secondary School: English and the Content Areas.* Urbana, IL: National Council of Teachers of English.

Atwell, Nancie. 1987. *In the Middle: Writing, Reading, and Learning with Adolescents.* Portsmouth, NH: Boynton/Cook.

Barnes, Douglas, James Britton, and Harold Rosen. 1969. *Language, the Learner, and the School.* Harmondsworth: Penguin.

Barone, Thomas. 1992. A Narrative of Enhanced Professionalism: Educational Researchers and Popular Storybooks about Schoolpeople. *Educational Researcher* 21:8, 15–25.

Bateson, Mary Catherine. 1989. *Composing a Life.* New York: Plume of Penguin.

Bauman, Richard. 1975. Verbal Art as Performance. *American Anthropologist* 77: 290–311.

Belenky, M.F., B. M. Clinchy, N. R. Goldberger, and J. M. Tarule. 1986. *Women's Ways of Knowing: The Development of Self, Voice, and Mind.* New York: Basic Books.

Bishop, Wendy. 1990. *Something Old, Something New: College Writing Teachers and Classroom Change.* Carbondale, IL: Southern Illinois University Press.

———. 1990 "Traveling Through the Dark:" Teachers and Students Reading and Writing Together. *Reader* 24: 1–20.

Bleich, David. 1988. *The Double Perspective: Language, Literacy, and Social Relations.* New York: Oxford University Press.

Bloome, David, C. Cassidy, M. Chapman, and D. Schaafsma. 1988. Reading Instruction and Underlying Metaphors in Jane Davidson, ed. *Counterpoint and Beyond: A Response to Becoming a Nation of Readers.* Urbana, IL: National Council of Teachers of English. 5–17.

Briggs, Charles. 1988. *Competence in Performance: The Creativity of Tradition in Mexicano Verbal Art.* Philadelphia: University of Pennsylvania Press.

Britton, James. 1982. *Prospect and Retrospect.* Portsmouth, NH: Boynton/Cook.

———. 1990. *Language and Learning, 4th ed.* Portsmouth, NH: Boynton/Cook.

Britton, James, T. Burgess, N. Martin, A. McLeod, and H. Rosen. 1975. *The Development of Writing Abilities 11–18.* London: Macmillan.

Britzman, Deborah. 1986. Cultural Myths in the Making of a Teacher: Biography and Social Structure in Teacher Education. *Harvard Educational Review* 56:4, 442–472.

Brodkey, Linda. 1987a. Writing Ethnographic Narratives. *Written Communication* 4:1, 25–50.

———. 1987b. Writing Critical Ethnographic Narratives. *Anthropology and Education Quarterly* 18: 67–76.

———. 1987c. *Academic Writing as Social Practice.* Philadelphia: Temple University Press.

———. 1990. *Acts of Meaning.* Cambridge: Harvard University Press.

Bruner, Jerome. 1986. *Actual Minds, Possible Worlds.* Cambridge: Harvard University Press.

Calkins, L. M. 1985. Forming Research Communities Among Naturalistic Researchers. In T. R. Donovan, and B. W. McClelland, eds., *Perspectives on Research and Scholarship.* New York: Modern Language Association.

Carter, Kathy. 1993. The Place of Story in the Study of Teaching and Teacher Education. *Educational Researcher* 22:1, 5–1, 18.

Chilcott, J. J. 1987. Where Are You Coming From and Where Are You Going? The Reporting of Ethnographic Research. *American Educational Research Journal* 24:2, 199–218.

Chiseri-Strater, Elizabeth. 1991. *Academic Literacies: The Public and Private Discourse of University Students.* Portsmouth, NH: Boynton/Cook.

Clifford, James, and Marcus E. George, eds. 1986. *Writing Culture: The Poetics and Politics of Ethnography.* Berkeley: University of California Press.

Coles, Robert. 1989. *The Call of Stories: Teaching and the Moral Imagination.* Boston: Houghton Mifflin.

Conant, James. 1959. *The American High School Today: A First Report to Interested Citizens.* New York: McGraw-Hill.

Cooney, Barbara. 1990. *Hattie and the Wild Waves.* New York: Viking.

Cremin, Lawrence. 1961. *The Transformation of the School.* New York: Random House.

Daniels, Harvey and Steven Zemelman. 1985. *A Writing Project: Training Teachers of Composition from Kindergarten to College.* Portsmouth, NH: Heinemann.

Dewey, John. 1938. *Experience and Education.* New York: Macmillan.

Dillard, Annie. 1974. *Pilgrim at Tinker Creek.* New York: Harper's Magazine Press.

———. 1989. Write Till You Drop. *The New York Times Book Review.* May 28.

Dooley, D. A. 1990. Essay review of Grumet, M. (1988). *Harvard Educational Review* 60: 527–533.

Durst, Russell K. 1990. The Mongoose and the Rat in Composition Research: Insights from the RTE Annotated Bibliography. *College Composition and Communication.* 41:4, 393–408

Eisner, Elliott, ed. 1975. *Learning and Teaching the Ways of Knowing.* Eighty-fourth Yearbook of the National Society for the Study of Education, Part II. Chicago: University of Chicago Press.

_____. 1990. Keynote speech at New Hampshire conference on assessment, Merrimack, NH, November 8.

_____. 1991. *The Enlightened Eye: Qualitative Inquiry and the Enhancement Of Educational Practice.* New York: Macmillan.

Elbow, P. 1973. *Writing Without Teachers.* London: Oxford University Press.

_____. 1981. *Writing with Power.* New York: Oxford University Press.

_____. 1990. *What is English?* New York: MLA and Urbana, IL: National Council of Teachers of English.

Fine, Michelle and P. MacPherson. 1993. Over Dinner: Feminism and Adolescent Female Bodies. In S. K. Biklen and D. Pollard, eds., *Gender and Education: Ninety-second Yearbook of the National Society for the Study of Education, Part I.* Chicago: University of Chicago Press.

Freire, Paulo. 1970. *Pedagogy of the Oppressed.* New York: Continuum.

Fulwiler, Toby. 1987. *The Journal Book.* Portsmouth, NH: Boynton/Cook.

Geertz, Clifford. 1973. *The Interpretation of Cultures.* New York: Basic Books.

_____. 1983. *Local Knowledge: Further Essays in Interpretive Anthropology.* New York: Basic Books.

_____. 1988. *Works and Lives: The Anthropologist as Author.* Stanford: Stanford University Press.

Gere, Anne Ruggles. 1987. *Writing Groups: History, Theory, and Implications.* Carbondale, IL: Southern Illinois University Press.

Gilligan, Carol. 1982. *In a Different Voice.* Cambridge: Harvard University Press.

_____. 1990. Girls at 11: An Interview with Carol Gilligan. *Harvard Education Review.* VI: 4, 5–7.

Glassie, Henry. 1982. *Passing the Time in Balleymenone: Culture and History of an Ulster Community*. Philadelphia: University of Pennsylvania Press.

Goffman, Erving. 1983. *Forms of Talk*. Philadelphia: University of Pennsylvania Press.

Goldberg, Natalie. 1986. *Writing Down the Bones: Freeing the Writer Within*. Boston: Shambhala Publications.

Gomez, Mary Louise. 1990. The National Writing Project: Staff Development in the Teaching Of Composition. In G. E. Hawisher and A. O. Soter, eds., *On Literacy and Its Teaching: Issues in English Education*. Albany: SUNY Press.

Goodenough, Ward. 1957. Cultural Anthropology and Linguistics. In P. L. Garvin, ed., *Report of the Seventh Annual Round Table Meeting on Linguistics and Language Study*. Washington: Georgetown University monograph series on languages and linguistics, 9: 167.

———. 1981. *Culture, Language, and Society*. Menlo Park, NJ: Benjamin/Cummings.

Goodlad, John T. 1984. *A Place Called School*. New York: McGraw-Hill.

Goswami, Dixie and Peter Stillman, eds. 1987. *Reclaiming the Classroom: Teacher Research as an Agency for Change*. Upper Montclair, NJ: Boynton/Cook.

Graham, Robert J. 1991. *Reading and Writing the Self: Autobiography in Education and the Curriculum*. New York: Teachers' College Press.

Graves, Donald H. 1983. *Writing: Teachers and Children at Work*. Portsmouth, NH: Heinemann.

———. 1984. *A Researcher Learns to Write*. Portsmouth, NH: Heinemann.

———. 1990. Unpublished seminar paper and personal communication.

———. 1991. *Build a Literate Classroom*. Portsmouth, NH: Heinemann.

Green, Judith L. and Amy Zaharlick. 1990. *Ethnographic Research*, unpublished handout, research roundtable. National Council of Teachers of English Annual Convention, Atlanta, Georgia.

Greene, Maxine. 1990. Relationality in the Humanities: A Perspective on Leadership. *Language Arts* 67:4.

———. 1989. The Teacher in John Dewey's Works. In Philip W. Jackson and Sophie Haroutenian, eds. *From Socrates to Software: The Teacher as Text and the Text as Teacher.* Eighty-fourth Yearbook of the National Society for the Study of Education, Part I. Chicago: University of Chicago Press.

———. 1988. *The Dialectic of Freedom.* New York: Teachers' College Press.

Grossman, Pamela. 1989. A Study in Contrast: Sources of Pedagogical Content Knowledge for Secondary English. *Journal of Teacher Education* September–October, 24–31.

Grumet, Madeline. 1988. *Bitter Milk: Women and Teaching.* Amherst: University of Massachusetts Press.

Handelman, Don. 1990. *Models and Mirrors: Towards an Anthropology of Public Events.* Cambridge: Cambridge University Press.

Hatton, Elizabeth. 1989. Levi-Strauss's Bricolage and Theorizing Teachers' Work. *Anthropology and Education Quarterly* 20:2, 74–96.

Heath, Shirley Brice. 1983. *Ways with Words: Language, Life, and Work in Communities and Classrooms.* Cambridge: Cambridge University Press.

Heilbrun, Carolyn. 1988. *Writing a Woman's Life.* New York: W.W. Norton.

Hymes, Dell. 1975. Folklore's Nature and the Sun's Myth. *Journal of American Folklore* 88: 346–349.

Hynds, Susan and Donald Rubin, eds. 1990. *Perspectives on Talk and Learning.* Urbana, IL: National Council of Teachers of English.

Irving, John. 1989. *A Prayer for Owen Meany.* New York: W. Morrow.

Jaeger, Robert M., ed. 1988. *Complementary Methods for Research in Education*. Washington: American Educational Research Association.

James, William. 1907, 1969. *Pragmatism and Four Essays from the Meaning of Truth*. Cleveland: Meridian Books.

Johnson, Susan Moore. 1990. *Teachers at Work: Achieving Success in our Schools*. New York: Basic Books.

John-Steiner, Vera. 1985. *Notebooks of the Mind*. Albuquerque: University of New Mexico Press.

Joseph, S. 1988. Feminization, Familism, Self, and Politics: Research as a Mughtaribi. In S. Altorki and C. El-Solh, eds., *Arab Women in the Field: Studying Your Own Society*. Syracuse: Syracuse University Press.

Kantor, Ken J. 1984. Classroom Contexts and the Development of Writing Intuition: An Ethnographic Case Study. In R. Beach and L. Bridwell, eds., *New Directions in Composition Research*. New York: Guilford.

Kelly, George A. 1963. *A Theory of Personality*. New York: Norton Library.

Knoblauch, C. H. and Lil Brannon. 1988. Knowing our Knowledge: A Phenomenological Basis for Teacher Research. In L. Z. Smith, ed., *Audits of Meaning: A Festchrift in Honor Of Ann E. Berthoff.* Portsmouth, NH: Boynton/Cook.

Lakoff, George and Mark Johnson. 1980. *Metaphors We Live By*. Chicago: University of Chicago Press.

Langland, Joseph. 1988. *Twelve Poems with Preludes and Postludes*. Sudbury, MA: Water Row Books.

LeFevre, Karen Burke. 1987. *Invention as a Social Act*. Carbondale, IL: Southern Illinois University Press.

Leslie, Craig. 1984. *Winterkill*. Boston: Houghton Mifflin.

Lester, Nancy B. and Cynthia S. Onore. 1990. *Learning Change: One School District Meets Language across the Curriculum*. Portsmouth, NH: Boynton/Cook.

Lightfoot, Sara Lawrence. 1983. *The Good High School: Portraits of Character and Culture*. New York: Basic Books.

Lloyd-Jones, Richard and Andrea Lunsford, eds. 1989. *The English Coalition Conference: Democracy Through Language*. Urbana, IL: National Council of Teachers of English.

Lord, Albert. 1960. *The Singer of Tales*. Cambridge: Harvard University Press.

Lortie, Dan. 1975. *Schoolteacher: A Sociological Study*. Chicago: University of Chicago Press.

Lytle, Susan L. and Marilyn Cochran-Smith. 1989. Teacher Research: Toward Clarifying the Concept. *The Quarterly* 11:2, 1–3, 22–27

Macrorie, Ken. 1984. *Writing to be Read*, 3rd ed. Upper Montclair, NJ: Boynton/Cook.

———. 1988. The I-Search Paper: Revised edition of *Searching Writing*. Portsmouth, NH: Boynton/Cook.

Mayher, John S. 1990. *Uncommon Sense: Theoretical Practice in Language Education*. Portsmouth, NH: Boynton/Cook.

McLaren, Peter. 1988. The Liminal Servant and the Ritual Roots of Critical Pedagogy. *Language Arts* 65:2.

Mishler, Elliott G. 1990. Validation in Inquiry-Guided Research: The Role of Exemplars in Narrative Studies. *Harvard Educational Review* 60, 415–439.

Moffet, James. 1968. *Teaching the Universe of Discourse*. Boston: Houghton Mifflin.

———. 1981. *Coming on Center: English Education in Evolution*. Portsmouth, NH: Boynton/Cook.

Morrison, Toni. 1987. The Site of Memory. In William Zinsser. *Inventing the Truth: The Art and Craft of Memoir*. Boston: Houghton Mifflin.

———. 1979. Meaning in Context: Is There Any Other Kind? *Harvard Educational Review* 49, 1–19.

Murray, Donald M. 1968. *A Writer Teaches Writing.* Boston: Houghton Mifflin.

———. 1982. Teaching the Other Self: The Writer's First Reader. *College Composition and Communication* 33: 140–147.

———. 1989. *Expecting the Unexpected: Teaching Myself—And Others—To Read and Write.* Portsmouth, NH: Boynton/Cook.

———. 1990. "Pushing the Edge," unpublished notes, Durham NH, July 16.

Myerhoff, Barbara. 1974. *Number Our Days.* New York: Simon & Schuster.

Myers, Miles. 1985. *The Teacher-Researcher: How To Study Writing in the Classroom.* Urbana, IL: National Council of Teachers of English.

*NCTE Guidelines for the Preparation of Teachers of English and Language Arts.* Urbana, IL: National Council of Teachers of English.

Neilsen, Lorri. 1989. *Literacy and Living: The Literate Lives of Three Adults.* Portsmouth, NH: Heinemann.

Newkirk, Thomas. 1979. *Proposal for New Hampshire Writing Program,* unpublished manuscript.

———. 1983. Is the Bay Area Model the Answer? *English Education* 15: 161–166.

———. 1989a. *More Than Stories: The Range of Children's Writing.* Portsmouth, NH: Heinemann.

———. 1989b. *Critical Thinking and Writing: Reclaiming the Essay.* Urbana, IL: National Council of Teachers of English and Education Resources Information Clearinghouse. *Monographs on Teaching Critical Thinking #3.*

———. 1990a. Looking for Trouble: A Way to Unmask Our Readings. In Thomas Newkirk, ed. *To Compose: Teaching Writing in High School and College.* 2nd ed. Portsmouth, NH: Heinemann.

———. 1990b. personal communication.

————, ed. 1990c. *To Compose: Teaching Writing in High School and College.*, 2nd ed. Portsmouth, NH: Heinemann.

————. 1992. The Narrative Roots of the Case Study. In Patricia A. Sullivan and Gesa Kirsch, eds., *Methods and Methodologies in Composition Studies.* Carbondale: Southern Illinois University Press.

Newkirk, Thomas and Patricia McLure. 1992. *Listening In: Children Talk About Books (and Other Things).* Portsmouth, NH: Heinemann.

Noddings, Nel. 1986. *Caring: A Feminine Approach to Ethics and Moral Education.* Berkeley: University of California Press.

North, Stephen. 1987. *The Making of Knowledge in Composition: Portrait of an Emerging Field.* Upper Montclair, NJ: Boynton/Cook.

Ong, Walter J. 1975. The Writer's Audience is Always a Fiction. *Publications of the Modern Language Association* 90:1, 9–21.

————. 1982. *Orality and Literacy: The Technologizing of the Word.* New York: Routledge.

Peacock, James L. 1989, 1986. *The Anthropological Lens: Harsh Light, Soft Focus.* Cambridge: Cambridge University Press.

Perl, Sondra and Nancy Wilson. 1986. *Through Teachers' Eyes: Portraits of Writing Teachers at Work.* Portsmouth, NH: Heinemann.

Plato. 1973. *Phaedrus and the Seventh and Eighth Letters.* Walter Hamilton, trans. London: Penguin.

Ponder, G., ed. 1990. *School Culture: Teacher Lore.* Kappa Delta Pi Record 26:4.

Powell, Arthur, Eleanor Farrar, and David Cohen. 1985. *The Shopping Mall High School.* Boston: Houghton-Mifflin.

Richards, Judith. 1977. *The Sounds of Silence.* New York: Putnam.

Richter, Conrad. 1953. *A Light in the Forest.* New York: Knopf.

Roemer, Marjorie. 1989. Literate Cultures: Multi-Voiced Classrooms. *The Quarterly* Winter.

Romano, Tom. 1987. *Clearing the Way*. Portsmouth, NH: Heinemann

———. 1990. Breaking the Rules in Style. In Thomas Newkirk, ed. *To Compose: Teaching Writing in High School and College.* 2nd ed. Portsmouth, NH: Heinemann.

Rosaldo, Renato. 1989. *Culture and Truth: The Remaking of Social Analysis.* Boston: Beacon Press.

Rose, Mike. 1989. *Lives on the Boundary: The Struggles and Achievements of America's Underprepared.* New York: Free Press.

Rosenberg, Pearl. 1989. *The Empowerment Educator as Disguised Ruler: The Paradox of Negotiating Power and Status in a College Classroom.* Doctoral dissertation, University of Pennsylvania.

Rosenblatt, Louise. 1938/1983. *Literature as Exploration*, 4th ed. New York: Modern Language Association.

———. 1978. *The Reader, the Text, the Poem.* Carbondale: Southern Illinois University Press.

Ruby, Jay, ed. 1982. *A Crack in the Mirror: Reflexive Perspectives on Anthropology.* Philadelphia: University of Pennsylvania Press.

Santino, Jack. 1983. Miles of Smiles, Years of Struggle: The Negotiation of Black Occupational Identity Through Personal Experience Narrative. *Journal of American Folklore* 96: 393–410.

———. 1986. A Servant and a Man, a Hostess or a Woman: A Study of Expressive Culture in Two Transportation Occupations. *Journal of American Folklore* 99: 304–396.

Schechner, Richard and W. Appel, eds. 1990. *By Means of Performance: Intercultural Studies of Theatre and Ritual.* Cambridge: Cambridge University Press.

Schön, Donald. 1983. *The Reflective Practitioner: How Professionals Think in Action.* New York: Basic Books.

———. 1987. *Educating the Reflective Practitioner.* New York: Jossey Bass.

Schulman, Judith H. 1990. Now You See Them, Now You Don't: Anonymity Versus Visibility in Case Studies of Teachers. *Educational Researcher* 19:11–15.

Schultz, L. M., C. H. Laine, and M. C. Savage. 1988. Interaction Among School and College Writing Teachers: Toward Recognizing and Remaking Old Patterns. *College Composition and Communication* 39:2, 139–153.

Shannon, Patrick. 1990. *The Struggle to Continue.* Portsmouth, NH: Heinemann

————. 1989. The Struggle for Control of Literacy Lessons. *Language Arts* 66: 625–34.

————. 1988. *Broken Promises: Reading Instruction in 20th Century America.* Granby, MA: Bergin and Garvey.

Simon, R. I. and D. Dippo. 1986. On Critical Ethnographic Work. *Anthropology and Education Quarterly* 17:4, 195–202.

Simmons, Jay. 1991. Unpublished doctoral dissertation, Writing Process Lab, Education Department, University of New Hampshire.

Sizer, Theodore. 1984. *Horace's Compromise: The Dilemma of the American High School.* Boston: Houghton-Mifflin.

Smith, Louise, ed. 1988. *Audits of Meaning: A Festschrift in Honor of Ann E. Berthoff.* Portsmouth, NH: Boynton/Cook.

Stafford, William. 1986. *You Must Revise Your Life.* Ann Arbor: University of Michigan Press.

Strong, William. 1988. Report: Inside the New Hampshire Writing Project. *The Quarterly.*

Sunstein, Bonnie. 1994. Teachers' Tales as Texts: Folklore and Our Profession. In Trousdale, Ann, ed. *Give a Listen.* Urbana, IL: National Council of Teachers of English.

————. 1989a. *The Pit and the Persona: Genres and Contexts of Teacher's Tales,* unpublished manuscript.

————. 1989 b. *The Write Words: Literacy, Language, and the Re-Socialization of the English Teacher,* unpublished manuscript.

————. 1990. *The Nature of Lore and a Writing Teacher's Culture.* unpublished manuscript.

————. 1991. Notes From the Kitchen Table: Disabilities and Disconnections. In S. Stires, ed., *With Promise: Redefining Reading and Writing For "Special" Students.* Portsmouth, NH: Heinemann.

Taylor, Denny and Catherine Dorsey-Gaines. 1988. *Growing Up Literate: Learning from Inner-City Families.* Portsmouth, NH: Heinemann.

Thomas, Lewis. 1990. *A Long Line of Cells: Collected Essays.* New York: Book of the Month Club/Viking Penguin.

Toelken, Barre. 1979. *The Dynamics of Folklore.* Boston: Houghton-Mifflin.

Tomlinson, Barbara. 1988. Tuning, Tying, and Training Texts: Metaphors for Revision. *Written Communication* 5:58–81.

Turner, Victor. 1982. *From Ritual to Theater: The Human Seriousness of Play.* New York: Performing Arts Journal Publications.

Van Maanen, John. 1988. *Tales of the Field: On Writing Ethnography.* Chicago: University of Chicago Press.

Vibert, Anne. 1990. Unpublished doctoral dissertation, Writing Process Lab, Education Department, University of New Hampshire.

Vygotsky, Lev. 1978. *Mind in Society: The Development of Higher Psychological Processes.* Cambridge: Harvard University Press.

Weathers, Winston. 1980. *An Alternate Style: Options in Composition.* Rochelle Park, NJ: Hayden.

Welty, Eudora. 1984. *One Writer's Beginnings.* New York: Warner Books.

Wilde, Jack. 1993. *A Door Opens: Writing in Fifth Grade.* Portsmouth, NH: Heinemann.

Williams, Raymond. 1982. *The Sociology of Culture.* New York: Shocken Books.

Wilson, David. 1988. *Teacher Change and the Iowa Writing Project,* doctoral dissertation, University of Iowa.

# Also available from Heinemann-Boynton/Cook . . .

*Attempting Change*
*Teachers Moving From Writing Project to Classroom Practice*
David E. Wilson, University of Nebraska-Lincoln

Hundreds of thousands of teachers have participated in writing projects offered around the globe. James Moffett has referred to the writing project movement as "the most positive development in English education" since World War II. But what happens when teachers leave their summer writing projects and return to their classrooms?

In *Attempting Change*, Dave Wilson answers this question and many others. He examines the post-project lives of secondary English teachers who participated in Iowa Writing Project institutes during two different summers. Using surveys, interviews, case studies, and classroom observation, Wilson describes the complex relationship between these teachers' practices and beliefs when they attempted to change their approach to the teaching of writing.

Alive with the voices of classroom teachers and their students, *Attempting Change* tells the stories of teachers like Robin, Wilma, Eileen, and Hal, moving inside their homes and classrooms as they try to make sense of their experiences in the writing project and their lives as teachers. Often, teachers' participation in a summer writing project is a turning point in their careers. Many teachers leave feeling guilty about past practices and excited to try new ones in their classrooms. Wilson lets readers see and understand the guilt and excitement, the successes and difficulties experienced by these teachers.

*Attempting Change* is invaluable for teachers, teacher educators, and writing project instructors and directors wanting a better understanding of the ways writing projects influence classroom teachers and the realities of these teachers' post-project lives.

0-86709-340-4 / 1994 / Paper

*Contact your local supplier, favorite bookstore, or call us direct.*

Boynton/Cook Publishers
HEINEMANN
361 Hanover Street
Portsmouth, NH 03801-3912
(800) 541-2086

————. 1994. *Attempting Change: Teachers Moving.* Portsmouth, NH: Boynton/Cook.

Witherell, Carol and Nel Noddings. 1991. *Stories Lives Tell: Narrative and Dialogue in Education.* New York: Teachers' College Press.

Yeats, William Butler. 1962. In Rosenthal, M. L., ed. *Selected Poems.* New York: Macmillan.